Teaching
With
Heart

In Memory
of

Willard B. Spalding, D.Ed.
1903–1981

A lifetime of commitment
to Public Education

~

The gift
of his loving family

DATE DUE

Teaching With Heart

Making Healthy Connections With Students

Judith A. Deiro

CORWIN PRESS, INC.
A Sage Publications Company
Thousand Oaks, California

For information address:

Corwin Press, Inc.
A Sage Publications Company
2455 Teller Road
Thousand Oaks, California 91320
E-mail: order@corwin.sagepub.com

SAGE Publications Ltd.
6 Bonhill Street
London EC2A 4PU
United Kingdom

SAGE Publications India Pvt. Ltd.
M-32 Market
Greater Kailash I
New Delhi 110 048 India

Printed in the United States of America

Library of Congress Cataloging-in-Publication Data

Deiro, Judith A.
    Teaching with heart: Making healthy connections with students /
author, Judith A. Deiro.
        p.   cm.
    Includes bibliographical references and index.
    ISBN 0-8039-6344-0 (cloth: acid-free paper).—ISBN
0-8039-6345-9 (pbk.: acid-free paper)
        1. Teacher-student relationships—United States.   2. Teachers-
United States.   3. Teaching—United States.   I. Title.
    LB1033.D44   1996
    371.1′023—dc20   95-50203

This book is printed on acid-free paper.

96   97   98   99   10   9   8   7   6   5   4   3   2   1

Corwin Press Production Editor: Diane S. Foster
Corwin Press Typesetter: Andrea D. Swanson

Contents

Foreword

Judith Deiro's book joins a growing number of important studies that demonstrate convincingly that caring is possible in schools and that there is no recipe for accomplishing it. In the pages of this book, we meet six very different teachers working in six different situations. Some are overtly friendly and warm; others are more formal and cool. But all six care deeply about the growth of their students as whole persons, and all of them consistently treat their students with dignity and respect.

Because there is no precise recipe for caring, we should not conclude that there are no strategies associated with it. Deiro gives us a powerful, detailed description of the strategies these teachers use to establish relations of care and trust with their students. Most important and universal is the effort to make time for one-to-one connections. All of these very busy teachers find time to let individual students know that they are recognized, watched, and appreciated. Furthermore, they all take seriously the responsibility to nurture their own growth. They believe what some of us have been preaching for a long time: Caring implies competence. When we care, we want to do our best for the recipients of our care. Thus, caring teachers study, experiment, reflect, and find ways to augment their energies.

If anyone ever doubted it, this study makes clear that teaching requires tremendous amounts of physical and psychic energy. We often think of teachers as needing the patience of saints and their work as an energy-depleting plodding through prescribed courses of study with reluctant students. But here we see vibrant people infecting their students with their own excitement for both intellectual work and life itself. Sharing their interests and occasionally disclosing their own mistakes and failures, these teachers show their students that it is possible to live a life of commitment, to recover from failure and disappointment, and to have fun along the way. All of them have found ways to renew the energy that can be so quickly used up in teaching. Paradoxically, most of them get energy from teaching. They supply energy, but they also receive energy from their responsive students.

The schools in which these teachers work are, for the most part, supportive of their efforts to nurture and care. Like the teachers, the schools are very different. Some are broadly and consistently supportive of nurturing attitudes and activities; others are more cautious and even legalistic, supporting a determined teacher in his or her effort to nurture but maintaining a more formal position with respect to most teachers. Studies like this one may encourage more openness in schools now afraid to support closer relationships between teachers and students.

My greatest hope, when I read a book like this one, is that educators at every level will begin to think more deeply about what they are doing and why. Cases like these are not to be copied or "replicated." Rather, they should inspire reflection and experimentation: How can I establish relations of care and trust with my own students? How can I increase my own supply of energy? How can I make lessons more interesting and useful? What can I do to know my students better without intruding in their private lives and violating their dignity? How can schools encourage and protect teachers who want to create caring relationships? This book encourages us to explore these questions with greater courage.

Nel Noddings
Stanford University

Foreword

"Teachers in elementary schools teach children and those in secondary schools teach subject matter"—or so the folklore goes. However, in *Teaching With Heart*, by following six teachers in three different schools, we learn that establishing important connections to students and their families is critical to teaching—no matter what the age of the student. The book describes in rich detail how this most vital part of the teaching/learning process takes place, even as we come to understand that different teachers have different ways of making it happen.

Being responsible for the education of as many as 140 students a day seems almost an impossible task, yet secondary teachers do it, bonding to their students in ways that help connect them to school, learning, and better and more wholesome relationships with their peers and their families. How does this happen? What is it that some teachers do to make this happen? And what can we learn about their strategies that can benefit the teaching profession?

Building trust with students means letting them know that you are there for them. Some teachers do this by making themselves available before, between, and after classes, leaving the classroom open so that students feel comfortable dropping by to talk or visit on their way to other classes. Some teachers design their curriculum to create opportunities for contact with small groups or on a one-to-one basis. Sometimes, by interweaving the personal and academic, connections are made in a natural and ongoing way; and sometimes a caring comment on a student's work tells students that the teacher cares about *them* as well as their ideas. These kinds of strategies, and the teachers who implement them, give us a view of teaching in secondary school that, unlike the lore, makes us appreciate the importance to learning of teachers who reach out to "make healthy connections" with students.

While this book should be of interest to anyone who cares about teaching and learning, teachers and would-be teachers will find much that is especially stimulating and valuable. Student teachers, struggling to make connections to their students while teaching their subject, can see how the integration of these activities helps to form an effective teaching style. Teachers, working hard to engage students distracted by concerns that seem far more powerful than their class material, can compare and reflect on their own attempts to build trusting and caring relationships embedded in the organization of the curriculum—relationships that strengthen the social and academic experience, enhancing classroom, individual, and group learning.

At a time when the political and social conditions in our society are rapidly changing, schools are being asked to raise standards—of learning and of social and individual behavior. It is more important than ever that nurturing students is seen as a critical part of what it means to be a good teacher. Some do it intuitively, some have models they emulate, and some will be fortunate enough to read this book, which will help them to see how it is that the everyday, seemingly obvious ways of relating to students are, in the long run, what connects students to learning and to their world.

Ann Lieberman
Teachers College, Columbia University

Preface

A healthy relationship with students is the key to fostering prosocial behavior among students. It is also an essential component of the teaching process. Yet many educators are unsure of the skills and attitudes that make this vital relationship work. Some assume that the skills to build a healthy relationship are innate to an individual's personality. Banking on student teachers gaining these skills while growing up or through common sense, teacher education programs fail to teach these vital skills. As a result, learning about this essential component in the teaching process is left to fate. Yet today, faced with the responsibility to teach upwards of 150 students, some of whom are emotionally and socially needy, teachers often feel incapable of nurturing healthy teacher-student connections.

I had the opportunity to carefully observe six competent secondary teachers develop close and trusting relationships with their students within their role as teacher. I took those observations and translated them into vignettes of actual teachers nurturing and working with their students. The result is a rich and detailed description of teachers building healthy connections with students.

Importantly, the six nurturing teachers you will meet in this book are not superstars. Quite the contrary. They are typical teachers who confront the standard demands every teacher faces. These six dedicated individuals use some techniques that allow them to significantly touch their students lives—each within the framework of a teacher's role, not as a parent or a counselor. One message of this book is that it is possible to accurately describe and classify what these six teachers are doing.

Who Would Benefit From Reading This Book?

Teaching With Heart provides important information for teachers, teacher educators, educational administrators, and prevention specialists working within schools. In general, it provides teachers with a rationale for building close and trusting relationships with students. It also offers specific suggestions on how to build those relationships. For teachers already making healthy connections with students, this book validates their efforts. For other teachers, the information in this book gives some new ways of thinking about the teacher-student relationship. It debunks some myths held about who teachers have to be and what they have to do to make healthy connections with students.

For teacher educators, this book provides a valuable conceptual framework for teachers' nurturing behavior. It discusses skills, knowledge, and sensitivities necessary to make healthy teacher-student connections, and it provides some key curriculum components to include in teacher training so that nurturing connections with students are enhanced.

For educational administrators interested in hiring teachers who make healthy student connections, this book gives a description of teacher qualities to look for when hiring. And it can alert administrators to the workplace resources necessary to support nurturing teachers.

For prevention specialists, especially those who work with schools, this book reframes how educators can be effectively involved in prevention efforts. It provides ideas for involving teachers in prevention activities in ways that are not add-ons to a teacher's already busy schedule.

Overview

Chapter 1 discusses the importance and value of developing close and trusting relationships with students for their overall healthy development. Chapter 2 presents the strategies used by the six nurturing teachers to form close and trusting relationships with their students. Chapter 3 illustrates the quintessential attitude needed to encourage student openness to a teacher's caring—treating students with dignity and respect.

Chapters 4, 5, and 6 discuss the personal and workplace resources that nurturing teachers use to revitalize their professional energy. They also identify personal characteristics that the teachers hold in common that enhance competence and engender student trust and acceptance. And they discuss workplace resources that support and facilitate teachers making healthy connections with students.

Finally, Chapter 7 summarizes the findings of the research. In addition, it addresses some common concerns of teachers, teacher educators, and educational administrators with the ideas and insights presented in the book.

Acknowledgments

There are a number of people I wish to acknowledge and thank for their help and support in writing this book. First, I want to thank the six key informants for providing me the opportunity to sit in their classrooms and observe them teaching and relating to their students. It was not a difficult task; rather, it was emotionally moving to see the commitment, dedication, and high regard these teachers have for the students and the teaching profession. Out of courtesy, I do not use their real names or the real name of anyone introduced in the text.

I want to express my appreciation and gratitude to several individuals who spent a significant amount of time editing the drafts of this book and giving me valuable feedback—Linda Knapp, Ann Baye, Linda Reisser, Barbara Hudson, Shellie Mueller, and Steve Robbins. The hours they spent editing and talking with me were very helpful. Their belief in me and the book was inspiring.

This book is the result of a qualitative study I did for my doctoral degree. I am forever grateful to my dissertation chair, my doctoral adviser, and my mentor, Michael Knapp. Throughout the study, he always treated me and my ideas with the utmost dignity and respect. Michael exemplifies what this book is about. His enthusiasm for the findings and encouragement of me to get them published inspired me to translate the dissertation into a book for educators. I feel very fortunate to have him as my mentor.

Finally, my deepest appreciation to Tom Sergiovanni, Nel Noddings, Ann Lieberman, Bonnie Benard, and Steve Glenn for their support and encouragement of my writing and their continual wisdom and inspiration.

A special thanks to Tricia Bennett, Alice Foster, and Diane Foster at Corwin Press for all the work they did to make this book a reality.

About the Author

Judith A. Deiro has worked as a teacher and counselor for 25 years. She is presently a full-time tenured faculty member at Whatcom Community College in Bellingham, Washington. She has a keen interest in prevention of high-risk behaviors among young people, and is a certified chemical dependency counselor actively involved in community prevention efforts. As a consultant and trainer, she has given numerous presentations and training sessions on prevention of chemical dependency and other high-risk behaviors among young people. She received her Ph.D. in Education from the University of Washington, with an emphasis on prevention and education. She is a recipient of the Washington State Exemplary Women in Community Colleges Award and the Whatcom Community College Full-Time Faculty Excellence Award.

1

Changing Role of the Teacher

❋ ❋ ❋ ❋ ❋

In Suburb Junior High School in the mid-1990s, Richard, a seasoned counselor, slips inside the classroom doorway of the seventh-grade social studies teacher's room. It is the end of the school day, and Richard collapses against the wall with a heavy sigh. Pam, the teacher, is tidying up getting ready to go home. From across the room she looks at the 55-year-old bearded and balding counselor and empathetically says, "Rough day, huh Richard!"

Pam is aware that an eighth-grade girl had lost a dear friend and neighbor that morning due to suicide. While still in bed, he had put a gun to his head and pulled the trigger. The suicide victim had been the girl's mentor as well as her friend. Understandably, the young student was distraught and confused about her mentor's behavior.

"I swear," Richard utters, "In the 1960s, I had to work with one crisis a month. In the 1970s and 1980s, it picked up to one a week. Now, it seems like every hour I have a crisis. It can be anything—sexual harassment, drug problems, suicides, or guns on the school grounds."

Pam and Richard briefly discuss other crises occurring at the school. Then Richard pushes himself away from the wall and starts to walk away. He pauses, turns back toward Pam, and says, "My job has really changed over the years and what's worse, all too often this school is some of these kids' only home!"

❋ ❋ ❋ ❋ ❋

Changing Student Needs
and a Teacher's Role

There is little doubt that educators face more intense challenges with students today than they did 30 years ago. Students come to school socially and emotionally depleted and ill-prepared to learn. At home, students live with parental indifference, social isolation, hopelessness, and even physical and emotional abuse and neglect. Some students deal with even more difficult home situations such as parental mental illness, alcoholism, drug addiction, or criminal behavior. All these unfavorable social conditions place young people at risk of becoming involved in unproductive or even self-destructive behavior. An at-risk or high-risk youth is defined as one who is facing two obstacles to healthy development: the inner obstacle of unmet needs and the outer obstacle of increasing environmental stresses (Burns, 1994). Even young people who come from loving, supportive homes can become at risk, especially during adolescence, because of negative peer pressure or antagonistic environmental conditions. Adverse living conditions are threatening the healthy emotional and social development of children. They are obstacles that young people must successfully overcome if they are to grow up to be productive, well-adjusted adults. Unfortunately, many young people simply survive these adverse situations by engaging in their own self-destructive activities, such as drug and alcohol abuse, dropping out of school, or gang activities. Such self-destructive behaviors place these kids at risk for perpetuating the cycle of poverty, abuse, or criminal activity with which they grew up. The doors to what otherwise may have been bright futures close.

As educators, we are all too familiar with the adverse situations students deal with daily and with the feelings of hopelessness and powerlessness as we watch young people set themselves on a pathway to self-destruction. We know the problems. Frustrated, disheartened, and sometimes overwhelmed, we want answers. We need to learn effective, appropriate ways to deal with the complicated human situations we must face daily in the classroom.

This book describes appropriate, effective ways for teachers to help students deal with the adverse situations they face. It illustrates ways teachers can make a difference for the growing number of students living in high-risk situations or living at-risk lives. Based on a qualitative study completed in 1994 (Deiro, 1994), this book illustrates an appropriate role teachers can assume to help these students. This role is not another add-on to further overload a teacher's current busy schedule. The suggested role involves teacher behaviors that are natural, intrinsic parts of a teacher's responsibilities. In essence, this book suggests ways for teachers to simultaneously improve their teaching skills and help at-risk students.

The book begins with a discussion about ways teachers can make a difference for students by presenting evidence that demonstrates the importance of building meaningful connections with young people. It affirms that the most powerful and effective way teachers can help young people overcome the negative impact of adverse situations and become productive citizens is by developing a close and trusting relationship with their students. The book first establishes that the healthy development of children in today's society is dependent on more adults becoming meaningfully involved in children's lives. Then using this premise, it explores an appropriate role teachers can assume that allows them to become meaningfully involved in the lives of their students.

Bonding as a Key to
Healthy Adolescent Development

Bonding with prosocial adults has been identified as the key protective factor buffering children against the influence of adverse situations (Benard, 1991; Brook, Brook, Gordon, Whiteman, & Cohen, 1990; Hawkins, Catalano, & Miller, 1992). Prosocial here refers to individuals who obey the laws of society and respect our social norms. For example, bonds with a parent who smokes marijuana or who disrespects the law do not foster healthy social and emotional development, whereas bonds with a parent who models good work habits, chooses not to abuse drugs, and shows active concern for the welfare of others do promote healthy development. It does not seem to matter what the adverse situation is (e.g., living in poverty or a high-crime area, with parental indifference or social isolation); being bonded with at least one prosocial adult mediates the negative impact of such adverse circumstances. Children value adults who value them. Thus, children who are living in seemingly intolerable situations but who have a prosocial adult outside their home environment who cares about them will adjust their behavior to carefully safeguard that relationship. In doing so, the child begins to internalize the prosocial value system of the caring adult. For that reason, bonds with prosocial adults are essential for a child's healthy social and emotional development (Bowlby, 1988; Bronfenbrenner, 1986; Brook et al., 1990; Glenn, 1982). Without appropriate relationships with prosocial adults, a child's opportunity for healthy social and emotional development is markedly impaired.

Decreasing Opportunities for Bonding

Today, there are too few prosocial adults actively involved in the lives of children. Our rapid-paced, geographically mobile lifestyle makes it difficult to find enough time and energy to develop meaningful connections with young people. As a result, the number of positive, productive adults available for relationships with children is eroding (Bronfenbrenner, 1986; Coleman, 1985b, 1987a, 1988; Glenn, 1989; Hodgkinson, 1991). No longer can a child expect to have a grandma or an aunt nearby to offer hugs and reassurance during difficult family times. No longer is there an uncle to attend a child's school play when mom has to work or dad is drunk.

Children need these networks of caring, prosocial adults actively involved in their lives in order to develop into well-adjusted, prosocial adults. As a result, the social and emotional needs of children today are not being met in ways that foster their healthy development. Without their social and emotional needs being met, young people are at risk of becoming involved in unproductive or self-destructive behavior. In essence, because of our urban lifestyle and the rapid-paced, geographical mobility of society, most young people today can be considered at risk.

Since 1940, U.S. society has undergone tremendous changes in demography, economic structure, and lifestyle. These changes have reduced the number of prosocial adults meaningfully involved in the lives of young people. Until the Great Depression, the United States was primarily a nation of people who lived in rural areas or small communities. By the 1950s, this census statistic had changed. Due to a combination of factors such as the baby boom, easy mobility, and job opportunities in cities, by the 1950s the United States was a nation of people who lived primarily in large cities or suburbs. With the migration to the cities, young families lost the nurturing and support of large extended families, lifelong friends, close neighbors, and the familiarity common among people in small rural communities. Along with the loss of extended family members living close by came the loss of multigenerational child-rearing practices. Other demographic changes, such as increases in the number of primary caregivers working outside the home and the number of single-parent families, have further depleted the number of prosocial adults actively involved in the lives of children.

The demographic trends of the 1940s and 1950s also brought changes in educational institutions, which further decreased the number of prosocial adults involved in the lives of children. The baby boom of the 1950s brought with it large, consolidated schools. Census statistics show that the numbers of high schools stayed relatively the same from 1930 to 1970 despite the population boom (Coleman, 1974). Schools were reorganized from small schools in small districts to large, consolidated schools in huge districts. Classroom size shot up from an average of 20 students per classroom to an average of 36 students per classroom (Glenn, 1989). More students per classroom and larger schools create fewer opportunities for students and teachers to make individual contact or engage in meaningful dialogue. These conditions decrease the opportunities for quality connections between teacher and student and further reduce the availability of prosocial adults with whom young people can develop close and trusting relationships.

Finally, advances in technology also have contributed to the decrease of quality connections between adults and children. Technological advances such as the television, videocassette player, and computer make life more pleasant but cut down on opportunities for meaningful interaction. Television is a passive, relaxing, low-concentration activity. The average American family spends 4 to 6 hours a day watching television. Twenty-five percent of all time spent at home by family members is spent watching television, not in talking to one another (Kubey & Csikszentmihalyi, 1990). Television is gradually taking the place of the social infrastructure that creates a sense of purpose and belonging—meaningful dialogue, bonding, and quality time with adults. Some child development experts proclaim the influence of television on children today has surpassed the influence of church, family, and schools. These institutions were once considered the teachers and shapers of our nation's children. Television producers and main TV characters hold that responsibility now.

These tremendous changes in demography, economic structure, and lifestyle apparent in today's society have diminished opportunities for adults to be meaningfully involved in the lives of children. In earlier times when we lived in small communities and had large extended families, networks of prosocial adults were readily available to form close and trusting relationships with children. Everyone knew their neighbors and their neighbors' kin. Young people spent time in the company of older, more mature members of the community. Communities took responsibility for raising a child. Children often worked side by side with their parents or other adults. Neighbors, friends, and extended family all provided guidance and support for the rearing of children. Bonds among older and younger group members developed more readily.

Now it is difficult for adults to find quality time to spend with young people. Intergenerational bonds are difficult to form. Without these bonds, the older generation has a hard time playing a key role in shaping the emotional and social development of young people. Of course, the past was not perfect and all children did not live in caring communities. But today there are fewer opportunities for adults to develop healthy bonds with children because of our rapid-paced, geographically mobile society.

For generations we relied, often unknowingly, on intergenerational bonding to nurture the healthy development of our young people. Now our nation faces the consequences of not having a network of familiar adults forming close relationships with young people. And painfully, we see the repercussions of that loss acted out in their behavior. Many problems that teachers face in their students today result from the lack of prosocial adults meaningfully involved in the lives of children.

Rebuilding the Network of Caring Adults

It is unlikely that the trends of modern society are going to reverse. In working toward a solution, we cannot plan on returning to the past when women stayed at home or the majority of Americans lived on farms or in small communities. Present economic demands, personal desires, and technological advances preclude that lifestyle. We need to discover ways to increase the number of caring adults actively involved in children's lives within our fast-paced, geographically mobile lifestyle. Those of us who are regularly in touch with young people need to discover ways to use the time we do have with children wisely and constructively. We need to understand how to develop close and trusting relationships with young people within limited time frames, with limited contacts, and with limited resources.

Parents, primary caregivers, extended family members, close friends, neighbors, community members, and youth leaders can all play important roles in rebuilding the network of caring adults surrounding young people. But of all the various professionals who have the potential to change young lives, probably no one has greater potential than a teacher. Besides parents and primary caregivers, teachers have the greatest access to the most children. Teachers are in touch with young people 6 hours a day for 9 months of the year. For this reason, teachers are potentially a rich resource for rebuilding the network of supportive, caring adults needed by young people.

To be a rich resource for young people though, we educators may need to reframe our primary professional responsibilities to include making healthy connections with students. Educators may need to think about teaching and schooling in unfamiliar ways. More teachers need to discover and advocate appropriate ways to become meaningfully involved in students' lives. Educational administrators need to find ways to support and encourage teachers who are developing caring relationships with students. School restructuring efforts need to include development of caring school environments as a priority. If this is done, teachers can help buffer the negative impact of high-risk situations that students face and, in turn, enhance the healthy development of at-risk young people. And we educators will play a fundamental and significant role in making a difference in their lives.

Meeting Students' Emotional and Social Needs

As discussed earlier, because of societal conditions, most young people today are at risk of becoming involved in unproductive or self-destructive behavior. The obstacles young people face that interfere with their healthy, prosocial development are both the increasing environmental stresses and unmet developmental needs. Aware of these developmental difficulties, educational researchers and administrators have been exploring approaches to addressing the problem. In an effort to relieve some of the environmental stresses, some schools or school districts are developing collaborative relationships with social service agencies. In these situations, social workers, chemical dependency counselors, nurses and physicians, law enforcement officers, and so on work on school grounds in efforts to reduce a particular environmental stress as well as to promote student prosocial development.

Other educational theorists and researchers choose to focus on the unmet developmental needs of students. They are advocating that schools become places that nurture the emotional as well as the academic needs of students (Martin, 1992; McLaughlin & Talbert, 1990; Noddings, 1992; Sergiovanni, 1993). These theorists believe that it is time to take full account of the changes that have swept our culture in the past 50 years. It is time for educators to acknowledge that the traditional, extended family is quickly becoming an anachronism. Alone and isolated, today's families cannot meet the social and emotional needs of their children. Other societal institutions need to step up and support families in their efforts to meet these needs.

Educational theorists argue for teachers to take a more active role in nurturing students. They contend that school success is as dependent on caring and nurturing students as it is on promoting academic achievement. For instance, Noddings (1988) claims that when schools focus on what really matters in life—the social and emotional needs for caring—the academic success teachers strive for so diligently will happen naturally. She says, "It is obvious that children will work harder and do things—even odd things like adding fractions—for people they love and trust" (p. 10). And this is true. Research bears out that when students' emotional and social needs are met they learn better (Coleman, 1985a, 1987b; Earls, Beardslee, & Garrison, 1987; O'Donnell, Hawkins, Catalano, Abbott, & Day, 1995).

The need for teachers to assume a role in meeting the social and emotional needs of children is clear. What that role may look like is not so clear. Teachers are not social workers or parents. A teacher's primary responsibility is for the academic development of students, not their social and emotional development. As such, questions arise about the nature of the teacher's role and the place and function of nurturing behavior in it. One concern is that if teachers assume a more nurturing role, they will essentially become counselors or social workers. Or even worse, teachers will enable parents to abdicate their responsibilities by doing the parents' job for them.

The next section addresses these concerns. It examines where the responsibility for nurturing students falls within the teacher's role. To distinguish the teacher-student relationship from others, it describes four types of social relationships and identifies criteria for determining what type of nurturing behavior is appropriate for teacher-student relationships.

The Nurturing Teacher

When one attempts to visualize an appropriate role for teachers in nurturing the needs of at-risk students, images are foggy. More often than not, images involve adaptations of the role of social worker, counselor, or parent. There is no clear picture of how teachers can meet the social and emotional needs of students without taking on one of these other roles. When teachers assume a more active role in promoting the overall development of students, there is a potential for role confusion. Therefore, it is important for educators to discover ways to nurture developmental needs that do not compromise their primary academic responsibilities.

Teacher-Student Bonding
and the Role of a Teacher

Developing positive personal relationships with students is now recognized by many as a valued and important part of a teacher's responsibilities (Goodlad, 1990; Lieberman & Miller, 1984; Noddings, 1988, 1992). Building caring relationships is one way teachers enhance their primary responsibility for the academic development of students and, at the same time, promote the healthy social and emotional growth of students. As such, developing healthy teacher-student bonds is a natural and integral part of being a teacher. Teacher-student bonding means the teacher and student have developed a close and trusting personal relationship involving an emotional connection with a sensitivity about what the other thinks and feels (Hirschi, 1969). Focusing on the student side of the relationship, when students are bonded to a teacher they are confident that the teacher cares for them. They enjoy being near the teacher, and they orient their behavior toward the teacher's likes and dislikes, even in the teacher's absence. And they become distressed when something threatens to disrupt the relationship.

Recent research on bonding is helping educators define an appropriate role for teachers in working with the social and emotional needs of their students. As discussed earlier in the chapter, children need networks of caring, prosocial adults actively involved in their lives in order to grow and develop into well-adjusted, prosocial young adults. If bonding with prosocial adults facilitates healthy development, then teacher-student bonding may promote the healthy development of students.

The Potential Power of Teacher-Student Bonding

Although research is limited, the few studies done suggest that teachers who do bond with students make powerful impacts on their lives. For example, in a 30-year longitudinal study with Asian American children living in adverse and discordant home conditions, Werner and Smith (1992) traced factors that helped these children grow up to be successful, well-adjusted adults. They call these children *resilient*, which means they have the ability to rebound or recover from adversities that have the potential for serious psychological harm. The successful adults in this longitudinal study most frequently mentioned a favorite teacher as the person who really made a difference for them. This teacher was not only an academic instructor but also a confidant and positive role model for students.

Another study (Moskovitz, 1983) also identified caring, responsive teachers as having positive, long-term effects on their students. Moskovitz did a follow-up study with 24 Nazi concentration camp survivors who were children when held captive by the Nazis. These individuals were sent to an orphanage in England at the end of World War II. In follow-up interviews with these survivors 37 years later, Moskovitz was amazed at the positive feelings they had about life. The survivors attributed these positive feelings to a teacher in their orphanage who provided them with warmth and caring and encouraged them to treat others with compassion.

Other studies acknowledge the impact of caring teachers on students. One study reveals that a caring, prosocial first-grade teacher helped children from a disadvantaged, urban neighborhood overcome adversity and become successful, prosocial adults (Pedersen, Faucher, & Eaton, 1978). Another study (O'Donnell et al., 1995) found that bonding to teachers is associated with a decrease in delinquency or behavioral problems, an increase in social and academic skills, and higher scores on a standardized achievement test. A study by McLaughlin and

Talbert (1990) suggests personal bonds with adults in the school have greater capacity to motivate and engage students academically than do the more traditional forms of social controls that emphasize obedience to authority or conforming to rules. Finally, Rutter (1987), in his study of the impact of adverse home conditions on children, concluded that children from disadvantaged and discordant homes are less likely to develop emotional problems if they attend schools that have attentive personnel and good academic records. All the studies mentioned above give evidence of a positive association between a connection with a caring, supportive teacher and the prosocial development of young people.

In addition to the studies just mentioned, prevention specialists have identified bonding with prosocial secondary caregivers such as teachers as the key protective factor (Brook et al., 1990; Glenn, 1982; Hawkins et al., 1992). Prevention specialists are theorists and researchers who seek ways to prevent high-risk behaviors (e.g., drug usage, dropping out of school, illicit sexual behavior, teenage parenthood) that interfere with the healthy emotional and social development of young people. Seeking to understand and identify factors that protect young people from high-risk behaviors, prevention specialists also have affirmed the importance of caring relationships with teachers. Models for preventing high-risk behavior designed by prevention specialists advocate bonding between teacher and student as a strategy for promoting prosocial behavior in young people.

In light of the above research, as well as what we as educators know intuitively, there is little doubt of the potentially powerful influence of a caring and supportive bond between teacher and student. As such, identifying an effective way for teachers to help students overcome adversity may be as simple as describing role-appropriate ways to build close and trusting relationships with students. It sounds simple, yet when we set about to explore possible role-appropriate ways to build close and trusting relationships, information is disturbingly scant. Despite teachers' need to understand how to develop this vital relationship, little energy has been put into understanding the dynamics of building caring, emotional connections. This becomes even more disturbing when we acknowledge how difficult it really is to make this relationship work. As Goodlad (1990) points out, the skills, understandings, and sensitivities necessary to make such a relationship work often are not automatically acquired as one becomes a mature adult.

If we could understand more about what makes the teacher-student relationship work, we might be able to equip teachers with some principles and practical skills for building close and trusting relationships. Equipped with the necessary skills, understandings, and sensitivities, more teachers could be nurturing and shaping the social and emotional development of young people.

Appropriate Ways to Develop
Close and Trusting Relationships

Understanding appropriate ways for teachers to develop close and trusting relationships with students is contingent on understanding the unique characteristics of teacher-student relationships as compared with other social relationships. These unique characteristics help clarify what is appropriate nurturing behavior for a teacher. The next section distinguishes four types of social relationships, highlighting the distinct characteristics of the teacher-student relationship.

Four Types of Social Relationships

One way to distinguish between different types of social relationships is to look at the purpose for the relationship. Using this approach, Bennis, Schein, Steele, and Berlew (1968) describe four distinct types of social relationships: expressive-emotional, confirmatory, instrumental, and influential. An expressive-emotional relationship is formed for the purpose of fulfilling itself. It is enacted in the form of friendship, romance, love, and marriage. We commonly think about this type of relationship when discussing social or intimate relationships. In fact, we are bombarded daily with reference to the expressive-emotional relationship. Songs proclaim its virtues; books and films are created around the theme.

On the other hand, a confirmatory relationship is formed for the purpose of confirming information about self or clarifying social realities or beliefs. For instance, acquaintances in the same church or social club are confirmatory relationships. They affirm one another's belief systems and help establish one another's identity. Norms within social groups help establish appropriate behavior and thus confirm a social reality for group members.

The third type of relationship is the instrumental relationship. It is formed in order to achieve a goal. The main focus of an instrumental relationship is a task. Colleagues and peer work-related relationships and collaborators on research projects or political campaigns are examples of instrumental relationships.

Finally, the influential relationship is formed for the purpose of creating a change in one or both parties in the relationship. A teacher-student relationship is an example of an influential relationship. Parent-child, counselor-client, doctor-patient, and parole officer-parolee relationships are other examples.

Nurturing behavior within an influential relationship is the focus of this book. The next section discusses the distinct characteristics of an influential relationship in detail. Knowing these characteristics is essential to define appropriate teacher behaviors that nurture and support the building of close and trusting teacher-student connections.

Characteristics of an Influential Relationship

Influential relationships are distinguished from other social relationships by several distinct characteristics (Bennis et al., 1968). First, the central concerns are *change, growth,* or *learning.* A pivotal concern of the change-agent (e.g., teacher) in an influential relationship is acquisition or modification of behaviors or attitudes of the change-target (e.g., student). In addition, the change, growth, or learning produced in influential relationships is *planned and not usually spontaneous or accidental.* Second, when the relationship reaches the point in which continuation will not lead to significant advances in learning, it should be discontinued as an influential relationship. Therefore, learning that began in the relationship needs to be internalized by the change-target so that it will continue after the influential relationship has been discontinued. In a healthy influential relationship, the goal is termination (e.g., graduation, discharge, parole). Third, healthy influential relationships have an asymmetrical distribution of power among participants. The change-agent holds more power than the change-target. With this asymmetrical balance of power comes responsibility. The change-agent is expected to give more, to know more, and to understand more than the change-target, rather than the other way around. As a rule, students learn from teachers, clients learn from counselors, and patients learn from doctors. In influential relationships, the needs of the change-target must take precedence over the needs of the change-agent. In a teacher-student relationship, the needs of the student take precedence over the needs of the teacher. In summary, the characteristics of healthy influential relationships are intentional promotion of growth and change, fostering independence through encouraging internalization of learning, and respectful use of an asymmetrical balance of power.

The Parameters and Ethics of
Nurturing Behavior in Influential Relationships

The type and purpose of a social relationship provide a useful guideline for defining what behavior is nurturing within each type of relationship. The four types of relationships mentioned are governed by different norms and codes of behavior. What may be considered nurturing and appropriate behavior in one type of relationship may not be nurturing and appropriate in another. For instance, whispering sweet nothings in the ear of a spouse may be nurturing behavior, whereas whispering sweet nothings in the ear of a student may be grounds for a sexual harassment or sexual abuse suit. Because the purpose of an influential relationship is different from that of an expressive-emotional relationship, it follows that behavior considered nurturing in an influential relationship also may be different. When determining if a teacher's behavior is nurturing and appropriate, the characteristics of a healthy influential relationship—intentional promotion of growth and change, empowerment of students through internalization of learning, and respectful use of power—become criteria for determining appropriate nurturing behaviors for teachers.

Because the influential relationship of a teacher and student has the unique characteristic of being asymmetrical in nature, a possible ethical dilemma is introduced for teachers who bond with students. This is particularly relevant and important in today's society in which sexual abuse and harassment are prominent concerns. As stated earlier, teachers are expected to be more mature and to give more in the relationship. Student needs are to be prioritized first. Altering the purpose of the relationship to be more in tune with an expressive-emotional relationship—a relationship formed for the purpose of friendship, romance, love, and marriage—is inappropriate and unhealthy. One should ask whose needs are being met. The asymmetrical nature of an influential relationship always defines the student as the more vulnerable member of the dyad. Because of the vulnerability of the student, behaving in a teacher-student relationship as the teacher might in an expressive-emotional relationship is not only not nurturing but unethical. Teachers need to remain cognizant of the imbalance of power when bonding with students and in maintaining relationships beyond the classroom.

Although a goal of an influential relationship is termination, the purpose of the relationship may be redefined to that of an expressive-emotional, confirmatory, or instrumental relationship after termination. There are many hazards involved in making such a change, however. Before such redefinition, the original purpose for forming an influential relationship should be explicitly completed. Such completion is usually signaled by a ritual, process, or formal activity. Even then, some influential relationships are not appropriate for redefinition. For example, with parent-child relationships, children throughout their lives usually hold a special esteem for their parents. Even when children move into adulthood and their relationship with their parents takes on the characteristics of an expressive-emotional relationship, a parent still holds a place of honor and esteem in the adult child's eyes and the child still holds a place of responsibility in the parent's eyes. The same is true for the teacher-student relationship. Even though students may mature and move into full adulthood, teachers from their past continue to hold a place of honor and esteem in their eyes because of the important role the teacher once played in the adult's individual growth and development.

Redefining an influential relationship as a confirmatory or instrumental relationship is usually ethically less sensitive than redefining an influential relationship as an expressive-emotional relationship. Only when two individuals who were involved in an influential relationship are separated for a significant period of time, usually 2 years, and then meet again on an equal footing is the development of an expressive-emotional relationship ethically defensible. Even then, care must be taken that the relationship is on an equal footing. Usually if a relationship originally started as an influential relationship, it is ethically safest to behave as if the relationship is still on such a basis—even though no learning is being consciously planned and produced.

A Teacher's Nurturing Role

We now know that healthy bonds with prosocial adults are essential for a child's healthy prosocial development. Because teachers have a responsibility to build effective connections with students, such healthy bonds can be formed with young people as a natural, intrinsic part of the job of a teacher. Thus, teachers who so desire can play a vital role in prosocial development of young people. As such, teachers provide a rich pool of prosocial adults to whom young people can bond. We also know that some teachers do form such bonds with students and that these bonds have had a powerful effect on the prosocial development of students. Such bonds have made a difference for many young people living in adverse or discordant conditions.

Though research suggests a natural, intrinsic role for teachers in shaping the prosocial development of young people, it gives us little information on how teachers accomplish this task. Developing caring relationships requires an adult to give individual-focused time, attention, and support to the child. So then what do teachers do to make caring, emotional connections with a whole classroom of students? What skills and sensitivities are helpful in developing close and trusting relationships with students? Do these skills and sensitivities help students accept the nurturing of the teacher? With these primary questions left unanswered, how can teachers who are interested in helping young people reach their highest potential assume such a role with confidence and some assurance of success?

This book, and the research study it describes (Deiro, 1994), attempts to answer these central concerns for educators. The particular focus of this book is on secondary schoolteachers because they are faced with the greatest environmental obstacles when they assume the task of developing close and trusting relationships with students. Unlike elementary- or postsecondary-level teachers, secondary-level teachers' workdays are usually scheduled around 50-minute segments of time with 25 to 30 students. These workbound restrictions leave the secondary teacher little time to give individual students the attention and support necessary to nurture a bond. Still, some are able to do it successfully.

In addition, whatever secondary teachers do, it is not clear precisely how they communicate caring to students. No matter how hard teachers try to connect with students, if students do not interpret what teachers do as caring, bonds between teachers and students will not develop. Therefore, it is essential to identify not only what secondary teachers do that nurtures bonds but also what communicates to students that they are cared for by the teacher.

Finally, given the constraints under which they operate, secondary schoolteachers who attempt to build close and trusting relationships with students clearly face a difficult, and sometimes overwhelming, task. There is little research that addresses the personal characteristics and resources enabling secondary teachers to overcome environmental obstacles and develop nurturing relationships with students. The study recounted in this book describes the personal characteristics, beliefs, and skills of teachers who successfully bond with students despite the environmental restrictions placed on them. Given that teacher-student relationships are asymmetrical and that nurturing teachers can easily become emotionally drained, the book examines how teachers who bond with students replenish their emotional reserves. Teachers are expected to give more, if needed, than they receive from students. How do teachers who nurture students all day long maintain their own professional and personal energies? Knowing these personal resources may give a window to understanding teachers who nurture students despite what may seem like impossible barriers.

Although student response to a teacher's caring is significant in the forming of a teacher-student bond, this book does not examine the many student variables that moderate a teacher-student bond. Nor does it focus on the dynamics of the bonding process between teacher and student. Students enter school environments with different degrees of vulnerability to adverse conditions. A student's degree of social and emotional neediness plays an unpredictable role in his or her receptiveness to a relationship with a prosocial teacher. Some students bond more easily than others. Because of the many possible student variables, students are silent partners in the teacher-student relationship in this book. The focus here is only on the behavior of teachers who nurture healthy teacher-student relationships.

The next chapter answers some of the questions presented here by describing strategies that six nurturing teachers use to develop close and trusting relationships with students. (A characterization of each of the teachers and of their schools and a description of the research strategy for the study are located in Appendix A.) Chapter 3 discusses how these six teachers communicate caring to their students so that students interpret the teacher's behavior as nurturing. Chapter 4 identifies personal beliefs that motivate and encourage nurturing behavior, which these teachers hold in common. It also discusses strategies that these teachers use to revitalize themselves after

particularly stressful days. Chapter 5 describes the personal characteristics and skills the six nurturing teachers hold in common. These
characteristics and skills appear to sustain and revitalize these teachers in their efforts to nurture students. Chapter 6 identifies an ideal
school environment for supporting teachers who want to nurture
students. Using the parts of the ideal environment that are present
within the workplaces of the six teachers, it shows how specific
environmental characteristics might support nurturing teachers. Finally, Chapter 7 summarizes the strategies for nurturing students
and the personal and workplace resources that support and revitalize nurturing teachers. It discusses implications of the strategies for
nurturing and resources for revitalization and answers key questions
that may concern the reader.

Making Healthy Connections
With Students

🕸 🕸 🕸 🕸 🕸

*It is a late Thursday afternoon right before spring break at Suburb
Junior High. The familiar electrifying energy common before a spring break
is in the air. The children are excited; the teachers are eager. Pam, a social
studies teacher at Suburb Junior High School, is staying late after school to
be interviewed by me. She was identified by her supervisors, colleagues, and
students as a well-respected teacher who develops close and trusting relationships with her students. Pam is one of six teachers from three different
secondary schools I have selected to observe and interview as part of a study
on teachers' nurturing behavior. This is the fourth and final interview. Pam
is leaning back in her chair in a relaxed position as she responds to the
questions.*

"The last question is open-ended . . . anything you would like to add?"

Pam thinks for a moment. "You know, I never really considered myself
a very nurturing teacher until you showed up. I never thought of it one way
or another. So I'm just really surprised that you would even want to talk to
me about this stuff!"

"What is your image of a nurturing teacher?"

"I don't know." *Pam pauses while she thinks. Then she begins again.*
"I get this feeling . . . like my kindergarten teacher was real nurturing." *Pam*

laughs as she reminisces. "She used to feed us cookies and we'd have naps. That's what I think of when I think of nurturing . . . like a mom, you know." Pam laughs again, pauses, and then quickly adds, "I mean, I'm not like these kids' mother. I mean, I get the image of this kind of round, gray-haired matron, right, . . . who always smells like fresh-baked bread or something."

※   ※   ※   ※   ※

Strategies for Bonding With Students

Pam's image of a nurturing person is not unusual. Neither is the idea that she did not see herself in that image. Every teacher has personal impressions and beliefs about behaviors that nurture. These impressions tend to color their thoughts on the topic. Pam associated nurturing with gentle mothering. Others believe nurturing is more loosely connected with warmth, empathy, and gentleness. This study uncovers something quite different. Two fundamental questions addressed by this study are the following: What do secondary teachers do to nurture bonding with students? What lets students know that teachers care for them? Six teachers from three different secondary schools were selected to be interviewed and closely observed working in their classrooms. These six teachers were identified by their supervisors, colleagues, and students as excellent teachers who develop close and trusting relationships with their students. (A brief description of the research methodology plus a characterization of each of the teachers and the schools in which they work can be found in Appendix A.) This chapter offers vivid illustrations of the strategies for bonding used by the six nurturing teachers. Then, the next chapter describes the behaviors in which these teachers engage that communicate caring to students and encourage student openness to effective connections with teachers.

The six teachers observed use one or more of the following six strategies for bonding with students:

1. Creating one-to-one time with students
2. Using appropriate self-disclosure
3. Having high expectations of students while conveying a belief in their capabilities
4. Networking with parents, family members, friends, and neighbors of students

Table 2.1 Teachers and Their Strategies for Bonding

	One-to-One Time	Self-Disclosure	High Expectations	Networking With Parents	Community Building	Rituals and Traditions
Dale	X			✓		
Dean	X	✓				
Gail	X			✓		✓
Pam	✓	X				
Ruby	✓	✓			✓	✓
Tom	✓	X	X			

NOTE: X = Primary strategy used; ✓ = Augmenting strategy used.

5. Building a sense of community among students within the classroom

6. Using rituals and traditions within the classroom

As indicated in Table 2.1, three strategies are used as the primary ways for a teacher to bond with students: (a) creating one-to-one time with students, (b) using appropriate self-disclosure, and (c) having high expectations while conveying a belief in students' capabilities. Creating one-to-one time with students and using appropriate self-disclosure are the most common strategies employed by the teachers.

One-to-one time is used by all the teachers, with three teachers relying on this strategy as their primary technique for bonding. Appropriate self-disclosure is used by four teachers, with two teachers relying primarily on this strategy as their principal technique. One teacher uses the strategy of having high expectations while conveying a belief in students' capabilities as a primary strategy for bonding with students.

Four other strategies also are evident, although these additional four strategies are not used as primary strategies by any of the six nurturing teachers. Instead they are used to augment the primary strategy. Or as illustrated by Ruby, who had no primary strategy for bonding, they are used in combination with each other so that together they create enough influence to facilitate bonding. These six strategies for bonding suggest there is a repertoire of nurturing behaviors for teachers that builds close and trusting connections with students.

The strategies outlined are assumed to be the basis for the bond that has developed between student and teacher. There is no way to verify that the behavior observed and identified actually creates bonds. However, what is clear is the following: (a) There is a bond between these teachers and their students, as evidenced by the inventories students took measuring closeness and trust with the teacher (see Appendix B); and (b) theoretically, these behaviors do develop feelings of closeness and trust among individuals.

Creating One-to-One Time

Psychologists have long suggested that when individuals spend one-to-one time together while engaged in a caring or responsive dialogue, a bond develops between those individuals. Familiarity and trust form a basis for the bond. The more time one spends with another, the more one has the opportunity to know and trust the other. The more experiences individuals share in a caring and supportive atmosphere, the more likely a bond is to develop. This argument suggests that the more time a teacher spends with a student showing caring and concern for that student, the more that student will develop feelings of closeness and trust with that teacher. Time spent sharing the same or similar experiences and caring about each other should provide a familiarity and a common history that allows a bond to develop and grow.

Common Ways Teachers Create One-to-One Time

With more than 140 students, creating one-to-one time with each seems like an impossible task for a secondary teacher. Yet all six nurturing teachers use some variation of this strategy. Although there are many differences in how this strategy is employed, there are some key similarities. All six teachers make themselves accessible to students before class, between classes, and after school. They arrive early to open their rooms for whomever wants to drop in to talk with them. They stay after school for students to drop by and talk. They station themselves by the classroom door when the bell rings to make themselves accessible to students entering and leaving the classroom. They reach out and clasp the hands of students who reach out for them. They talk to students or connect with them nonverbally in the halls between classes. In essence, these teachers remain focused on students throughout the day.

> As I walk to lunch or somewhere else, [I] could be focused on
> where I have to get and what I'm going to do, and *not* say hello
> or anything to any of the kids. But [I stay alert], especially in
> junior high, because they are so social. I mean, if you walk by
> and don't say anything, they take that as an insult. (Tom)

Extensive involvement in extracurricular activities is another way all
of the observed teachers create more one-to-one time with students. In the
interviews, each teacher identified extracurricular activities as a key way
to create one-to-one time with students. Therefore, they extend themselves beyond the classroom in a variety of school-sponsored activities
such as coaching, field trips, dramatic plays, or sporting events.

Finally, these teachers are open for conversations with students.
The teacher's openness to conversation encourages students to connect
with teachers on a one-to-one basis. None of these teachers are uncomfortable having students talk to them about whatever is on the students'
minds. These teachers establish trust and credibility by keeping confi-
dentiality with students, which encourages one-to-one conversations.
They have learned how not to take responsibility for solving student
problems but rather how to be good listeners, be supportive, and make
referrals whenever possible. They know how important it is for students
to feel free to talk about whatever they want to share. And they remember the influence on their own lives made by teachers who listened to
them when they were students.

> I want kids to feel okay talk[ing] to me about anything. Other
> [teachers] might not want that. . . . It goes back to my own
> personal [educational] experience with having a couple of
> people with an educational background really help me out
> when I was really going through tough times. And if they
> had put those walls up and said, "I can't talk to you about
> this. . . . This has nothing to do with class. . . . I don't want to
> talk to you about this," that could have really affected how
> I turned out. I don't have any problems with kids talking to
> me about issues. I want them to feel safe if they want to write
> that they've experienced something. (Ruby)

These teachers give freely of their time, which encourages conversations with students. Students know they can have the teacher's time
if only they ask for it.

She just holds out her arms for anybody and welcomes new people and just is there for anybody who ever needs to talk. (Peter, student)

She goes out of her way to get to know some people. . . . I remember when I first went into her class. She kind of let you know that she was there to listen to you and she's just a real sweet person and she goes out of her way to get to know kids. (Sally, student)

These general techniques, such as making oneself accessible to students, being open for conversations with students about anything, and giving freely of one's time for individual conversations with students, are used by all the observed teachers in their efforts to create one-to-one time with students.

Distinct Ways Teachers Create One-to-One Time

Although all of the teachers use the in-common ways described above to create one-to-one time with students, three distinct techniques for creating one-to-one time emerged: (a) designing curriculum that maximizes individual or small-group contact, (b) interspersing personal and academic talk, and (c) using direct personal dialogue during nonclass time. One of these three techniques was used when the strategy of one-to-one time with students was the primary way a teacher built bonds with students. When other primary strategies were used to build a bond with students, two additional distinct techniques for creating one-to-one time with students were observed: (a) using written comments and (b) using nonverbal communication of touching and physical closeness. These two additional techniques were used to augment or reinforce other strategies employed for bonding with students.

The following section characterizes each of these distinct techniques for creating one-to-one time with students. Along with each characterization is an extended illustration or pertinent example of the technique being used by a teacher.

Designing curriculum to maximize individual or small-group contact. One way for creating one-to-one time with students when there are 25 to 30 students in a classroom is to design curriculum so students work on projects in small groups of three or four people during class time. The teacher then interacts with these small groups, giving individual attention to each group. With only six to eight groups to interact with, the teacher is able to focus attention on and engage in meaningful dialogue with each group or particular members of a group. When one member of the small group is addressed, all members tend to feel involved in the conversation, especially when the dialogue focuses on the project for which the entire small group is responsible.

Dean, a biology teacher at Inner-City High School, provides an example of designing curriculum to create one-to-one time with students. He designs his curriculum to be small-group oriented, consisting primarily of experiential activities and exercises. He arranges his classroom so students work in clusters of three, four, or five, creating about 7 to 10 small pods. He spends little class time lecturing. At the beginning of class, he briefly describes and assigns a group activity. Then he races around to all the tables responding to individual student concerns, interacting on a one-to-one basis or with a small group. When asked how he sees himself creating quality time with each student he says,

> You just gotta rush around and it's hard. You know something? You saw those classrooms. Second and fifth periods are less rowdy because there are less kids. I can get to more [students], and there are more [students] on task. Third and sixth periods I have a helluva lot of kids. There are 35 and 36. That's too many kids in a science classroom. And it's too many inner-city kids. . . . That third period is 35 ninth graders. Friggin' ninth graders! Oh my god! Their hormones are crazy. They're just going crazy all the time.

When talking with a student in a group, he often squats to bring himself eye-level with the student. Or he may place his elbows on the table and brace himself with them, his body in a bent-over position in order to be eye-to-eye with the student. Dean is able to remain focused on the student he is working with fairly well even though others are shouting at him and the classroom is noisy. He always uses a soft voice. Dean's ability to remain intensely focused aids him in establishing personal contact.

Dean often leaves the last 5 to 10 minutes of class for open time to socialize with students, teasing playfully or talking earnestly. This free time creates more time for Dean to establish personal contact with his students, although this is not his primary reason for structuring his lesson plans to allow for such interaction. Dean empathizes with students' need to socialize. He believes social time helps to keep his students coming to class, a chronic concern at Inner-City High School.

> I never, ever forget what it was like when I sat in that seat. I never forget that the most important thing to me wasn't learning the life cycle. The most important thing to me was the social aspects of school, and if I can somehow incorporate those into a learning environment, then I'm going to be better off.

Interspersing personal and academic talk to create one-to-one time. When teachers intersperse personal and academic talk, students are informally and personally acknowledged intermittently during a traditional lecture or during other academic activities. The dialogue with a student may or may not be regarding the topic of the lecture or activity at hand. Although these teacher-student connections may be brief, as the following example demonstrates, they can still be meaningful for students.

Dale provides an example of adapting the traditional lecture mode to create one-to-one time with students. He teaches the class Fundamentals of Mathematics to freshmen and sophomores at Rural-City High School, using primarily a traditional lecture mode when teaching. He may take a few minutes to explain a mathematical concept on the blackboard. Then he will turn around, walk forward, and softly say something personal to a student or respond to a social question. After a moment of personal contact, Dale smoothly returns to his academic presentation. Dale does this or similar behaviors many times during a class period. The following is an example from a classroom observation:

> On the board, Dale works another problem. He stops and says to a female student, "New boots?" She answers, "No." Dale responds, "They were just shined?" She replies, "Yeah." Dale comments, "I need to get some new shoes." Other students pipe in about good types of shoes to buy. Dale listens, nods in acknowledgment, and then continues with his lecture as if it was never interrupted.

Here is another example from classroom observation:

> All of a sudden Dale says, "Did anyone see my picture in the paper?" Several students say, "Yes!" Dale says with a big grin, "You guys pass!" He returns to his lecture and adds a few more points about math and then pauses again and says, "Jane, you got your hair cut." She smiles and nods. Another female student who had her hair in a ponytail says, "I got my hair cut but you didn't notice." Dale humbly replies, "You're right. I didn't notice." He returns to the lesson at hand.

Dale uses this strategy throughout an entire class period, stopping his presentation every couple of minutes to connect with students. The class period rolls by with a unique blending of academic material and social comments. He presents a few minutes of academic material and then pauses to say something personal to a student. Or he may ask that worksheets be handed forward and during the shuffle of papers he will talk to some students. He may stop by a student's desk and ask how the new home that his or her family is building is coming along, while other students are working on math problems. He may stop to check with a quiet student making sure he or she understands the material.

Students are aware of his distinct way of establishing personal contact with them. Often they will interject a social question or comment for Dale before Dale can. For instance, after Dale has completed a problem on the board or asked for homework to be handed in, students will pipe in with a personal comment. As an example, after showing the class a trick to use to learn percentages, Dale turned to face the class. A student said, "If I buy a new pair of cleat shoes, can I play baseball?" Dale answers, without missing a beat, "Anyone can play if you can hit, run, field, and throw. Can you hit?" "Yes." "Can you run?" "Sometimes." "Can you field?" "Yes." "Can you throw?" "Yes." "Three out of four. What percentage is that?" he asks the whole class. And they smoothly returned to the lesson for the day.

In interviews, both students who sere selected commented on Dale's style of communication.

> Well, every day he tries to, and he tells us that he tries to make it a point to talk to every one of the students in his class.

And he'll be like, all of a sudden he'll stop and he'll go, "Wait! You know, hi _____. I haven't said hi to you today." And then he'll go, "Okay" and then finish what he was doing. So I mean, that makes you feel good because that shows that he cares. (Annette)

Well, he tries to talk to every person in the classroom every day. He'll ask, "How ya doing?" We all, most of the guys in there, almost everybody plays sports in there. He always asks them how their game went and who won. He knows something about every person in the classroom outside, which is nice. And he talks to everybody. (Danny)

Surprisingly, Dale was unaware he uses this style for creating one-to-one time. It comes naturally for him. And even more surprising, Dale does not lose his original train of thought when interrupted by a social comment. He simply responds or sincerely comments and then returns to his original thought without losing a beat or even appearing flustered. And surprisingly, the interruptions do not get out of hand or make the lecture seem disjointed. There just appears to be a natural, easy flow to the process.

Dale is aware that he wants to connect with each child; the motivations for his behavior are conscious and intentional.

I ask more than just "How ya doing?" "Well, what's going on? What are you going to do this weekend?" Or I find out a little bit about each kid. I try to find out something about him. Where they live, what they're doing, what do they like to do after school? Sometimes I ask them just to talk. And one time I asked that of a kid, and I found out that he flies airplanes. A 15-year-old kid who's up flying airplanes. And I thought "That's really cool!" because my dad was a pilot. And I thought "Gee, you would never know it if you just get them in class and get them out." Each of these kids has lives that—some are good. They do great things. And some are really harsh. And I figure if I can get one of them harsh kids to maybe open up just a little bit and just get something out they'll feel better. Not to use it against him, not to do nothing, just to show him that one person might care.

Using direct personal dialogue during nonclass time to create one-to-one time with students. Another way for creating one-to-one time with students during the school day is to use direct personal dialogue with students between classes, before and after school, and at school events. With this technique, the teacher retains the classroom as a quiet, academically focused environment. There is little social interaction between teacher and student during class time. Between classes and before and after school, however, the classroom becomes a hub for playful interaction and meaningful dialogue between teacher and student.

Gail provides an example of a teacher using direct personal dialogue during nonclass time to create one-to-one time with students. She teaches primarily the language arts to freshmen at Inner-City High School. Gail does not design her curriculum to create time with students, and her delivery style does not incorporate personal connections with students. In fact, in the classroom Gail runs a tight ship. She has high expectations of her students and strictly enforces the rules of class conduct. You can hear a pin drop in the classroom when students are working independently. Dean, her colleague, has much respect for her. He calls her "Iron Woman" and says, "She's as tough as nails." There is little one-to-one social interaction between her and her students during class time.

However, Gail creates quality time with students primarily by direct, personal dialogue with them before and after class, between classes, after school, at school events, and during off-hours. She gets involved in their lives. She talks to them about their personal problems or things that have happened to them over the past evening. She enjoys the students; she enjoys being part of their lives. She sits with them at sporting events. She invites them to her home. She lives within their community, so they see her in stores in the evenings and on the weekends. She has fun with students and views this added time she spends with them as pleasurable and revitalizing. Gail says, "I enjoy their company. They have a lot of interesting things to say. Some are really funny, really witty. I just like being with them."

Students gather in Gail's room before and after school and between classes, and not just to talk to Gail. Sometimes they come to talk to each other. Gail joins in on the fun. She interacts with her students much as an old-fashioned mother or big sister would, telling them what to do and how to straighten out their act. One morning before school, Gail was sweeping the floor, getting ready for the day to begin. She was chatting with a student, Susan. They were verbally ribbing back and forth. Gail was quizzing Susan about her new boyfriend. Apparently Susan's boyfriend got caught carrying a weapon and fighting at a school game the night before. "Is he a smart student?" Gail quizzed. "Uh huh!" Susan responded. Gail said, "That is what you said about the last one." Gail continued razzing the student more about her choice of boyfriends, asking more questions about the relationship. When the bell rang and the students started to take their seats, she quietly said to Susan, "Don't stay with this one."

Gail makes personal connections with students by "being nosy." Once during an interview session with me, a student interrupted the conversation. She turned her attention fully on him. After responding to his concerns, she directly asked him a question about his personal life. Afterward she turned back to the interview and said, "See, I'm nosy. That's why I know everything going on in everybody's life." When students were asked how Gail learned about them, one student said, "She just asks people. She talks to everybody. She's got a way of staying aware of her students and how they're . . . if they're screwing up or not" (Jake). Another student said, "Just talking to her. You know, I talk to her and she asks me about my family" (Abe).

Students appreciate a teacher who takes an interest in their personal lives. "You can really talk to her. . . . You can talk to her and that's the teacher who cares—that will communicate with the students" (Abe). One student giving advice on how to be a nurturing teacher says,

> Just take a little extra time out to care because there's a lot of things going on with a lot of the students these days—like parents or boyfriends. Just take some time out to understand that everyone has problems and just might be having a bad day. (Susan)

Using written comments and nonverbal communication to create one-to-one time with students. Two other techniques for creating one-to-one time were also observed: using written comments and nonverbal communication. These two techniques were observed being used primarily to augment other strategies for bonding with students. Using written comments and using nonverbal communication were not observed as primary strategies for developing bonds with students.

Ruby uses written comments to enhance her personal connection with students. Ruby is a health teacher at Rural-City High School.

Because Ruby's teaching style and curriculum design do not facilitate verbal connection with each student every day, she reaches out to them through written comments and writing assignments. In her classes, students do worksheets that are submitted at the end of the class period. Ruby often connects with them through writing personal comments on their worksheets.

> Sometimes it's really hard to get around to every student during a given class day. But I just try to make them feel wanted and noticed and appreciated in here. They do lots of worksheets and things, so I'll write a lot of little things on them like, "Good effort today," or "You had some great thoughts today," or "That must have been a rough experience to go through. I'd like to talk to you more about this." I'll try to put little personal messages to them.

Students often make personal connection with Ruby through the different worksheets and daily writing assignments.

> I felt comfortable with her, you know, like from the beginning of her class. I felt real comfortable writing down how I really felt and stuff. And like, if I had anything to hide from my family, I could write it down. Because I knew she cared and she wouldn't go around telling. (Sally)

Ruby knows that many students who cannot connect with her verbally can connect with her through their writing.

> Most kids are real willing to connect, if not to say something verbally. They're real willing to at least write it on paper. I mean every conceivable thing that can happen to a kid has been written. So I feel that they know that I care and that I'm someone they can talk to in one way, shape, or form.

For Ruby, student writing is a powerful tool to create one-to-one time with students that helps establish personal contact within the classroom.

Nonverbal communication, such as direct eye contact, personal touch, standing next to a student, and nonverbal acknowledgments, can be a way to create one-to-one contact with students. Nonverbal cues communicate an acknowledgment and connection between teacher and student. Gail, Tom, and Ruby provide examples of using nonverbal communication to create one-to-one time with students.

Gail's classroom nonverbally reflects her interest in her students and her efforts to establish personal contact. She creates a homey atmosphere in the classroom. Clipped to the front blackboard is a picture of one of her students as a toddler. She has four 2′ × 2.5′ multipicture frames resting on the chalk rail of her blackboard. Each one is filled with snapshot photographs of students. Her walls are decorated with collages created by the students about themselves, sharing such things as their favorite foods, how they prefer to spend Saturday morning, current steady, favorite performers, and so on. These pictures remind one of how a mother displays her child's work on the refrigerator. Students are treated like family members. Because student lockers have been removed from the halls of Inner-City High School, many students have no place to leave their belongings. They use Gail's room for a northwing locker. Bookbags line the front wall of Gail's classroom.

> My room is sort of a locker room. I have certain drawers that certain students use. I have sweats and lunch kits, and all kinds of things in those drawers.

Tom and Ruby's teaching styles also provide examples of the use of nonverbal communication to create one-to-one time with students. Their teaching style is primarily the traditional lecture mode with open discussions. This style limits the amount of personal, one-to-one time they can spend with students. Tom and Ruby recognize the importance of one-to-one time for bonding but acknowledge the overwhelming task of employing it as a key strategy for developing a bond. Tom, a social studies teacher at Suburb Junior High School, says,

> You have 25 to 30 kids in a class, 55 minutes. If you break it down per minute, that's maybe 2 minutes per kid. Not a whole lot of quality you can do in that time.

Ruby says,

> I try to get around to every kid and I don't come anywhere close to that. To be able to talk to every kid . . . there's just no

way it happens. You know, you can physically walk by them, and I'll do that much more so than I'll verbally acknowledge every single kid.

The primary nonverbal communication cue that Tom and Ruby use is touch. Sometimes when walking by a student, Ruby will touch his or her shoulder as a technique of acknowledging the student.

I do get around the room a lot and I do do human contact, put an arm on the shoulder, or whatever—safe contact—just to let them know that I appreciate their effort and just to let them know that I know that they're there. They're not just a face or a name or a number but they're a real human being. (Ruby)

Touch is also part of the way Tom makes one-to-one contact with students. He strongly believes in appropriate touch with students.

When you talk to my students, one of the things they'll probably . . . I hope they mention, and if you watch me in class you'll see me go around and pat kids on the back, the kids who like to wrestle, the junior high age stuff. You know, that all has to be a part of it too because to them that's part of the contact. (Tom)

Both Ruby and Tom are aware of the controversy around touching students in today's cultural environment. They both acknowledge the need to limit touch but also believe it is an important element in nurturing students. Ruby feels it is a little safer for female teachers to touch students than male teachers but limits her touch to a student's shoulders. Tom believes there is a big difference between a groping hug and just a warm hug that conveys caring. He tells his students at the beginning of the year that he is Italian and was raised with a lot of touching and hugging. He lets the kids know that he is going to touch and hug them. And he gives his students the option not to be touched. "If [touching is] something [you] don't like, just tell me, and that's okay." Tom holds touching too valuable to give it up altogether.

The big thing today that they say is so dangerous to do is the physical contact that you have with the kids. It's become more and more difficult because of individuals that wreck it for the good people. You've watched how I walk around the class and . . . hands on the shoulders of the kids and things like that. They seem pretty comfortable with that. That's a quality that I really like, in terms of developing trust and nurturing. (Tom)

Both male and female students come up to Tom and ask for a hug. Tom hugs kids, teases them, and gently touches them when they are not feeling well. At one point in a lecture, he reached out and touched a girl next to him. "Poor _____. You are not feeling very well. You are not giving me a bad time today." Then he touches her on the head and gently rocks it. She weakly smiles and the other students smile also.

Eye contact is another nonverbal cue used to enhance contact with students. Tom specifically arranges students' desks in his classroom in a way that encourages easy eye contact (see Figure 2.1). This arrangement also permits closer physical presence for the teacher when lecturing or facilitating a group discussion. The desks are in a semicircle, with two rows of desks dissecting the center of the semicircle. Tom teaches from the center of the semicircle sitting on his desk or standing in front of it, right in the midst of the students.

Summary of Techniques
for Creating One-to-One Time

In summary, all six nurturing teachers use several techniques for creating one-to-one time. For instance, they make themselves accessible to the students and remain focused on student needs throughout the day. They are open for conversations with the students about any topic, inviting students to talk to them and giving freely of their time for personal dialogue. In addition to these similarities in approaches to creating one-to-one time, several teachers use distinct techniques, including (a) designing curriculum to maximize individual or small-group contact, (b) interspersing personal and academic talk, (c) using direct personal dialogue during nonclass time, (d) using written comments on student papers, and (e) using nonverbal communication such as touching and physical closeness. All of these techniques appear to help create one-to-one time with students for these secondary schoolteachers.

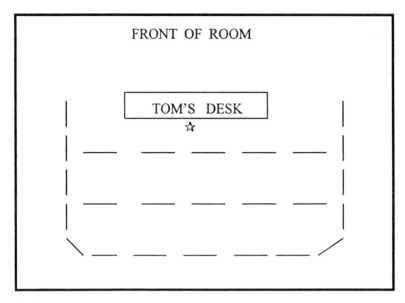

☆ Tom

Figure 2.1. Arrangement of Tom's Room

Using Appropriate Self-Disclosure

In his classic book on interpersonal effectiveness, David Johnson (1972) discusses self-disclosure as the key to building a close personal relationship. "To like you, to be involved with you, to be your friend, I must know who you are" (p. 9). Without self-disclosure, a truly close personal relationship is difficult to form (Johnson, 1972; Jourard, 1964). However, a teacher's role is to develop effective connections with students, not necessarily a close personal relationship. Students need to feel an emotional link to a teacher and to trust that the teacher will be attentive and responsive to the student's needs. But in an influential relationship such as a student-teacher relationship, a close, intimate bond is inappropriate. When used appropriately, the strategy of self-disclosure can foster the development of healthy connections with students without the intimacy found in expressive-emotional relationships.

Self-disclosure appropriate for an influential relationship is defined as the act of sharing and exposing the teacher's own feelings, attitudes, and experiences with students in ways that are helpful to them. When used inappropriately, a teacher self-discloses information to satisfy the teacher's emotional needs to confess, cathart, grandstand, or manipulate. When used appropriately, a teacher self-discloses information about himself or herself that is pertinent, in both content and context, to the needs of the students. Teachers exercise discretion regarding the personal information they share, and they have some idea of how students can use the information to enhance their learning process. The personal information shared by a teacher is used to enhance the learning process and to build a bridge between teacher and student, connecting them on a common human level. Sometimes the self-disclosures provide examples to illustrate a concept the teacher is discussing. Sometimes the self-disclosures are used primarily to develop trust and build a personal relationship.

A primary strategy that Tom and Pam use to develop healthy bonds with their students is appropriate self-disclosure. They provide powerful examples of appropriate self-disclosure, with each employing this strategy in a little different style.

Pam does a lot of teaching by analogy, using her personal experiences as examples. She tells of her failings and mistakes as well as successes if it serves a purpose to emphasize and clarify a point: "I tell them things that aren't all that great sometimes [laughter] about myself . . . failings and mistakes and stuff like that, if I think it serves a purpose." Some of these self-disclosures about her failures are disarmingly honest and revealing, as classroom observations and a vivid example will illustrate.

Pam shares stories about herself that could happen to anyone, but she does not share intimate, personal information. The self-disclosures she makes are stories students can relate to and identify with.

> I do a lot more self-disclosure than I think a lot of people do with my students. But I am selective about what I talk about too. I almost never talk about my personal life, really, except some anecdotes that illustrate issues that come up. . . . I do the analogous kinds of reasoning with them and illustrate it with my own personal stories. But you know, they're not real

self-revealing. . . . They're kind of the "everyman" kind of stories. . . . I think they could happen to anybody. It could happen to any of [the students].

Pam is clear that the purpose of self-disclosure is to enhance the students' learning process and to be genuinely and authentically human with students.

You know, the goal is to bridge the gap between us as people but not become intimate. . . . I want them to relate to me. I want to be able to relate to them. But I don't want to be on intimate terms with them. Nor do I want them to be on intimate terms with me.

Fortuitously, one of the days on which Pam was observed, the seventh and eighth graders had an assembly on sexual and personal harassment. On this occasion, Pam skillfully and powerfully used self-disclosure to promote learning as well as bonding. The assembly was 45 minutes long, with four college students enacting 8 to 10 short vignettes depicting different types of harassments that seventh and eighth graders deal with daily. The vignettes were poignant and sometimes even painful to watch. After the assembly, no time was allotted for students to discuss with an adult how they felt, what they learned, or what implications their learnings may have in their lives. Students were dismissed to return to their normal class schedules.

After the assembly, Pam put aside her preplanned lesson for the day and devoted the class periods to debriefing issues raised by the assembly. Before each class began, Pam checked to make sure that students had not had the opportunity to debrief what they had learned from the assembly in a previous class. No other teacher had taken time to discuss the ideas. Pam began with asking, "How many thought the assembly was realistic?" After a little discussion, most students timidly agreed with one another that the vignettes were true to life. Then Pam continued. She talked about how her stomach got tight during the vignettes and continued exploring by asking, "How many of us have been hurt by harassment or have hurt others?" Few students acknowledged their involvement. She then vividly told a story about how, when she was in the seventh grade, she had ridiculed a neighbor girl in an effort to gain the approval of a certain group of kids she was with. She disclosed how embarrassed and ashamed she felt about that incident, even to this day. The students began to talk. Students shared their own stories, talking about times when they were harassed or when they harassed others. They talked about how they could do things differently. They discussed possible reasons why human beings are so mean to each other. They talked about the difference between sexual harassment and flirting. They discussed what they could realistically do if they were sexually harassed or if they were caught up in peer pressure and harassing someone else.

Throughout the discussion, Pam skillfully interjected self-disclosures that kept the discussion focused, candid, and honest. For example, Pam did not let students give stock answers such as, "I would just walk on" or "It doesn't bother me." She recognized that students were trying to be tough or to have the right answer. She did not reject those answers either but said she had tried that but it did not work for her. She shared from her own experience how she has difficulty in similar situations doing the right thing. Pam shared how hard it was for her as a teacher to intervene in situations she overhears in the hallways. "Sometimes I am confused and don't know what would be best for me to do that you guys would want me to do. What do you want me to do?" Pam's self-disclosures helped the discussions stay open and sincere. Students honestly looked at the role of harassment in their lives and in society and how they could realistically cope with it. It became a valuable learning experience for students. At the end of the day, Pam's teaching assistant thanked Pam in front of the whole class for sharing her own life with them. She expressed how much easier it was to trust Pam and talk to her because Pam does share who she is with them.

Like Pam, Tom uses self-disclosure throughout the year using himself as examples of concepts he is discussing. But using examples with self-disclosures is not the only way Tom employs self-disclosure to develop closeness and trust. He also employs self-disclosure in another unique and effective way. Tom begins the school year by creating an opportunity for students to get to know him on a personal level.

> [On the first day], I don't hand out my rules, I don't create my seating chart, I don't hand out books. I pull up the stool. I ask them their names, and just on a sheet of paper jot it down so I can begin associating faces with names. . . . I start off by telling them a few things about myself and introducing the room more than anything else. And not necessarily

all the historical things but the other things in the room
which help give them clues about me and things that interest
me. And then I let them ask me any question they want. And
you know, they are pretty good. I always start out by saying,
"You know, I can walk down to the office and pull out your
permanent record file and read all kinds of stuff about you
but you don't have the right to go down and ask for Mr.
_____'s permanent record file and read all kinds of stuff
about me. So this is your opportunity—what do you want to
know?"

The students ask all kinds of personal questions. One common
question is, "I bet you were really a smart, good kid in school." Tom
tells them that is not who he was. He tells them about his father's death,
about dropping out of school, about his past drug-dealing history, and
about his shame in hurting people through his addiction. Tom's purpose for doing this is not to develop intimacy. Tom wants to develop
trust, rapport, and an awareness that he can understand them and their
problems. Tom uses self-disclosure primarily as a tool to begin developing rapport and to bridge the gap between him and the students,
showing their common humanness and developing a basis of equality.
Because of Tom's high academic and behavioral expectations for his
students, he needs to develop a learning environment in which students
have a clear understanding of his humanness and personal struggles.
This context helps foster the mutual respect he needs to motivate his
students to work hard for him.

You know, I try to be real honest and up front. They know
everything. I mean, there's not a whole lot they don't know.
They like that, I think. It makes it so that you start taking down
the walls and taking off the masks, you know, the kind of things
that everybody comes in with. And they see you more as a
human. Their common [belief about] a teacher is someone who
is always very good in school, never got in trouble. . . . It's good
for them to see that you're human, you made mistakes and
hopefully from those mistakes you can be a little bit more
understanding of the ones that they make too.

Tom demonstrated one other interesting technique for employing self-disclosure as a teacher. When working with the troubled

youth in the alternative school, Tom showed them his evaluation
report.

> When I was evaluated, after it was written up, I took it back
> to class, slapped it on the table, read it to them, explained to
> them what each part meant. They saw my report card! And
> so you take it down to where everybody's equal.

Having High Expectations of Students
While Conveying a Belief in Their Capabilities

A school culture of high expectations is a critical factor in increasing academic achievement (Hurn, 1985; McDermott, 1977; Rist, 1970).
Students from inner-city disadvantaged communities who choose to
go on to college often give the reason for their success as having one
person who believed they could do it (California Department of
Education, 1990). The dynamic appears to be the internalization of
high expectations by the students. When along with the high expectations the message is consistently "You can do it. You are a bright
and capable person!" one naturally sees oneself as bright and capable. Such a perception of oneself fosters a sense of purpose and a
meaningful future.

People like people who think highly of them. Students like
teachers who think highly of them; students enjoy being around
teachers who see them as bright and capable with bright futures in
front of them. It logically follows that if teachers have high expectations of students while clearly conveying a belief in their capabilities,
teachers would be more likely to develop positive emotional connections with students. The key seems to be conveying a belief in student
capabilities along with holding high expectations.

Creating bonds through having high expectations of students
while conveying a belief in their capabilities requires two distinct
behaviors on the teacher's part. First, teachers have to establish and
maintain high academic standards for their students. In addition,
teachers need to believe that students can meet these high standards.
The belief in students' ability to meet high standards is conveyed by
working from the assumption that students will accomplish whatever is expected of them. When there is evidence that students are
not meeting expectations, teachers problem solve from the perspec-

tive that something is blocking the student from using his or her innate abilities. In this way, they communicate belief in the student's ability. In other words, teachers convey a belief in the student's capabilities by focusing on his or her academic strengths rather than expressing discouragement and disappointment about what the student is not able or willing to do.

Tom provides an example of having high expectations while conveying a belief in students' capabilities.

> It doesn't matter what your socioeconomic class is, if you're going to lower your expectations you're being either racially, culturally, or economically bigoted. . . . You push for excellence. It doesn't matter, your strategy should always be to set high expectations. People rise to their expectations. If you set them high, they'll go high. If you set them low, they'll go low.

Tom perceives students as capable, and students respond positively to that perception. Even with the special education students mainstreamed into his classes, he holds high expectations, and students respond. According to his student teacher,

> Even the slowest . . . even with the groupings . . . I like the fact that [Tom] doesn't dummy down the curriculum. You see a lot of that when they make [student] groups up . . . this group works on different worksheets. But it's pretty much the same core material. He doesn't let them take advantage of their challenges. One kid was constantly . . . if you let him, he will fall farther and farther behind. Tom doesn't let him. [Tom] knows the student is having a problem, so he'll slow down, but he won't slow down so much that the kid is taking advantage of his disability. The kid may still complain, "I can't do it that fast. Let's slow down some more." Tom just tells him, "You know, I'm going to slow down this far. You are capable of keeping up."

Students *are* able to keep up. Tom's educational background, with special training for working with both the special education and the highly capable population of students, may give him additional skills and confidence to work with a variety of students.

The clearest example of Tom's belief in the capabilities of all students is from an earlier experience he had teaching in an alternative school. He held high expectations while believing in the abilities of these troubled youth.

> These were kids who had never read the classics at all. I read them *Treasure Island*—we read *Treasure Island* together. When I got the book, you know, other teachers said, "Well, those kids will never be able to read that!" I said, "Yes. It'll take a while, but we'll get through it." So we read *Treasure Island* and their day off was to watch the movie *Treasure Island*. Popcorn, you know, the whole 9 yards.

Tom had pretested these troubled young students at the beginning of the year. At the end of the year, they showed 2 years' average growth in reading and 3 years' growth in mathematics. Not one student had dropped out of the program that year. The year before, *every* student had dropped out of the program.

On one of the three observation days, Tom had students reading and analyzing Martin Luther King's speech on *The Philosophy of Nonviolence*. This speech has some complex ideas often difficult for adults to comprehend. Tom worked with the students, prodding them with questions and helping them understand difficult concepts by relating the ideas to events common in their own lives. "How many of you would find it hard not to strike back at someone who is hitting you?" "Why do you think this nonviolent approach works?" You could see students begin to understand the concept of nonviolence by the looks of disbelief and amazement on their faces.

Tom does not talk as though he has the answers but as though he is exploring ideas right along with the students. Tom talks *with* the students, not *at* them or *for* them. Although he has high expectations of students, Tom shows respect for them. The learning atmosphere is safe. Students feel free to make mistakes without ridicule or embarrassment while they are in the learning process.

A critical component of conveying the belief in students' capabilities is for teachers to have high expectations of themselves and their ability to teach. In this regard, teachers assume mutual responsibility for a student's confusion. This mutual responsibility conveys to students that the teacher believes they can understand when the message is clearly communicated. Tom holds high expectations of himself and his teaching abilities. He realizes that if students are having a difficult time learning, part of the responsibility rests with how he is teaching. Tom works hard to create lesson plans that make concepts easy to grasp because they relate to student experiences.

> I had one girl one year who was having a really hard time understanding the Great Depression and how everything collapsed. She posed the question to me right at the end of class. I thought about it literally all night long. Okay, what can I do with this kid? She really liked to go shopping at the mall. She was a real mall rat. So I came back to class and everything was in mall language and I turned everything around. The mall was the "country." The stores within the mall were the "states." That is how I explained the Depression to her.

Students recognize that high expectations and hard work are mutual expectations of Tom's. They appreciate Tom's shared efforts and hard work in order to promote their learning process. When questioned about Tom's style of teaching, one of his students, Jerry, said proudly, "He makes sure you do your work. He makes sure that you have a passing grade." Students know that Tom wants them to work hard, to learn, and to pass the course.

Networking With Family and Friends

James Coleman (1985a) describes a functional community as a community in which "a child's friends and associates in school are sons and daughters of friends and associates of the child's parents" (p. 529). This closure in a generational loop is called an intergenerational closure. With schools situated in functional communities, parents know the parents of their children's friends. Teachers know the family, friends, and neighbors of their students. The intergenerational closure allows for a flow of information that strengthens and supports parents and teachers in school-related activities.

Opportunities for close relationships between students and teachers are more available for teachers who live and teach within functional communities. These additional opportunities for building relationships with students are based on other possible affiliations than just those within the classroom. For instance, teachers may be friends with the child's parents, attend the same church as the child's family, or shop in the same grocery store. Teachers have an opportunity to become familiar with or be part of the community of people who are important individuals within the lives of their students. Teachers can build on these opportunities as a strategy for building bonds with students. A teacher networks with students' families and friends, finding common ground with students on which to develop a personal connection. The more significant people from a student's life with whom the teacher is acquainted, the more common ground the teacher has on which to build a bond. These personal connections among teacher, student, and the student's parents, extended family, friends, and neighbors provide an intergenerational closure for students. Such closures provide a sense of community or family with the teacher being part of that family or community.

It is clear that teachers can strengthen their connections with students by living within the communities in which they work and becoming acquainted with students' parents, relatives, neighbors, and friends. Dale provides an example of the bonding strategy of networking with a student's circle of family and friends. The community of Rural City provides an ideal opportunity to use this bonding strategy. Rural-City High School is situated in a small rural community with a population of about 15,000 people. It is the only high school in the small, self-contained community. Self-contained communities are characterized by long-term residents, extended families living within the same area, neighbors familiar with neighbors and their neighbors' extended families, and businesspeople and shopkeepers living within the communities in which they work (Coleman, 1985a). Many of the local residents' families have lived and worked in Rural City for generations.

Dale has lived and taught in Rural City for 14 years. In the first 4 years he taught at Rural-City Middle School; during the last 10 years he has been teaching at Rural-City High School. Dale believes it is important for teachers to reside in the community in which they teach. He says, "I've always felt that if you teach, I think you should be a resident of where you teach. I've always felt that."

By living within the community and actively participating in the community, Dale has many opportunities to meet his students' parents, family members, neighbors, and friends. Sometimes in the past he has had a student's older siblings or cousins as students. He meets parents and others through coaching his son's church-sponsored basketball team or through shopping. In the small community, he sees students about town shopping and meets their parents and family members then. "You know, I go downtown and I know everybody almost. Even though I wasn't a hometown boy; I wasn't born here."

Some of Dale's personal friends are parents of his students. He says he often mixes socially with the parents of his students. Some parents live right down the street from Dale.

> There have been times, like, we'll go to social things at their houses. [One student and his family] they just live a couple of doors down and our wives—his mom and my wife—are good friends. We go over there and they come over here. Ray comes over and plays basketball so I see quite a bit of him.

The extracurricular activities in which Dale participates also provide opportunities to get to know the parents. For instance, he takes tickets for wrestling matches and volleyball, soccer, and football games. At the door, he meets the parents, family members, friends, and neighbors: "When you're at the door you know all the parents. You know who's there. . . . They know me. So you build a little friendship that way." He is timekeeper for the girls' basketball games and coaches varsity baseball, which give him additional opportunities to meet parents and other significant individuals in his students' lives. The personal and community connections Dale develops by living in the community in which he teaches create an intergenerational closure for students. Such closures provide a sense of community and familiarity for students with Dale being part of that community. The following observation notes demonstrate this sense of community and familiarity.

> Before the next period starts, Dale and the students talk about the basketball game that sent them to the state basketball tournament. Several students asked where he sat at the game and if he had seen their parents. He said, "Yes, I saw your parents." The students seemed pleased.

> Dale gives them a harder math problem to work and then walks around the class to help. He pats a male student on the back and says, "Does your mom want to talk to me yet?" The student smiles and says something back to Dale that is not audible.

Dale knows the names of most of the parents and is on a first-name basis with many. Once during a class observation while Dale was taking roll, a student said it was her birthday tomorrow and she was having a party. Dale said, "We will all show up. I am sure Mike and Sue [parents of the student] will appreciate that." And he continued to take roll.

The fact that Dale knows their families, friends, and neighbors is important to his students. Annette, a student in recovery from alcoholism, said,

> He knows certain things. He knows that I had been doing bad in school but that now I'm trying and my grades are better and stuff. He's—like I said—he's talked to my dad so he knows what my dad's told me about me being at home and stuff, like if I've had problems and stuff.

In addition to providing a common circle of friends and acquaintances, these intergenerational closures create additional channels of communication that provide additional information on a student situation. These additional channels of communication help parents and teachers gain a different perspective on a child's school-related activities. A child's needs and behaviors are less likely to remain unnoticed and unattended because there are added communication channels and multiple sources of people for support who are familiar with the child. As evidenced by Annette's statement, the additional communication channel created by networking with her father provided opportunities for Dale, Annette, and her father to gain additional support and added information on Annette's situation. Networking with parents, family members, friends, and neighbors provides a common ground with shared histories, shared experiences, and a common understanding on which a teacher can build healthy connections with students.

Opportunities for bonding through networking with family and friends are not as available in less self-contained communities such as those surrounding Inner-City High School or Suburb Junior High. Suburb Junior High is surrounded by a rapidly growing residential area, a recent product of the urban sprawl from a nearby large metropolitan area. The school is situated in a typical residential bedroom community. Adults who reside there spend the majority of their day working or playing in other geographical locations. Few businesses are located within the jurisdiction of Suburb Junior High School. The population of the community is geographically mobile and constantly changing as families move in or out of the area. This constantly changing population and the lack of businesses within the community make it difficult for Suburb Junior High School teachers to bond with their students through networking with each student's circle of family and friends outside the school environment.

Like the community surrounding Suburb Junior High, the community surrounding Inner-City High School also does not provide the teachers the same opportunities for networking with family and friends as does Rural City. The reasons, however, are different from those just described for Suburb Junior High School. With Inner-City High School, 30% of the students do not reside within the community surrounding the school. These students are bused to Inner-City High School from other communities outside the Inner-City High School area. Also, some high school age students residing within the community surrounding Inner-City High School are bused to other high schools. Siblings or extended family members living within the community surrounding Inner-City High School may even attend different schools than their brothers, sisters, or cousins. Only 70% of the students attending Inner-City High School reside within the surrounding community. Even though the community surrounding Inner-City High School may have many of the characteristics of a functional, self-contained community, the potency of bonding through networking with family and friends is diminished for teachers because of busing.

Teachers who choose to live and work within the community surrounding Inner-City High School do have an opportunity, though limited, to become familiar with key people outside the school who are part of students' lives. For example, Gail lives and works in the neighborhood surrounding Inner-City High School. She recognizes the value of living and working in the neighborhood as a means of building personal connections with students.

> This is my neighborhood. These kids live around me, and it's important for me to do well here because it's important for my neighborhood, very important. . . . Because I live in the neighborhood, sometimes I see them [students] at the store on the weekends or at night. I just get into more things [with the students] on another level.

Networking with students' parents, kin, or neighbors is a bonding strategy Gail uses to augment a primary strategy of one-to-one time with students. She is able to bump into some of her students and her students' circles of family and friends while grocery shopping, getting gas, or walking the dog. But approximately one third of her students do not reside in the same community she does. This limits the number of students with whom she may build common ground by knowing their circle of family and friends outside of school.

Bonding through networking with parents, family, friends, and neighbors is more viable for Inner-City High School teachers than for the Suburb Junior High School teachers. But this strategy for developing bonds with students appeared most potent in the self-contained, functional community surrounding Rural-City High School, where there is no busing. Based on observations, the community of Rural City provides the most potent opportunities for bonding by networking with family members and friends.

Building a Sense of Community Among Students

Creating teacher-student bonds through building a sense of community among students is another useful strategy for developing effective connections (Corey & Corey, 1987; Peck, 1987). Community, as used here, refers to a relational community in which human interaction and social ties draw people together. Relational communities are defined as "networks of individuals who interact within formal organizations and institutions, and as members of informal groups" (Heller, 1989, p. 3). Common interests, histories, and experiences draw these individuals together and are the basis on which social relationships develop (Heller, 1989).

In relational communities, a special cohesiveness develops among members. A genuine sense of community comes after the group members have committed themselves to taking significant risks and shared personal pains and meaningful experiences. In relational communities, group members become tolerant and accepting of each other. A feeling of belongingness and relatedness among the members is developed (Corey & Corey, 1987). These feelings of belonging and relatedness extend to everyone in the group, including the group leader and potential new members. According to Peck (1987), in genuine communities boundaries are soft. "[Members] do not ask, 'How can we justify taking this person in?' Instead the question is 'Is it at all justifiable to keep this person out?' " (p. 61). This group dynamic of genuine communities is called *inclusivity*. Inclusivity means that there are no outcasts; everyone is welcomed.

Inclusivity may explain how building a sense of community among students may also enhance teachers' ability to build effective connections with students. As with other relational groups, when a teacher helps students bond to each other by encouraging risk-taking, honest self-disclosures, and sharing among class members, a sense of community develops among students. Students feel a sense of belongingness and relatedness among themselves. By inclusivity, the teacher is drawn into the student community. Students feel bonded to each other and bonded to the teacher.

Ruby provides an example for bonding through building community among students. She does so by designing her curriculum so that students share personal values, attitudes, beliefs, strengths, and insights with each other on a regular basis. Through these sharings, students get to know one another on a personal level.

> I think, at least within every month, there's opportunities for the kids to really talk about things about them, about where they're at, and what they're all about and why they're important. I try to do exercises and activities for them to acknowledge that out loud. And it's very hard for them to do that. It's very hard for them to reflect. And some of them look at it as exposing their strengths. They say it's much easier to talk about the bad things.

Students are aware that they can talk about their feelings and what is important to them in Ruby's class. One student commented on how Ruby has students share their feelings about important issues in their lives—one of the things Ruby does ritually to build community among students.

> She has you write down your feelings a lot of times on stress and stuff . . . like about how you would cope with stress and your problems and . . . she asks us how we'd cope with that and how we'd solve it. (Shelly, student)

As an example of how Ruby designs her curriculum to build community among students, for one class activity Ruby had students put their first name in the middle of a 5 × 7 index card. Then she asked that they write the name of an animal they would be if they could be an animal. In the top left corner, students identified their favorite food and, in the top right corner, a safe place to be. In the bottom left corner, students named their favorite singer, movie, or book and, in the bottom right corner, two positive qualities about themselves. Students then exchanged these cards with one another. Ruby had made a card for herself, and she exchanged with students she did not know very well.

Ruby often designs these activities so that students are writing their ideas first. She tells students they will be disclosing what they write with other students so that they are prepared to share. She establishes ground rules that help create a safe environment for students. When she notices that a student is having a difficult time sharing with another, she will gently approach him or her and volunteer to share what she wrote or to listen to what the student has written. This encourages students to share.

> Ruby asks the students to share something that made them angry and an appropriate way to communicate that anger. One student who is sitting in the back of the room is not sharing with anyone. Ruby gently approaches her and says supportively, "Why don't you share with me?" The student hesitates and then starts sharing with Ruby. Ruby patiently listens and responds encouragingly with questions. (observation notes)

Ruby works hard to get students to open up and speak out loud about themselves in class. At the beginning or end of the week, she saves time for talking about topics unrelated to the class focus as a technique to get students used to speaking up in class.

> At the beginning of the week or the end of the week we talk about nonclass-related things. . . . We'll talk about something other than the classroom, that is, movies, whatever, just to try and get them to relax and open up a little bit.

The environment that Ruby creates is very safe for and respectful toward students. This safe environment encourages students to connect with one another.

Ruby also encourages students to bond to the larger school community through involvement in extracurricular activities or supporting athletic events. She encourages students to go to games, to get involved with school activities, and to develop school spirit. This additional bonding increases the sense of community among the students.

Through the sense of trust and closeness Ruby builds among students, it appears that a general sense of connectedness to her emerges as well. There is no way of verifying that Ruby's efforts to build community among her students help to foster a sense of connectedness with her. Theoretically, it is clear that these behaviors develop feelings of closeness and trust among community members and their leader. Furthermore, students feel bonded to Ruby. Therefore, it seems reasonable to identify building community among students as one strategy Ruby uses to develop close and trusting connections with her students.

Providing Rituals and Traditions

Throughout the ages, providing rituals and traditions has been a common strategy to bond individuals to their families, communities, institutions, or even country. Rituals are activities that are done the same way each time they are introduced, such as having the last 15 minutes of class every Friday reserved for open discussion or beginning a social studies class with a current event introduced by a student. Traditions are customs, practices, or special events that are routinely acknowledged and honored, although how they are acknowledged and honored may be different each time. For instance, teachers may celebrate Martin Luther King Day, but they may create a different type of celebration each year in honor of the event.

Rituals and traditions help build a sense of community. They create a common experience for members, providing students with a common basis and a familiar routine. As the above examples indicate, teachers may incorporate rituals or traditions into their curriculum or as a nonacademic activity as a strategy to enhance their connections with students. Although rituals and traditions are not used as a primary strategy for bonding by any of the six observed teachers, two teachers use to enhance other strategies for bonding.

Ruby provides an illustration of how teachers can use rituals and traditions as a bonding strategy. At the beginning of her classes, Ruby reads or has a student read a "one-minute message" from a daily inspirational reader.

One of the little things that we try to do on a consistent basis is our one-minute message. We read different messages about life and living and hope and self-esteem, you know, every kind of issue that we deal with in our classroom. The kids are pretty good about reminding me about it if I forget. . . . There are some wonderful lessons for them to think about. It seems to have more of an impact on them than *they* will even acknowledge.

Ruby also periodically has her students stand at the end of class and yell what she calls the PMA (positive mental attitude) cheer. She asks them how is their positive mental attitude today and they give the answer: "Happy, healthy, feel fantastic, boy are we enthusiastic!" These small rituals and traditions in which everyone participates help these teachers develop close connections with the students.

Summary of Strategies for Bonding

The six strategies discussed in this chapter suggest role-appropriate ways for teachers to build close and trusting connections with students. The six strategies for bonding with students are the following:

1. Creating one-to-one time with students
2. Using appropriate self-disclosure
3. Having high expectations of students while conveying a belief in their capabilities
4. Networking with parents, family members, friends, and neighbors of students
5. Building a sense of community among students within the classroom
6. Using rituals and traditions within the classroom

These strategies are probably not the only role-appropriate ways for developing bonds with students, but they do demonstrate a variety of ways for secondary teachers to bond successfully with students without compromising a teacher's primary responsibility for the cognitive development of students. As such, teachers become a rich resource of prosocial adults to whom young people can connect in meaningful ways.

3

Communicating Caring
to Students

※ ※ ※ ※ ※

It is Dale's first interview with me. The principal had introduced us no more than 15 minutes earlier. We begin to learn about each other by exchanging small talk, slowly working through the awkward feelings we all have when we first meet. Dale teases me about my "heavy equipment." I have two tape recorders going this time, one as a backup to the other. I no longer depend on my skills at speedtyping as a fallback in case the tape recorder doesn't work. We start to chat about where Dale was trained to be a teacher and why he wants to be a teacher. Sitting in a student's desk directly across from me, Dale appears relaxed, as if he is enjoying this opportunity to reflect on his background.

"What experiences influenced your choice to be a teacher?" I ask.

Dale immediately responds, "Being able to share knowledge is a pretty key part for me." He pauses for a few seconds, pondering that idea, and then adds, "Well, it's strange because when I was in high school, I had a math teacher who was as intimidating as hell. He just would use big words; he'd talk right at you. He'd make you break into a cold sweat just looking at him because he would intimidate you. And I thought then, 'I don't really think I'm learning a lot, feeling this way.' He was an outstanding man. I mean, he was smart, brilliant. But boy, he just really scared the living daylights out of me."

*Dale pauses and looks directly at me. "I want to make people feel at ease
. . . and feel that they can do it—you know, that I'm not intimidating them
in the field of math, like I felt when I talked to this man."*

*I remain silent while Dale recollects his thoughts and continues with
his story. "We had another math teacher in my high school who was the
father of three kids who were boys. Everybody called him Pops B_____
because he was like a dad and he made you feel good. But boy, he earned your
respect when you were in his class. He helped you feel like you could talk to
him. You felt safe asking him anything, instead of feeling embarrassed to
ask 'Why?' when you didn't understand. That is the only thing that I've
really tried to carry with me—treat the kids with respect."*

☒   ☒   ☒   ☒   ☒

Treating Students With Dignity and Respect

No matter how hard teachers try to connect with students, if
students do not interpret what teachers do as caring, bonds between
teachers and students will not develop. Caring is a way of *being* in a
relationship; it does not emerge from a step-by-step formula (Noddings, 1992). In order to develop close and trusting relationships with
students, teachers need to convey caring for students and an openness to emotional connections. For example, the intimidating, critical
mathematics teacher that Dale described may have cared deeply
about students, but his mannerisms and nonverbal language kept
students at a distance. It is unlikely that he was able to develop close
and trusting relationships with students because students would
have a hard time perceiving him as open to a caring connection with
them. An important factor in these observed teachers' ability to bond
with students is the ability to be in relationship in such a way that it
is perceived as caring by students. What do nurturing teachers do
that helps students perceive they are really cared about?

Education literature has little to say about what teachers do to
communicate concern and caring to their students. The parenting
literature, though, is rich with research that provides insights and
guidance on communicating caring to children. Because a parent-
child relationship is another example of an influential relationship,

it seems reasonable to assume that ways of being in a relationship that promote closeness and trust between parent and child may also promote the closeness and trust between teacher and student. Most pertinent, behaviors and attitudes advocated by the authoritative model for parenting have been shown empirically to increase feelings of closeness and trust between child and parent (McNabb, 1990). In addition, authoritative approaches also foster self-reliance, self-control, a willingness to explore, and a sense of well-being in children (Baumrind, 1971; Glenn, 1982; Hoffman, 1970). Thus, this model provides us with insights on how to communicate caring to students.

A key criterion of authoritative parenting strategies is that children are treated firmly with dignity and respect (Glenn, 1982; Glenn & Nelsen, 1988). Dignity is a quality or state of being worthy of esteem or respect. Being treated with dignity means honoring an individual's position. Respect is the ability to communicate regard for the capability of others to manage their own lives successfully. In the authoritative parenting model, it is taken for granted that parents "have more knowledge and skill, control more resources, and have more physical power than their children, but they [parents] believe that the *rights of parents and children are reciprocal*" [italics added] (Cole & Cole, 1989, p. 383). Children are viewed as capable and significant and are treated respectfully (Glenn, 1982). The authoritative parenting model includes such parental behaviors and attitudes as the following (Briggs, 1977; Cole & Cole, 1989; Glenn, 1982):

1. Parents control their children through attempts to explain their rules and decisions and by reasoning with them.
2. Parents are willing to listen to their child's point of view even if they do not always accept it.
3. Parents set high standards for their children's behavior and encourage them to be individualistic and independent.
4. Parents' demands of their children are held within what is developmentally appropriate for the child.
5. Parents affirm what is right about the child; they separate the child's personal worth from his or her behavior.
6. Parents use discipline as an opportunity to teach the child so he or she can internalize the learning and become independent.

These authoritative parenting behaviors communicate thoughtfulness and respect for a child and promote the prosocial development of children (Baumrind, 1971; Glenn, 1982; Glenn & Nelsen, 1988; Hoffman, 1970). The same kinds of behaviors are appropriate for teachers and can help them communicate caring to their students. This chapter describes some of the ways nurturing teachers communicate respect for their students. Student responses also affirm that such respectful treatment provides a basis for the development of a caring teacher-student connection. Treatment with dignity and respect enhances student perceptions of caring and, thus, receptiveness to a teacher's caring.

The respectful treatment of students by the six selected teachers is inspiring to observe. These teachers treat students with dignity and respect in a variety of ways. They use a considerate tone of voice and receptive manner when speaking to and about students. For instance, Tom addresses the students as "sirs" and "ladies." Dale addresses them as "ladies and gentlemen": "Ladies and gentlemen, I am glad to see you. I am really glad to see you. We need paper, pencils, and books today" (observation notes).

Dale tells students at the beginning of the year, "I'm going to earn your respect. I'm going to work really hard to earn your respect. And I will respect you just as much as you respect me."

These teachers take time to listen to their students and take their concerns seriously. They trust that students are doing the best they can given their developmental level and life circumstances. When I talked to Dean at lunch one day, he said,

> These kids are adults. They've already made more decisions in their life than you or I have had to. You can't treat them like kids, but like adults. Take for instance the kid sitting up there studying. (He points to a small boy quietly studying.) He's a gang member and has been faced with situations you or I have not dreamed of.

Pam talks about her respect for students. "I relate to them as people. . . . I don't talk down to kids. I never have, I don't think, in a condescending way." These teachers see students as independent thinkers with important individual needs. Gail says,

> I see them as little people. I see them as independent thinkers, as very nice people. Even the ones that are sort of rough.

They are really nice but you have to cut through the roughness to get to the nice part.

When discussing with Tom's student teacher what he identified
that Tom did to show students that he cared, the student teacher said,

I think it comes down to respect. There is a definite two-way
respect in that classroom. You know, a lot of teachers expect
the kids to respect them, but it's not reciprocated.

These teachers acknowledge that they learn from students as
well as teach students. They extend to students the opportunity to
make their own mistakes and live with the consequences without
judgment. When disciplining students, these teachers do it respectfully, using discipline as an opportunity to teach rather than punish.
They truly enjoy their students and enjoy their jobs, communicating,
in effect, "You are more than a job to me."

The deep level of respect these teachers show communicates genuine caring. It communicates that they value their students and hold them
in esteem. They honor where their students are in life. These teachers
truly respect students and believe they have to earn their students'
respect. Such behavior is an illustration of the ethical use of a teacher's
power granted by virtue of his or her position (see Box 3.1, Appendix C).

The student responses illustrate the power of treating students
with dignity and respect. Students recognize that they are being
treated as assets rather than as objects. They feel respected and
reciprocate with respect. Their behavior changes in accordance with
those feelings. A clear example of this dynamic comes from Shawn,
a student of Tom's: "We treat him with respect because he treats us
with respect." A student of Dean's provides another example of how
being treated respectfully influences student behavior.

Well, everyone respects him. Like if people don't respect
you, the teacher, and the teacher tells them to do [some-
thing], they'll just talk back and then the teacher will have to
make them leave or something. And the people won't care.
(Rosie)

Students appear to thrive as learners in this caring environment.
They are open to paying attention and motivated to try. They care

about how they are doing in class when they feel respected. Annette, a student of Dale's, provides a powerful example. A troubled student, Annette communicates that she feels respected by Dale despite her behavior. She relates this respect in the following way:

> After being suspended for a while, you come back and it's like totally weird being in school again. And you know, I walked in Mr. _____'s classroom and he's like, "Hey Annette! You're back! Congratulations, you made it!" You know, he is like, "Have a seat. Come on. We're waiting for you" and stuff. You know, he like welcomed me. (Annette)

A minute later in the interview, she admits to trying harder and doing better in Dale's classes.

> I mean, he's the only math teacher I've learned from. I'm good at math but I usually don't get good grades in it. All my life I've gotten Ds and stuff, and this year I'm finally getting Bs in his class.

Students who feel respected by the teacher will reciprocate with respect (see Box 3.2, Appendix C).

Treating students with dignity and respect may be the key to promoting student perceptions of caring, supportive teachers. Students trust teachers who are respectful of them. As evidenced by the student inventories (see Appendix B), they feel safe sharing their thoughts and ideas, even sensitive situations, with these teachers. They believe that their teacher will listen to their concerns, hear their side of a story, and respond fairly when dealing with them. They trust that the teacher will help them with school problems, and they feel safe turning to the teacher when they need help. They *enjoy* being in the teacher's class.

Caring teachers are not afraid to have students talk to them about all kinds of topics, even sensitive ones. In fact, they invite student input. In a student's eyes, a caring teacher encourages dialogue and listens respectfully to a student's thoughts and feelings (Rogers & Webb, 1991). When a teacher treats students respectfully and with dignity, students are able to perceive the teacher's caring and concern and thus become more open and willing to develop a meaningful connection with the teacher. Student perceptions of a teacher as caring are built on mutual respect and the sharing that evolves from that respect (see Box 3.3, Appendix C).

Communicating Caring Through Discipline

Discipline is often viewed by teachers as an albatross, a necessary evil that comes with the job. These six teachers think of discipline as an opportunity to be respectful of students, promote student growth, and create learning experiences for students. Using discipline as an occasion to teach is an integral part of treating students with dignity and respect. Thus, how these teachers discipline is related to and mutually supports the overarching strategy for communicating caring to students—treating students with dignity and respect.

This section discusses how these teachers approach discipline and how their discipline strategies show respect for students. It includes classroom observations, examples, and responses from teachers and students to illustrate and support the points being described.

All six teachers approach discipline as another occasion to teach and promote student growth rather than as an onus. They view discipline as an opportunity to provide meaningful learning experiences. Tom provides a beautiful example. He had observed an A student cheating on an exam. Not singling her out, he led a class discussion on cheating the next day. He described cheating as compromising personal values of honesty and integrity. He hoped to instill within students the fact that they had choices that need not compromise their personal values. Then at lunch, he pulled the student quietly aside and asked her a series of questions about her perception of her efforts with the exam. At first she did not admit to cheating. Tom told her what behavior he had observed when she was taking the test, without accusing her of cheating. She then quietly acknowledged cheating. Once cheating was established, Tom asked her to give some serious thought to her value system, to her views of right and wrong, and to how difficult it is to live up to that value system. He gave her another day to think about this, saying that he was not sure yet what he was going to do.

The next day the student was remorseful and honest. She acknowledged that she should be treated like anyone else who had been caught cheating. She got a zero on the test, which dropped her tentative grade from an A to a C. Tom said to her,

You know you deserve respect for acknowledging that you should be treated like anyone else. I need to tell you that I'm going to call your parents and that you'll have to spend 2 hours with me next Thursday after school as part of the punishment, just like anyone else would. I don't hate you. I don't dislike you. I don't think any less of you. You made a mistake. Just learn from this and make this a valuable experience and everything will work out.

All six nurturing teachers view discipline as an occasion to teach or provide moral guidance (see Box 3.4, Appendix C). In this way, discipline is used to promote a good learning environment. During observations, these teachers were never seen using discipline for punishment or as a weapon in a power struggle with the students. The teachers did not discuss discipline in this manner either. These teachers understand that classroom management and caring are threads from the same tapestry. They use discipline as an opportunity to teach, which preserves the classroom as a safe place to learn, to make mistakes, and to grow.

Using Humor When Disciplining

These teachers use gentle humor often when disciplining students. Handling discipline with humor is a congenial way to treat students respectfully and still identify inappropriate behavior. These are some examples from in-class observations:

Gail quiets the class down to begin studying. "The more time you spend getting things together now, the more homework you will have to do tonight." She then says teasingly, "Any group who does the best work will get Rudolph's sandwich." "Oh no!" Rudolph cries. "You can't do that. . . . I'll sue." Everyone laughs, and Rudolph beams. The class then quiets down.

Tom goes over to a student who is making fun of him and places his hands on the student's shoulders to quiet him down. The student asks him to mess up his hair. Tom ruffles the student's hair and then looks disgustedly at his hand. "What weight of oil is that, 10 weight?" Everyone laughs.

Dale calls on a student who was not paying attention. "Matthew, what answer did you get for this problem?" Matthew says, "I don't understand how to divide this." Dale gently says, "Watch me and maybe you will get it." Matthew says, "I don't want to copy." Dale laughs. "I'm the guy in class that you can copy." Dale turns to me and says, "Matthew has a reputation for copying. We used to call him Xerox."

Dale has them work on a problem. Everyone starts working quietly. Students begin asking one another for help in understanding. The noise picks up. Dale says, "Don't shout out the answer because you will spoil all the fun for Erica, Jane, and Mary." The girls laugh. The class quiets down again.

Handling Their Own Discipline Problems

Curiously, these teachers seldom use the formal discipline system within the schools. Some of them never use the school discipline system. Gail says, "I may have sent two or three people in about 13 years [to the office]. I try to handle it myself." Dean sees discipline as solely his responsibility: "I don't even think of the discipline policies. You know why? Because what happens with me is within my classroom. I do my own discipline." Dean feels that if he cannot deal with the situation effectively, the administration won't be able to either. Ruby says, "[Discipline] is between the teacher and the student. It's not like for every little [discipline problem] you have to run outside the classroom and pull in an administrator. There's a lot that is left up to your discretion to deal with that student one-to-one, which I think is good." Pam explains why she chooses to use the formal discipline system as the last resort: "I use [infractions] as the last resort [because] . . . the kids don't take them seriously. . . . Part of the reason kids don't take them seriously is that some teachers use them too readily. They rely on the system as the first consequence." Tom volunteers to be in charge of after-school detention. "It gives me a way to connect with some of the tough students," and he is able to work with his own students. Dale makes the students walk around the building if they are acting up. He seldom uses formal discipline channels because he does not agree with the discipline policies and procedures. His students say they are applied unfairly. Dale says, "I don't think I agree with suspensions. It just gets the kid out of school."

Assuming responsibility for disciplining students rather than depending on the school's formal discipline system is another way these teachers communicate respect to their students. By managing their own discipline problems, these teachers are communicating that they believe in the student's ability and willingness to self-correct. If the teacher and student work together, they will be able to resolve the problem. Using discipline as an opportunity to provide moral guidance for students also helps to define and maintain the appropriate professional boundaries of the teacher as the change-agent in an influential relationship with the student. It demarcates the teacher's influence and authority with the student.

Creating a Safe Environment in Which to Learn

Because mutual respect facilitates creating a safe learning environment, creating a safe learning environment is also associated with treating students with dignity and respect. These teachers recognize the importance of creating safe learning environments for students (see Box 3.5, Appendix C).

When Gail was asked for the qualities of a healthy, caring relationship with students, she mentioned some of the behaviors that help to create a safe learning environment. "I guess their knowing that they can come and talk to me just about . . . anything. I'm not going to get mad at them or judge them." Dale recognizes the same quality of safety. He says,

> I call [students] by name or give them some kind of individual attention. I'm trying to get them to have confidence in me so they can ask me a question. A lot of kids seem embarrassed to ask questions, so I'm trying to eliminate that feeling so they can ask me about anything and feel real comfortable.

In a safe environment, students feel comfortable making mistakes or suggesting possible answers even when they are not sure of the correct answer. They can share their thoughts and feelings without fear of being put down, criticized, or ridiculed by the teacher or other students. On the first day that Pam was observed, she had planned the lesson around a simulated archaeological dig. Students forgot to bring items from home for the simulated dig. Pam did not criticize, nag, or tell them what to do. Rather, she turned what could have been a negative experience into an opportunity for students to practice problem-solving skills and teamwork. She had them brainstorm, in teams, a plan to ensure that they would remember to bring all the items for the assignment the next day. Each team shared with the whole class the strategies they had thought of to help them remember to bring the needed items. Teams could adopt one another's good ideas.

A safe environment encourages students to take a stand or have an opinion different from the teacher's. A safe learning environment promotes student perceptions of a teacher's caring because students see that the teacher encourages, supports, and affirms students rather than judges, criticizes, or belittles. These perceptions of the teacher are reinforced daily in safe environments.

In a health class where students talk about sensitive topics, Ruby believes it is critical that students feel safe.

> I want kids to feel okay to talk to me. Within the realm of the health class, we talk about so many issues in there. I guess I want them to feel safe if we're going to do a writing assignment and they're going to talk about particular issues that relate to teens. I want them to feel safe if they want to write that they've experienced something. . . . I just let them know that it remains confidential between us.

For minority students, a safe learning environment is also a culturally relevant environment. Teachers with classrooms composed primarily of students of color can create a culturally relevant classroom environment by providing a curriculum that reflects the cultures of the student (Ladson-Billings, 1992). Culturally relevant teaching requires the recognition of minority cultures as value experiences on which to build a classroom curriculum. In doing so, students are appreciated and celebrated both as individuals and as members of a specific culture. Students can experiment with new behaviors for social change with encouragement and support while critically examining the society. At Inner-City High School, Gail provides an example of offering a culturally relevant curriculum. Her readings in literature often have people of color as primary characters or in lead roles. She draws her examples from minority cultures. For instance, on the first day of observation, students were reading a short story titled *Farewell to Manzanar*, which is about an Asian American family. The second day of observation, students were analyzing Martin Luther King's speech, *I Have a Dream*. The third day of observation, students were reading a play about African Americans that was written in the jargon of African American people.

Summary of Communicating Caring

In summary, treating students with dignity and respect is an overarching strategy for communicating caring to students that crosscuts the data. Treating students with dignity and respect enhances a student's perception of caring and concern on the teacher's part. In addition to treating students with dignity and respect, two closely related and mutually reinforcing strategies also are used to communicate a teacher's caring: (a) using discipline as an opportunity to teach students and (b) creating safe learning environments for students.

4

How Nurturing Teachers Revitalize Themselves

Dean is sitting in a chair catty-corner from me, using the large library table next to us as an armrest. It is lunchtime. The Inner-City High School library is mostly unoccupied, except for the students who intermittently enter and stop to chat with Dean. Between interruptions, Dean is intensely focused on the interview process, animatedly answering the questions. He seems to radiate an energy that is contagious. This is my first interview with Dean. I have not yet observed him teach.

"Any thoughts of leaving the teaching profession?" I query.

"I thought about counseling," Dean responds. "I really truly believe that there is going to be a time in my life when I'm not going to be as effective with kids . . . when it's time to let the younger person do the actual teaching part and me doing more of a support role. At 60 years old, leading a classroom can take the life out of you. When you come observe these kids, you'll realize you've got to give a lot of energy if you're going to make it happen. At 60 years old, I'm not going to be able to do that. I know I'm going to want to be in a support role. I know that."

Silently I nod in acknowledgment, although inwardly I wonder if a counselor's role is any easier.

Dean leans forward and continues to talk, animatedly waving his hands. "Since I've been here, I swear to God, there's only one person in my entire 6 years that has retired on a nonmedical. All eight of the other people were medical. They had heart problems. Oh my God! They just reached this frazzled point. They hauled this one dude out on a stretcher. I'm not lying! On a stretcher! I remember because he grabbed the principal and said, "It was that f_____ English class!" He had been a math teacher. For years he taught math and driver's ed. and they made him teach an English class! They needed someone to teach English 101."

Dean chuckles, "It was almost funny after he got better. He came back and retired at the end of the year. The dude just said, 'I can't do this anymore. I'm leaving on a medical leave before I kill myself.' "

❈   ❈   ❈   ❈   ❈

What It Takes to Revitalize Oneself

Clearly, teachers need support and care themselves. As caregivers in asymmetrical, influential relationships, they are presumed more mature and capable of dealing with the world. Teachers are expected to give, even when they receive little in return. It is not the heavy emotional involvement with students that drains a teacher; rather, it is the involvement with few dividends (Heifetz & Bersani, 1983). The asymmetrical quality of the teacher-student relationship is the source of an emotional drain for teachers who nurture. It creates an incompletion in the caring cycle. The caring cycle is the reciprocal connection between two human beings involving a mutual giving and receiving of caring. Caregivers are worn down by the lack of completion in this caring cycle.

Understandably, working closely with 150 students can be an emotionally draining experience for nurturing teachers. How do these six teachers sustain and revitalize their personal and professional energy? How do these teachers maintain their enthusiasm for their jobs year after year? To shed some light on these concerns, this study explored both personal and environmental resources that provide support for these teachers in their efforts to bond with students. It seems logical that knowing these resources could help educators develop and support teachers who nurture. Knowing that there are effective ways to take care of oneself may reassure teachers who are contemplating taking a more active supportive role in the lives of young people.

In order to identify the personal and environmental resources that support the six nurturing teachers, the study explores their personal beliefs, traits, experiences, and skills and identifies similar characteristics. These shared qualities may well be the personal resources that enable these teachers to interact continually with students on such an intense level. This chapter and Chapter 6 discuss these personal resources—the similar beliefs, experiences, intrapersonal traits, and interpersonal skills—that seem to facilitate a teacher's ability to make healthy, rewarding connections with students. Some of these personal resources seem to help teachers in their efforts to nurture students such as developing trust and acceptance in students. This increased ability increases competence and confidence and thus mediates stress (Farber, 1991). Other skills and traits discussed are employed for the specific purpose of reducing stress and revitalizing personal and professional energy.

This chapter begins by identifying common beliefs about teaching held by the six nurturing teachers, illustrating each with specific examples. The chapter then discusses and illustrates the skills associated with revitalization strategies—the specific skills for mediating stress. Most of the beliefs and skills discussed are ethereal in nature and therefore difficult to illustrate through brief examples. The pervasiveness of each of the qualities among the teachers is demonstrated by brief examples or quotes for each teacher and recorded in the boxes in Appendix C. Finally, the chapter discusses the personal relational experiences that provide these teachers with tools for successful relationships.

Beliefs About the Role of a Teacher and Teaching

Observations and interviews with nurturing teachers reveal six common beliefs and practices about teaching and the teaching profession. They are the following:

1. Student growth is a primary educational goal.
2. Service to young people is the key motivation for becoming a teacher.
3. A teacher's power must be handled ethically.
4. The curriculum is a means to promoting student growth.
5. Teaching is a valued and valuable profession.
6. Classroom teaching is more desirable than an administrative position.

These six beliefs shared by all the teachers provide fundamental direction and purpose to a teacher's nurturing behavior. Thus, these beliefs provide cognitive support for bonding with students.

Student Growth Is a Primary Educational Goal

For all six teachers, a primary educational goal is student personal growth. Research (e.g., McLaughlin, 1990) suggests that the most valued educational goal of nurturing teachers is the personal growth of students. When given a choice of eight educational goals, student personal growth being one of them, all six teachers ranked it as one of their top three choices out of eight:

1. Basic academic skills
2. Good work habits
3. Academic excellence
4. Personal growth
5. Human relations skills
6. Citizenship
7. Occupational skills
8. Moral and ethical development

Four of the teachers chose student personal growth as their top choice for an educational goal, one teacher ranked it as second most important next to moral and ethical development, and one teacher ranked it as third, next to moral and ethical development and citizenship. Even the first and second choices of these two teachers encourage student growth by promoting their social and moral development. These teachers care about the personal, emotional, and moral development of students, as well as their cognitive development. They commit their energy, time, and curricula to nurturing student social and emotional development. They view the nurturing responsibilities of a teacher as an important and valued aspect of their jobs.

> Of all the things that your kids come away with in the classroom, all of the knowledge and the skills, I think one of the greatest things that they can come away with is just the fact that there's a human being that cares about them. (Ruby)

> The [nurturing relationship] is the most important thing. . . . I am either going to speed up the process of student failure or speed up the process of success by what I do. And the relationship is really what it is all about. (Dean)

Although these teachers view the role of a teacher broadly to include responsibility for the social, moral, and emotional development of students, it is not at the expense of their primary responsibilities as a teacher—the cognitive development of students. These teachers view student growth holistically. They do not see cognitive development happening independently of social, moral, and emotional development. They believe social, moral, emotional, and cognitive development happen synergistically. In other words, they view the cognitive development of students as part and parcel of their goal for student personal growth.

> I think that the bottom line for all teachers that are nurturing is that you really care about your student outcomes, what happens to every one of your students—when you start and when you finish with them. Everything else is like a different means to the same ends . . . a better individual. (Dean)

These teachers are committed to student learning and work hard at helping that happen. Dale provides an example by his willingness to teach a basic mathematics course, the Fundamentals of Mathematics, because he saw too many basic mathematics students failing the competency test. Dale believes these students can learn mathematics. He wants to try some new teaching strategies with these students to help them learn the subject. It is his first year of teaching Fundamentals of Mathematics in his 14 years of teaching.

> I don't have a textbook because I felt that that's the same old thing they've always done. So I'm trying to do new things, to be real creative with those guys. So I create things as I go in that class. What I do is, like on Sunday evenings, I'll come in and plan my week.

Dale would like to develop a mathematics lab for his basic math students.

> I'd like to get more computers in here. I'd like to be able to get a lab kind of, where we could put all these kids on their own computer and let them kind of go and explore things on the computer. . . . I think the kids would probably take off a lot quicker than just looking at a blackboard. I know they would.

Dean gives another good example of commitment to student cognitive development in his willingness to spend personal money to provide his students with the learning materials they need.

> Man, I probably spend $1500 a year out of my own pocket just to buy everything. . . . We have no budget. We ran out of paper! If I want to ditto something I have to bring my own reams of paper. [laugh] Today we looked at jellyfish. I had to buy those jellyfish. The next thing we look at is squid, and I'm going to have to go down and buy squid. A lot of things like jellyfish, I have to send to a biological supply house, and that's like a *bank!*

(See Box 4.1, Appendix C, for some brief examples illustrating the pervasiveness of a commitment to student learning among all teachers.)

Service to Young People Is the
Key Motivation for Becoming a Teacher

With a primary educational goal to promote student growth and development, these teachers broadly view the role of an educator as a human service professional. All six teachers were motivated to become teachers to be of service to other human beings in a meaningful way.

> Probably the thing that attracted me most was the desire to try and have some kind of influence on bettering our society. . . . [Teaching] gives me the opportunity to have what I think is a tremendous impact upon the future. (Tom)

Monetary interests were not a major consideration for any of the key informants. In fact, Pam and Dean changed careers as adults, leaving well-paying positions in the business world to return to college and become teachers. Both were seeking career positions that satisfied a personal need to be of service to others. For another example, when Dale was asked what his purpose is as a teacher, he says,

> To turn that light on in each kid. We used to call it "your paycheck." You get a paycheck when that kid's eyes light up, "I got it. I understand!" That's the paycheck. . . . Too, I think that the purpose that we have at the high school is to turn out people who are ready to go out and fend for themselves, to understand what it takes to support oneself, to give them at least a boost in that direction.

Tom, when describing what qualities he tries to project to students, says, "Money isn't the overall motivation in life. There's satisfaction in helping someone. You're not paid for everything." When asked what their purpose as a teacher is or what characteristics about the teaching profession are most attractive to them, invariably the responses of these teachers embody the theme of being of service to others and making a difference in the lives of others (see Box 4.2, Appendix C).

The Teacher's Power Must Be Handled Ethically

These teachers are keenly aware of the potentially powerful effect they have on students' lives. They acknowledge the power that their actions, words, and attitudes may wield with young, developing human beings. They believe it is the moral and ethical responsibility of teachers to be aware of how they use that power. They recognize that how they interact with students influences a student's self-perception and self-esteem. These teachers are aware that their behavior impacts a student's social, moral, and emotional development. Gail relates a story using the blue eyes/brown eyes experiment demonstrating the power of a teacher. With the blue eyes/brown eyes experiment, a teacher arbitrarily pigeonholes all students with a specific color of eyes as inferior, ignorant, and second-class citizens. Students with all other eye colors are considered superior, bright, and capable. The teacher interacts and reacts to students according to the labels. It is a powerful experiential exercise to demonstrate the power of stereotyping, but Gail relates how she became keenly aware of the responsibility she carries with her power as a teacher after using the exercise.

> We have a lot of power, a lot of power. [Teachers] don't realize it until they've done something damaging or until someone has come back after 10 years and said, "I've become this because of you." I didn't recognize it really, until 4 years ago when I did an experiment with my class—the blue eyes/brown eyes experiment. It took me about 7 minutes to make half the kids really mad, really upset, and doubt their abilities. *About 7 minutes!* And these are kids that I've had for 4 or 5 months and just that fast I was able to make them think they were stupid, and they couldn't do well on tests, and the other side of the room was better than they were. It took me another 20 minutes to tell them that this was all a test, not for real.

As a child, Ruby was powerfully impacted by the teachers in her life. She knows the power of an educator from firsthand personal experience and recognizes that a single teacher can make a difference in students' lives. She acknowledges that in today's society she, as a teacher, plays a powerful role in the social and emotional development of young people.

> It breaks my heart to think that for some of these kids who sit in my class for 50 minutes, that they see me more than they would see an adult in the home or that we might interact more than they interact with their adults at home. Kids really need and want attention, want validation that they're good people, that they are important . . . and I see that as being a huge, huge issue within our system today with our kids.

As a result of her personal experiences, Ruby believes students' awareness of her caring for them is the most important knowledge that she gives to students as their teacher.

With the primary goal of student personal growth and the awareness of power that comes with their position, these teachers have a
keen appreciation and compelling motivation for nurturing students. They *know* that teachers can make a difference (see Box 4.3,
Appendix C).

Curriculum Is a Means to
Promoting Student Growth

Conscious of the power of their words and actions, these teachers
carefully design and deliver their curricula to influence student
growth. They view their subject matter content as a vehicle, a means
to an end, not the end. The end purpose for these teachers is to help
students function successfully in society. They believe that the content knowledge they hold so dearly is not the most important lesson
for students to learn in order to lead productive lives or become
better people (see Box 4.4, Appendix C). Pam says,

> I mean, I love history and I believe it's real wonderful and
> all that. But is a seventh grader's life really going to change
> if they know who the rulers of Mesopotamia are? No. What's
> more important is that they learn how to be successful as
> people and they learn how to get along with each other. You
> know, they learn how to retrieve information that they are
> going to need. They learn how to work cooperatively. Those
> are some of the things important to me in teaching kids. That
> they have a sense of responsibility about being citizens and
> contributing and about being human beings and having
> compassion for one another. That's a lot more important to
> me.

Dean reflects the same sentiments as Pam.

> A kid's got to be able to read; a kid's got to be able to write;
> a kid's got to be able to do math; he's got to be able to work
> in a group; he's got to be able to respect his peers and deal
> with people, even people he doesn't like or she doesn't like.
> They got to be able to have pride in themselves and self-
> respect and real pride and respect in their community and
> the people around them. My whole approach to teaching is

to take a person and use the academic part to direct all of this—the reading and writing and the math and stuff like that. I use biology like a vehicle to try to make those other things occur, self-respect, all that kind of stuff.

Teaching Is a Valued and Valuable Profession

These teachers value their profession and perceive the teaching profession as valued by others. They are advocates for the profession. They demonstrate their commitment to the profession by their pride in their level of expertise and their continual efforts to upgrade their skills and knowledge in order to become better teachers.

All of the key informants have a high level of expertise in their content area and work to stay abreast of new developments in their chosen subjects. For example, Pam says,

> I think I have a very confident grasp of the subject. I bring to this more depth and a broader knowledge base than—this is going to sound conceited but—almost everybody, well, certainly in this building. And that's just because I've read history for almost all of my life, certainly all of my adult life. And I think about it in different ways and how it can be applied.

Ruby proudly says, "I am knowledgeable about what it is that I teach." Knowledgeable in his content area, Dale works hard to stay abreast of changes in his field.

> I do go—I try to go to a lot of the Educational Service District [ESD] math conferences. I try to keep up on that. I try to pride myself in being abreast with the new standards. I do support the new standards that the NCTM [National Council of Teachers of Mathematics] has come up with. I'm on the math curriculum writing committees [for the ESD]. . . . I've done some work to upgrade my math level past the calculus and things like that.

All these teachers are lifelong learners, actively seeking new learning experiences that will help them become better teachers. Gail seeks courses outside her content area that will help her be a better teacher.

> I have taken classes from [local universities] like how to incorporate humor in your classroom or courses on conflict management or courses dealing with alcoholism, "Here's Looking at You Two Thousand." Those kind of courses I find very beneficial. . . . I enjoy what is relevant today and I enjoy courses which help me help the kids today—help them deal with their problems and make my course more relevant to their lives.

Dean has traveled out of state to a large prestigious university for summer studies in the area of biology. He was selected as an exchange teacher to Japan. He sees this experience giving him a different perspective and new insights for teaching science. Tom is a social activist. He is energized by school renewal efforts and stays on the cutting edge of school reform within his building and his district. He is working on implementing team teaching and now is designing curriculum to teach to multiple types of intelligence. Tom expresses frustration with faculty members who are uncomfortable with change or doing things differently, saying,

> What I want to do is to go to a new school where I can use and have the structure to use and the ability to try and implement more lessons and programs designed to reach multiple intelligence. Right now, the way the structure is around here, it's real tough. I'm tired of trying to drag people kicking and screaming into the 21st century who are living in the 19th century.

Such enthusiasm for their subjects and their profession helps make these teachers good stewards of the profession. They see themselves as professionals, and they continue to grow professionally. They value education, promote the teaching profession, and advocate school renewal (see Box 4.5, Appendix C).

Classroom Teaching Is More Desirable Than an Administrative Position

None of these teachers has an interest in becoming an administrator. These teachers plan to remain in the classroom or in direct service to students for their whole career. Not only are they not interested in advancing in their careers through the administrative channels, but they also all state quite passionately their distaste for administrative positions. Here are some examples of responses to being asked if they ever thought of being an administrator:

> You could never get me to be an administrator. I don't have the personality for that. I don't have the patience. I have patience for kids but man, you put me in a room with parents not willing to do a thing and they're chewing on you because you suspended their kid for doing something—*No way!* I won't do that. I'd rather shoot myself before I become an administrator. (Tom)

> No! No! No! I have no desire to be an administrator. It involves too much politics and not enough kids. (Gail)

> I wouldn't touch that with a 10-foot pole. I think administration, especially when you come in at entry level and start out as a vice-principal, that so much of the contact with kids is the discipline. I don't think I would get a lot of positives from working with kids like that. In the classroom, you are going to deal with things like that but on a much, much smaller basis. The positive contact you have with the kids will greatly outweigh that. I am going to stay put in the classroom. (Ruby)

All the teachers observed responded to this question similarly. These teachers enjoy working closely with kids in a classroom situation. Foremost, they value the relationship with young people and do not see administrative positions offering them the same opportunities for relationships with kids as the classroom situation offers. Relationships with young people give their careers meaning so they have no desire to move up an educational career ladder to an administrative position.

Special Skills and Traits
That Help Teachers Mediate Stress

These beliefs about the role of teachers and the teaching profession provide teachers with a cognitive framework that gives direction and purpose to the professional energy they give to nurturing students. Such purposeful motivation helps sustain and revitalize professional commitment. Besides holding in common these personal beliefs, these teachers hold in common several coping strategies that ease their stress level and help them cope with the demands of the job. These include the following: (a) coping skill of detachment, (b) talking with someone they trust, including professional help if necessary, and (c) feeling effective at their jobs. These skills are identified in the research literature on burnout prevention among human service workers and teachers as healthy ways to cope (Edelwich & Brodsky, 1980; Farber, 1991).

Detaching

Detachment is the ability to acknowledge stressful events but not to take personally the happenings surrounding stressful events. Individuals who are able to detach from the stressful events of the day and keep a balanced perspective are less affected by their stressful work (Edelwich & Brodsky, 1980). Detachment is a primary psychological coping mechanism for these teachers. For instance, Dean says, "I am real good at detaching, as far as not taking it personally. . . . This is part of life. You are going to have conflicts occur at our level [high school]. Just deal with it." Ruby and Dale had to learn to detach. Ruby says she used to want all the students to like her and was really upset when she had a conflict with a student. "Now I just have resolved that there are some kids that, for whatever reasons, are going to have personality conflicts with you or they're not going to like the activities and things that you're doing, and that's okay." When asked about his strengths as a teacher, Dale mentions communication and detachment. "I've learned not to take everything personally. A lot of things are like water off a duck's back." All the key informants mentioned how much easier their job is when they detach personally from the stressful happenings.

Other evidence that demonstrates that these teachers detach is that they do not assume responsibility for students' well-being. Even though they view nurturing students as an important way to accomplish their educational goals, they are able to let go of the consequences of their nurturing efforts toward students. They do not have to be successful all the time. These teachers just do it, even if students choose not to respond favorably to the teacher's efforts. Letting go of the consequences of one's nurturing efforts is a way to avoid stress and frustration. These teachers acknowledge that students who refuse to respond to their nurturing efforts are difficult students with whom to work, but they also do not inappropriately assume responsibility for the decisions that these nonreceptive students make. These teachers appear to continue reaching out to these students in the same manner even though their nurturing efforts may seem in vain.

Finally, not taking things too seriously, another form of detachment, is additional evidence that these teachers use detachment as a coping mechanism. These teachers use healthy humor to lessen the impact of stressful days. These teachers have a good sense of humor. They are playful and funny and able to laugh at themselves. They have fun with their students and their peers.

> I've had more fun time teaching here than in any school . . . great practical jokers, a lot of humor. And people realize that the way that we keep our sanity is through laughing. And that's real important. (Tom)

A willingness to laugh at oneself and create humor helps keep stressful events in perspective and thus mediates stress.

Talking

Talking about stressful events with supportive peers, friends, or family is another helpful coping technique used by these teachers. These teachers turn to family, peers, and friends as sounding boards. Suburb Junior High teachers use their lunch period with their peers to relieve stress and talk about the stressful events of the day. Pam says, "It is a nice chance to kind of let off some steam and have some adult talk. . . . Usually it is peppered with a lot of four letter words and phrases. . . . We talk shop a lot during these lunches." Tom talks about how he learned to dialogue as an effective coping technique.

> I don't keep my feelings in like I used to. I think I did fit the typical male stereotype of just hold in everything and don't show the emotion for a long time. Things started to change when I was in my mid-20s, I'd say, and I think today I talk a lot more. Sometimes it takes a little prodding still. I've got a

> wife who's pretty good at the prodding. She gets me to talk
> about it so instead of bottling things in, so I let things out.

All these teachers made reference to someone they trust with whom
they can talk about the stresses of the day and mentioned talking
about stressful events as a technique to mediate stress.

Several teachers indicate that during really traumatic times, they
seek professional assistance for sorting out their problems. For instance, one teacher mentioned having been diagnosed with cancer
several years earlier and seeking professional counseling to help her
cope with the psychological aspects of the threatening disease while
she underwent medical treatment. Another teacher mentioned seeking professional counseling to help her resolve some childhood
issues that were unnecessarily complicating her life as an adult.
These teachers recognize that traumatic situations may be better
handled by involving a professional than by depending on family
and friends as confidantes, and they are willing to ask for professional assistance.

Feeling Effective in Their Jobs

The root of burnout for teachers may be feeling ineffective or
inconsequential in their jobs (Farber, 1991). These teachers feel effective and know they make a difference in student lives. They believe
their work matters. They feel appreciated and recognized for their
work both by parents and by students. They see the payoffs for their
work in the positive student or parent responses and the student
growth they witness. For instance, Ruby's back wall is decorated
with a 10-foot mural filled with student compliments to her in short,
clipped phrases such as, "You are the greatest!" or "I could never
have done it without you!" In the few days of observation of these
teachers, several times older students returned to say hello to a
"favorite" teacher. Some of these students had already graduated
and were just stopping by to visit. Tom says,

> I've lost track of the kids, to tell you the truth. I know I've
> made a difference, you know, in kids. I've lost track of a lot
> of them, in terms of who they are and who they were. They
> come back to see me, like the kid yesterday. He's entering
> the Marines, the music program for the Marines. And yet all

he wanted to talk about was his ninth-grade year. You know, and it's scary sometimes to think that you have that much impact. It's terrifying.

Once while I observed Dean, a previous student came into his classroom. She had been a teaching assistant for Dean and was home on break from college. She reiterated how important Dean had been in her life. Likewise, while interviewing Dale, he talked about the parents who talk to him about what a difference his teaching made for their child.

[Parents say,] "You did a hell of a job" or "You did a great job for us. My son or daughter really enjoys being in your class. You're teaching them something. They never liked math before." I get that. And that, to me, makes it worth-while. (Dale)

These feelings of effectiveness and consequentiality at one's job are important resources that support and sustain these teachers in their efforts to nurture students.

Past Childhood Experiences With Bonding

The common personal beliefs discussed provide the needed direction, support, and motivation for successfully developing close and trusting bonds with students. The coping skills ease stress levels and help these teachers handle the demands of their jobs. In addition to these personal resources, the research literature identifies another important personal cognitive resource affecting a teacher's effectiveness at developing healthy relationships—familial experiences with bonding as a child. Having positive bonding experiences with primary caregivers as a child cultivates a natural ability to form positive connections with others as an adult (Bowlby, 1988; Main, Kaplan, & Cassidy, 1985). Positive experiences provide individuals with intrinsic healthy mental patterns for relating with others (Bowlby, 1988).

Psychological theorists contend that a high percentage of children with abusive parents develop negative, unsuccessful patterns of relating. These negative patterns for relating make it difficult to form healthy relationships as adults (Bowlby, 1988; Karen, 1990;

Main et al., 1985). Thus, the skills for bonding and developing meaningful connections with others are passed from one generation to the next (Main et al., 1985).

In addition, psychological theorists contend that positive patterns for relating to others also can be developed in cases in which childhood bonding experiences were negative if there is some therapeutic intervention. Individuals reared in dysfunctional, abusive families are inadequately prepared both emotionally and socially to deal with the closeness and responsibilities of a personal relationship—unless these individuals therapeutically work through these negative experiences. In other words, teachers with childhood histories of chronic abuse may have difficulty forming healthy relationships with their students unless there is a therapeutic intervention resulting in personal insight and awareness (Main et al., 1985). They may also find these close relationships stressful. Without the social and emotional foundations and the resulting relational skills, the dynamics in a close relationship become a personal burden (Bowlby, 1988).

This study supports the assertions of the psychological theorists. Four of the six key informants appear to come from happy, stable childhoods. Their familial experiences were described as nurturing and supportive. When asked about their upbringing, they said such things as the following:

> I had a real nurturing upbringing. I had a real supportive mother and father and brothers and sister and we were all real tight. (Dean)

> I wouldn't trade it for anything. . . . All the people who were associated with me, my uncles were supportive, my aunt, my coaches that I had, the friends of Dad that I had were always just willing to help us. (Dale)

Healthy, familial bonding experiences as children appear to provide these individuals with positive relational skills that enhance their competence at forming healthy relationships as adults (Bowlby, 1979). In addition to equipping these teachers with healthy relational skills, these families are a major source of support and encouragement for them today. Such support is a personal revitalizing resource for these teachers in their efforts to develop close and trusting relationships with students.

Two teachers, Ruby and Pam, defined their families of origin as dysfunctional. In their families, there was physical and sexual abuse, abandonment, violent rage, and alcoholism. These teachers acknowledge that as children their parents did not provide them with an emotionally "secure base." Both Ruby and Pam have been through intense therapy to help them rework negative patterns for relating and integrate painful childhood experiences. Both teachers now draw on their therapeutic experiences in ways that are helpful for developing meaningful connections with others. Their abusive family backgrounds and therapeutic experiences have become an asset rather than a liability. These therapeutic experiences have given them a depth of insight and understanding into human behavior that is uncharacteristic of the general population. Both Ruby and Pam indicate that they would not be able to work with students the way they do if they had not gone to therapy. Understandably, these teachers depend on close friends and support groups as personal support systems for emotional renewal and revitalization rather than families.

Summary of Personal Beliefs, Coping Skills, and Experiences

Personal beliefs, coping skills, and positive childhood relational experiences provide some of the inner resources these nurturing teachers need to accomplish successfully their educational goals for the students. The common personal beliefs are the following:

1. Student growth is a primary educational goal.
2. Service to young people is the key motivation for becoming a teacher.
3. A teacher's power must be handled ethically.
4. Curriculum is a means to promoting student growth.
5. Teaching is a valued and valuable profession.
6. Classroom teaching is more desirable than an administrative position.

These six beliefs provide fundamental direction and purpose to a teacher's nurturing behavior, providing cognitive support for bonding with students. The coping strategies of detaching, talking about stressful events, and feeling competent in their jobs relieve stress and help these teachers deal with the demands of their jobs. Finally, positive childhood bonding experiences or reevaluated negative familial experiences provide nurturing teachers with the relational experiences needed to thrive when in intense relationships with many demands.

5

Characteristics of Nurturing Teachers

✄ ✄ ✄ ✄ ✄

Tom's voice becomes softer and he speaks more slowly as he continues to answer the question I had just asked: "What experiences influenced your decision to be a teacher?" I diverted my eyes downward as I listened to his answer. The lump in my throat tells me that if I make eye contact with Tom, my eyes would instantly well-up in sentimental tears. His response to my question stops me short. "All my lousy teachers . . . and one man by the name of Francis M_____. He was my literature teacher when I was a sophomore and a junior. He knew I had a lot of problems, but he always believed I was a good person and could do good things. I credit him with my life, literally. Without his belief in me, I couldn't have stopped doing the things I was doing."

I glance up at Tom and say, "That's exactly what this study is about . . . teachers who make a difference in students' lives."

Tom's eyes are red with tears as he gazes back at me, but he doesn't seem embarrassed. Tom continues, "Mr. M_____ was sort of a geek. He was the typical stereotype of an intellectual—horn-rimmed glasses, short, the works. Some students made fun of him, but we all knew he cared. The other teachers did not help me at all. They all knew I was having problems, but they didn't seem to care or believe that I could be different."

Tom pauses, glances away uncomfortably, and then looks directly at me and confidently says, "Even though I was doing some really outrageous things, and some I definitely shouldn't have been involved in, Mr. M_____ still somehow could see through all the dirt and recognize that there was a good person inside. Mr. M_____ believed in me."

Tom had been using drugs and even selling them to his classmates. In the first week of his senior year, he was forced to drop out of school. The day he dropped out of school, Tom was required to fill out a form identifying what he planned to do in the future. All his teachers had to sign this form. Never fully comprehending why, Tom indicated he was going to become a teacher. "They all laughed . . . except Mr. M_____. Mr. M_____ actually told me he believed in me. He said he knew I would do what I said I would. I knew I could teach better than most of the teachers I had. And I know teachers make a difference in a child's life because Mr. M_____ had made a difference in my life."

❦ ❦ ❦ ❦ ❦

Personality Traits Held in Common

The teachers observed have distinctly different personalities and different approaches to teaching. Some are strict and detached with high academic expectations; others are warm, spontaneous, and passionately involved. Some use traditional lecture modes for curriculum delivery; others use cooperative learning or small-group strategies or a combination of several delivery strategies. Some maintain very quiet classrooms; others have rowdy and loud classrooms. Some are intellectuals. Some are athletes. Some are regal and sophisticated; others are fun-loving and boisterous. Even with different personalities and teaching styles, these teachers are making a difference in many students' lives. Are there any common personality traits and skills among all the teachers? Are there special personal resources that help them nurture students? It seems logical that if there are common traits and skills, these qualities could provide windows to understanding the personal characteristics that support and advance nurturing behavior.

This chapter describes and illustrates the intrapersonal characteristics that all of these teachers share. Each characteristic also includes suggestions about how it may be a revitalizing resource for teachers who nurture close and trusting connections with students.

Predominant Intrapersonal Characteristics

Several intrapersonal characteristics held in common by the teachers appear to support and advance nurturing behavior:

1. Genuineness and authenticity
2. Inner locus of control
3. Tolerance for ambiguity
4. Humor
5. Nonjudgmental stance
6. Potency
7. Enthusiasm
8. Androgyny

Genuineness and Authenticity

The most vivid intrapersonal qualities that stood out early in the analysis are the genuineness and authenticity of the teachers. Genuineness and authenticity are defined as being fully and freely ourselves without overwhelming other individuals (Carkhuff, 1987). None of the six nurturing teachers presents a facade or phoniness that would misrepresent them. They do not hide behind their position of teacher to define themselves in relation to their students. They present themselves to students, first, as human beings and, second, as teachers. They appear unpretentious and unaffected.

> Ruby pauses during a lecture and says, "Gosh, I am talking a lot. Am I talking too much?" she asks the class. Some in the class respond "no" and others respond "yes." Ruby listens to the feedback and says, "I hear several yeses, so let's move on." She moves to a group activity. (observation notes)

Tom asks, "How many of you would find it hard not to strike back at someone who is hitting you?" Students raise their hands. Tom acknowledges that he would have a hard time also. (observation notes)

Dale provides a fun example of this intrapersonal characteristic. One student asked him why he always writes two math problems on the board for the class to work out rather than just one. Dale humorously rattled off a series of reasons, "I am on a roll, besides I don't want to break up my thought process and this is easier." Then he paused for a second and said sincerely, "Actually, I don't have a real valid reason." He laughed and so did the students.

These teachers recognize the importance of being genuine and authentic with students as a quality of a nurturing relationship. Dean says,

No matter what you do you got to be honest. You got to be yourself. You have to show them yourself. Your teaching style has got to be you. If I try to be anything but myself, I am not going to be a nurturing, caring-type teacher. If I try to be something different, it would just fail.

Stressing the same point, Pam says,

To develop nurturing relationships with students, you've got to be yourself. Don't try to force anything because kids can smell bullshit a mile away. Nothing's more painful to me than watching a teacher try to force something that isn't—I mean, some people fall into it. It's just natural for them to be warm and loving and show that. And other people may want to do it, but they can't. They're either not confident or comfortable enough with their own selves to do it.

Students appear to acknowledge the genuineness of these teachers. When describing qualities he liked in Gail, a student said,

It's really hard to explain. You'd have to see it for yourself. See it in her. You can't really put it into words. It's a lot—it's a lot in just watching her be herself. (Jake)

Genuineness and authenticity on a teacher's part support the bonding process by creating a basis for trusting the teacher and promoting student self-acceptance (see Box 5.1, Appendix C). Genuine and authentic responses solicit genuine and authentic responses. This cultivates trust and self-acceptance in individuals (Carkhuff, 1969, 1987; Rogers, 1961).

Inner Locus of Control

An inner locus of control is defined as the belief that an individual's destiny is his or her own responsibility and is not controlled by external events. Individuals are accountable for what happens in their lives (Farber, 1991). It becomes apparent that an individual has an inner locus of control when he or she assumes responsibility for how he or she is behaving and engaging in life.

The observed teachers readily assume responsibility for what is happening in their lives. They acknowledge ownership of choices that create change or turmoil in their lives. Individuals with inner loci of control are not easily swayed from personal convictions by the disapproval of others. They do not project blame on others. These teachers do not accuse or blame the administration, students, or others for negative events that are happening in their professional lives. Tom provides a good example with how he handled a political situation in his work environment.

A couple years ago, I submitted my name to be department head. A teacher who's pretty meek and mild said to me after I had lost, "You know, I would have voted for you, Tom, if you could do a better job in terms of when you disagree with people." And that made me think a lot and it was a stressful time. . . . The hardest thing for me to deal with is people who just simply don't try to improve themselves, just simply want to keep things the exact way they are, you know. I think I've done a better job at just kind of sitting back and not reacting to it. I've gotten a lot of compliments too from people. I'll go and sit in with the other side and listen to them and other people that were in our camp in terms of wanting to go forward in teaming and weren't willing to go unless some of the other people's points were considered. I took it upon myself to just go and do that.

Tom examined his behavior and took it on himself to make the necessary changes. Tom is now head of the social studies department at Suburb Junior High School. Gail provides another example of inner locus of control.

> If I have a class that's either not focused or not managed the way I like to see it managed, then I take responsibility for that. I need to find out what to do to manage it or what I need to do to help students get focused. I've been around teachers who always put the blame on the child, the child's home, and this and that. . . . You need to focus on what you can do to change it. My daughter's teacher is that way where it's, "Well, she plays around and she does this or she does that." My question to her is, "What have you done to make her attentive? Have you changed your plans? Have you changed your classroom management style?"

An inner locus of control is identified as the key characteristic of individuals who are least likely to experience stress and burnout (Farber, 1991; Fielding, 1982; Marlin, 1987; McIntyre, 1984). Research in psychology suggests that the most important factor for stress management is controllability. Inner locus of control places the control of events or reactions to events squarely in the hands of the individual. Teachers who accept responsibility for what is happening in their lives are less likely to suffer burnout and are more successful at mediating stress. As part of their inner locus of control, they recognize that their reaction to stressful events is their responsibility and adopt strategies to mediate or alleviate their stress. This personal resource supports teachers in their efforts to make close and trusting relationships by enabling them simply to enjoy the connections with students. They know that they are responsible for their reactions to student behavior, not the students. These teachers do not experience these connections as an added responsibility that drains them of their personal and professional energy (see Box 5.2, Appendix C).

Tolerance for Ambiguity

Although a sense of control is an important factor in mediating stress, tolerating ambiguous situations is also important (Fielding, 1982). A tolerance for ambiguity is defined as being able to comfortably deal with situations out of one's control. This quality is essential for reducing stress when working with a variety of people on a variety of projects. The observed teachers recognize their limits and capabilities. They understand that not everything is clearly defined or within their control but that their reaction to the situation can be controlled. Most often, they can comfortably let go of control and adapt to an ambiguous situation when necessary.

Dean and Dale are masters at tolerating ambiguity. Their skills are demonstrated by how quickly they shift gears and move from one student's demands and concern to the next student's concern. They have a high tolerance for confusion, noise, and disorganization. Not only are they tolerant of these environments, but they thrive in them. After a particularly frazzling day with many different unplanned events happening, Dean said with a big grin on his face, "This is where I thrive—in places like this on days like this. It does not have to be this noisy, but I thrive in places like this."

Both Dean and Dale can remain focused in the midst of the confusion, responding to a variety of student questions seemingly at the same time. For instance, Dale was observed telling a teaching assistant how to fix a computer glitch, asking a student to sit properly in her desk, and suggesting that another use a calculator all without losing his concentration on the problem he was explaining or the student he was working with.

Dean and Dale have an open, adaptable classroom management style that many teachers would judge as too permissive. However, with both of these teachers, tolerance for ambiguity and flexibility *ends* when a student's behavior has negative long-term effects on the student or other students, such as shirking his or her responsibilities to get assignments in or interfering with another student's opportunity to learn. Dean points out that he really has "no trouble with situations out of his control except when kids are hurt."

For Dale, Gail, Tom, and Pam, ambiguous situations actually enhance their teaching styles. They enjoy capitalizing on teachable moments. For instance, Pam adapts very quickly to what happens in the classroom. She values flexibility and wants "to find more ways to fuse [her] curriculum with student-directed learning."

I'm not one of those teachers who has to be in control all the time, although I keep a pretty controlled classroom in terms of my students. I'm willing to give up my directing the flow

of what is going on in the classroom and let it be more
student directed or issue directed. (Pam)

Like Pam, Gail likes to use teachable moments and responds to
individual student needs. She says, "I wish I could individualize
more of my lessons." Teachable moments help Gail make her lesson
plans relevant for her students, an important goal for her. Dale uses
ambiguity to enhance his creative teaching style, taking advantage
of the teachable moments. "I don't have lesson plans that are written
out anymore. It's kind of in my head. Sometimes I like to go on the
fly. I have the general idea, and I just go from there because I kind of
know what these kids can and can't do."

Even when these teachers struggle with an ambiguous situation,
they are aware of the importance of "letting go" as a strategy for
managing their stress. For instance, Ruby, because of her unstable
childhood, initially had trouble dealing with ambiguous situations
on the job.

When anything would disrupt what I thought was a stable
situation, it'd be like, "Oh, what have we got to do to fix this,
calm it down!" Now, it's like, if there's nothing I can do to
help it, then it's going to ride its course. I need to let it go.
(Ruby)

Ambiguous situations give these teachers a challenge, an opportunity to learn and grow. Tom says, "I like to be in control, but I also
like the uniqueness of a situation for learning where you are out of
control."

Thus, a tolerance for ambiguity is a helpful characteristic for
revitalization by increasing adaptability to a variety of situations. A
tolerance for ambiguity seems particularly helpful for those teachers
who choose to bond with young people primarily through one-to-
one time with students during class time. This strategy of bonding
requires that teachers be able to shift gears quickly and thrive in
environments in which many different demands are being made on
them. It requires that a teacher enjoy doing a multitude of tasks at
what seems to be the same time and have *little* quiet, focused, concentration time, at least during the actual class period. A tolerance for
ambiguity lets these demands become opportunities, not emotional
drains.

A tolerance for ambiguity also aids bonding as well as mediating stress. It communicates to students an openness to their needs and concerns, allowing students to perceive the caring and nurturing side of teachers.

Humor

According to the *American Heritage Dictionary* (1993), humor is a quality that makes something laughable, amusing, or playful. It really needs no clarification except that humor expressed by these teachers appears not at the expense of others. They often laugh at themselves. As mentioned earlier, these teachers are humorous and playful. They enjoy their jobs, and you can see it on their faces when you watch them teach. You can feel it when you talk to them. They appear to value humor in the classroom and in the work environment. These teachers talk with students using humor, often playfully teasing. For instance, Tom's baby daughter had her adenoids out the week before this interaction with a student.

> A student asks Tom how his daughter is doing, knowing that Tom's baby daughter had been sick. They talk for a few minutes about the baby. Tom asked the student if he had had his adenoids out. The student asked, "What is that?" Tom laughed and said, "Is your voice higher?" and there was a twinkle in his eye. The kid responded horrified, "Oh no!" Tom laughed and told him what adenoids were. (observation notes)

The teasing goes both ways. One student, finding out that Tom was being observed, jokingly said, "So that is why he is being so nice to us! He hasn't taken his belt off once!" Everyone laughed and Tom enjoyed the teasing.

Lessons are presented with humor, students are motivated with humor, discipline is handled with humor, and classrooms are managed with humor. Several of these teachers are just one step away from being stand-up comedians. For example, Dale uses a constant banter of humor to discipline, to instruct, to motivate, and to acknowledge.

> Dale says, "Tell me why we are here." Students respond with, "To learn math," "To get a credit," "Because you are

such a cool guy." Dale says, "The reason we are here today is to learn percentages so that on the comp test we will see them and say POC—piece of cake." The class turns its attention on Dale. He grabs a student's notebook to illustrate percentages. He looks in the notebook and sees a sandwich. He examines the ham sandwich. "What percentage of this sandwich is bread and what percent is filling?" The class rattles off different answers. Dale shows them—two-thirds bread, one-third filling. Amused he says, "Maybe that's not true. There is a lot of mustard on this thing!" They laugh. Then he pulls out some magazine pages that are stored in the notebook and acts shocked and horrified, as if they are from a girly magazine. The students laugh. (observation notes)

When Pam was facilitating the discussion on harassment, she flashed, "I feel like Oprah Winfrey!" Then she quickly proceeded into a short, impromptu vignette mimicking Oprah. She races up and down the aisles, holding a make-believe microphone under the chins of different students while she facetiously asks questions.

Tom says, "The students think I'm nuts, and that is great! I like the kids to laugh and I like them to joke around." He is uninhibited, a comedian in his classroom.

Steve, another teacher, walks into the classroom. Students recognize that he and Tom are dressed like twins. Several students want to take a picture. Tom and Steve pose for the picture in a goofy pose. Tom asks that another picture be taken. At the moment the picture is snapped, Tom kisses Steve on the cheek. The girls squeal, and the guys hoot. The kids think that it was too wild, and they start talking about putting it in the annual. "Mr.____ kissed Mr. ____!" (observation notes)

These teachers appear to enjoy their jobs and their students. They are fun to be around. They tease students, and students tease them. Their light humor and easy-going, cheerful attitude toward life seem attractive to students. Students appear to enjoy spending time with them. They come in during class breaks just to tease and banter back and forth.

Between classes, one student came into Pam's classroom. He is not one of Pam's students. His head is shaved down the middle in a strip about 2 inches wide. He wants to show Pam and some of the students his haircut. He is laughing and so is everyone. They are all curious about the new hairdo, including Pam. (observation notes)

These informal, fun connections help make the time spent with the teacher enjoyable; thus, they are likely to encourage students to connect with the teacher on an informal basis. Humor helps create opportunities for students to see another side of their teachers, enabling them to recognize the common humanness they share with the teacher. Humor, when used good-naturedly as demonstrated by these teachers, helps communicate personal accessibility, thus encouraging personal connections (see Box 5.3, Appendix C).

Nonjudgmental Stance

Nonjudgmental stance means an individual does not shame or accentuate what is wrong with another person, recognizing the person is doing the best that he or she can at the given moment. They see student potential, not imperfections. These teachers are able to focus on what is good about a child even when a child's behavior appears inappropriate. They acknowledge and encourage the good in students. They model behavior that fosters resiliency in young people. These teachers continually demonstrate acceptance and unconditional regard for every student. The teachers do not raise their voices or criticize students when disciplining them. They see students as basically good.

Dean provides a powerful example of nonjudgmental behavior. The vulnerable, high-risk student population with which Dean works would tax most teachers' patience. Dean explains that he tries to figure out the rationale behind the student's behavior and react to that, rather than judge the child.

I had this kid once in real trouble stand up, and I said, "Man, you have got to start and get your book out!" He was like, "No! No! F___ you! F___ you, man!" He was like screaming at me. And I looked at him and said, I said, "Alright man, come on now. There is something up with you. Obviously you are angry about something else than this. Now you have two options. Do you want to like go down to the vice principal or do you want to go in my back room and we will talk it out." But it was more like, "There is something up here. You don't go off like that, just like that. I know you too well. Why don't you go in my back room and we'll deal with it." There was relief on his face. When we went back there, it was just like he busted down because of his family situation. Something was happening there.

A similar example is provided by Tom. He had a student who was showing up for class sporadically and whose behavior toward others was insensitive and disrespectful. As Tom explained it,

> I called him out in the hall on Friday, and I said, "You know, I see a kid who isn't doing his work. He's kind of rude. He isn't really talking back a lot but he's not being real polite in class—a kid who's always run down and tired." And I said, "I'm concerned. I am not going to do a lot of prying but a lot of times if you tell me and let it out it will get better." And you could just see the tears going down. He just broke down big time, you know, at that point.

These teachers appear not to hold grudges against students who misbehave. Students are disciplined and then the relationship is returned to the same level as prior to the infraction. Students who overstep their boundaries do not appear to have to earn the teacher's respect again. These teachers seem to recognize that their authority with their students comes not from their position per se but rather from student respect for them. They appear to believe that different behavior is not encouraged through criticism and negative judgments. Rather, they seem to believe that change in behavior is encouraged through understanding, modeling, and appropriate instruction. As Dean says, "I would rather not judge her. I would rather help her be better."

A nonjudgmental stance of a teacher communicates respect for students. It helps create a safe environment within which healthy relationships can develop. Students are better able to perceive a teacher's caring; thus, teachers are better able to make healthy connections with students (see Box 5.4, Appendix C).

Potency

Potency refers to an individual's charisma or magnetic quality, although it is not just a quality of a superstar. A potent teacher communicates a dynamic, involved attitude toward students. These teachers are in touch with their own personal power and serve as models of someone who lives effectively and productively with hope, care, and enthusiasm. Their potency helps students get in touch with their potential power. The best example of this personal trait comes from student responses. The following student comments about Dean illustrate his dynamic, involved attitude toward students.

> Well, just the way he acts. I mean he's always making sure everything is okay, making sure you do your work. And he makes you feel really good if you do do your work. (Rosie)

> Mr. _____ cares about all the kids, not only the ones he knows. He cares about all the kids. So it's like if anybody has a problem usually they'll go to Mr. _____ and Mr. _____ will then try to help them out. (Vinnie)

> I mean, Mr. _____'s homework is hard sometimes but he'll always help you out with it. He'll always ask. A lot of teachers are too busy correcting papers to help you out. (Rosie)

Gail offers other examples of potency in action. Students interviewed recognize her power and influence with students. Jake says,

> She has turned a lot of people around and sometimes she'll respect a person more if she can see that they can come around and realize that they are screwing up.

Jake sees himself as a student Gail is helping to turn around. Jake believes other teachers see him as irresponsible and not willing to work; he perceives Gail as seeing his leadership qualities and helping him develop these qualities.

These are powerful examples of a teacher's dynamic involvement with students and the effect of that involvement. They provide evidence that students see these teachers as models and are influenced by the teacher's energy and caring attitude toward them. The observed teachers are involved with their students. They attempt to nurture the students' potential personal power and encourage them to be accountable for their behavior. Students become validated as useful human beings. With continual support from the teacher, students may begin to act personally responsible, responding from their personal power source. Potency helps encourage students to connect with a teacher because it helps students see their personal capabilities and their individual significance. Students are more likely to want to spend time and be close to teachers who foster a student's positive self-image (see Box 5.5, Appendix C).

Enthusiasm

Enthusiasm is described as exhibiting energy and interest in what one is doing. All these teachers are enthusiastic about their jobs. When observing these teachers, one can literally see and feel the creative energy being expended. Pam describes herself:

> I bring a real high energy [to the job], and I'm very enthusiastic about what I do and the kids relate to that most of the time. I tire some of them out. . . . I always feel like if I can convey some of the excitement that I feel about the discoveries that I make when I read history, then I'm doing a good job.

These teachers appear to enjoy what they are doing. It is easy to see their enthusiasm. Dean says,

> I just realized I really love teaching because, you know what, you're like an actor who can get up there and do your stuff and you're really the one creating the stuff that you do. And that's what I really like. I've never been caught up in the hype of money or anything like that.

These teachers' enthusiasm conveys a message to the students that they are more than just a job. For instance, one of Ruby's students, Peter, said, "I think she probably would still do this job if she wasn't getting paid. I think she likes it enough that she'd do that." This enthusiasm helps students to perceive caring on the part of the teacher and encourages openness to healthy connections. It appears to enable students to see that they are part of something that is very rewarding and fulfilling for the teacher, not a burden or a drain.

Perceiving that their participation is valued, students are more likely to be open to a teacher-student connection (see Box 5.6, Appendix C).

Androgyny

These teachers exhibit characteristics of an androgynous personality. Androgynous personalities demonstrate a balance in caregiving traits commonly associated with the feminine side of the personality and the risk-taking characteristics commonly associated with the masculine side (Cole & Cole, 1989; Gelman, 1991). For instance, Dean was a college football player who describes himself as "always [being] a caring, sensitive person." He speaks confidently about breaking up fistfights, confiscating guns, or intervening in verbally explosive situations. He appears confident of his ability to protect himself. Yet he is caring and keenly sensitive to the needs of students around him. Pam was a very successful businesswoman in a competitive manufacturing business for 14 years before she became a schoolteacher. Four of these teachers are coaches (Dale, Dean, Pam, and Ruby). Gail, who typically would be described as the most feminine of the three female teachers, still carries the self-confidence, assertiveness, nonconformity, and independence characteristic of Afro-American women (Kochman, 1981). Even though working in an inner-city secondary school, she does not appear to be intimidated by her students. She steps right up to them toe-to-toe in discipline situations. In fact, as she stated in an interview, she has little empathy for teachers who cannot maintain control of their classrooms.

It is not clear what role, if any, androgyny may play in the ability to bond with students or sustain professional energy. It is a particularly interesting finding, though, because androgyny has been identified as one of the strong characteristics in resilient children (Gelman, 1991; Werner, 1990). These teachers may be resilient personalities. They hold characteristics in common with resilient children such as the inner locus of control, sense of humor, enthusiasm, and some social skills (to be discussed in the "Predominant Interpersonal Skills" section). This resiliency may be the characteristic that helps explain the unending source of energy these teachers exhibit. The very resiliency that prevention specialists and educators seek to nurture and sustain in at-risk young people may be a characteristic of the adults with whom young people are bonding. It may be the resilient adult who can foster resiliency in young people.

Predominant Interpersonal Skills

The teachers observed not only displayed these intrapersonal characteristics in common but also shared several interpersonal skills. The way a teacher interacts with students appears to play a key role in the teacher's ability to communicate caring to the students and engender trust and acceptance. A teacher's competence at developing effective connections with students primarily depends on a teacher's interpersonal skills (Johnson, 1972). These teachers displayed five predominant interpersonal skills:

1. Effective communication skills
2. Empowering skills
3. Problem-solving skills
4. Conflict resolution skills
5. Accountability skills

These skills may assist them in their efforts to bond with students. The following sections discuss each of these predominant interpersonal skills. They describe the skills and identify how they may assist teachers in their efforts to bond with students and thus help sustain their professional energy.

Effective Communication Skills

One of the most pervasive skills that these teachers hold in common is effective communication. Effective communication skills include communication techniques such as listening, paraphrasing, summarizing, reflecting, and clarifying. The ability to communicate effectively is basic to other interpersonal skills such as empowering, conflict resolution, problem solving, and accountability. These teachers demonstrate the ability to communicate effectively. They are good listeners. They value listening and know how important listening is for validating the other person and making effective connections with students. They work on their listening and paraphrasing skills. They practice summarizing student comments to ensure that they are understanding correctly. They reflect back to a student the question he or she asks, which allows the student to hear his or her own question and the opportunity to clarify his or her own thinking.

They check their understanding with students to make sure they have heard the student's concern correctly. And they communicate responsively to student needs. Students see this behavior as very caring. Student responses provide the best supporting evidence that these teachers use effective communication skills. For example, consider what students said about Gail when asked what they thought made her a nurturing teacher.

> She listens. She listens a lot. She asks a lot of questions and she tries to understand everything. (Jake)

> She's easy to talk to. She tries to understand your problems. . . . You can talk to her and that's a teacher who cares, one that will communicate with students. (Abe)

Gail asks about students when she perceives something is wrong. She encourages students to talk to her about what is going on in their lives.

> She asks about you. And she'll take you somewhere where it's just you and her so you can talk without anybody else knowing. And she always has the right answer and tries to make you feel better. And you tell her and stuff. After the first time I talked to her, it's usually, "I have something to tell you" or sometimes I don't feel like talking about it but I always end up telling her. I always feel better afterward. (Susan)

As with Gail, students notice that Ruby makes a special effort to get to know them.

> She goes out of her way to know you. She takes time to just talk to you. Like, when I have a problem with a friend and I go to her for something, she'll like set up a time where me and my friend can have a time to talk by ourselves, like in her room or something. (Sally)

One observation day, Ruby gave up about 15 minutes of her 30-minute lunchtime in order to talk with a student who was concerned about a classmate's sexual behavior. Ruby paraphrased, probed, clarified her understanding, made tentative suggestions, and listened intently. This student obviously felt comfortable talking to Ruby about this very sensitive subject.

Effective communication skills appear to provide a vehicle for developing a close and trusting relationship. They are basic to the development and maintenance of healthy relationships (Johnson, 1972). These teachers have, value, and practice good communication skills (see Box 5.7, Appendix C).

Empowering Skills

Empowering skills teach or enable others to act on their own behalf. With their focus on student growth, these teachers see empowering students as critical to the process. They believe students need to become self-disciplined and self-reliant in order to become productive, successful citizens. In these teachers' view, students do not learn self-discipline and self-reliance when others are continually directing them and making their decisions. Dean asserts, when disciplining students, that "dogging" them or calling their parents in order to discipline them is not effective in the long run. It does not encourage self-discipline and self-reliance.

> In our educational system in high school, it's all, "We're going to send you to the office" or "We're going to call your parents." "We're going to do this; we're going to do that." This kid responds, "Yeah, I'd better do this! This is how I'm going to succeed." We train them for failure because that child will go to a college and "Oh! I don't have any intrinsic guidelines, nothing inside me that's going to make me do it myself." In a job with a boss, they are only going to say so many times, "Hey man, you've gotta get to work. You can't sit around. You must get to work." After four or five times, that dude is going to say, "Do you know something, you need to find another job!"

A principle for empowering young people is to provide them with opportunities to perceive that they have influence over what happens to them (Glenn, 1982; Glenn & Nelsen, 1988). These teachers attempt to empower students by working with student perceptions of personal power through curriculum, classroom management, and discipline decisions. For instance, working with curriculum, Gail seeks to empower students by teaching a culturally relevant curriculum, which acknowledges and honors African American and Asian American culture. Gail also attempts to empower her students by giving them some choices regarding their grade for the course.

> I've gotten to the point where at the end of a unit, the student has a choice of a grade he or she wants just by the project he or she chooses. . . . And so I gear my lessons so that they have responsibility. They have choice; they have control over what they want, what kind of grades they want. And they know that just because they do it doesn't mean that they're going to get this grade. There has to be quality and all that is understood. But I think the choice is important; the control is important.

Several other approaches for empowerment through curriculum are used by these teachers. For instance, when Pam does not like how a lesson is going because students do not seem to be grasping the concepts, she asks students for suggestions—and she implements their suggestions. With new units, she has students brainstorm what they already know about the subject and then she writes down their ideas using an overhead. By doing so, Pam believes students develop confidence that they already have a basic understanding of the subject and are just moving to a higher level of understanding.

> It always is astonishing to them to see how much they already know about the subject. So that always fills them with a lot of confidence that they already have a basic understanding of some of the things, and we're just going to go on to a higher level of refinement or whatever.

Empowerment through discipline can also give students the perception that they have some influence over imposed discipline consequences. Pam gives a clear explanation of how discipline may empower.

> I just think if you're real clear with explaining the procedures to them and outline what the rules are, what the boundaries are, and then negotiate the consequences or somehow right

at the beginning set up what the parameters are. And then just be real consistent. And let them know all the way, you know, this is where we are with this. You guys have exceeded the boundary here. And what were the consequences that we all decided on? And I remind them of what they already know.

Pam negotiates ground rules and consequences prior to an infraction. By doing this, when rules are broken and consequences enforced, students are more likely to recognize that their behavior brought about the consequences imposed on them. Students are more likely to see that, if they choose, they may be able to affect what happens to them. It is more likely to be "I was kicked out of class because I was disrespectful" than "The teacher kicked me out of class."

Ruby also stresses that consequences for behavior are the student's choice. For another example, when asked about an assignment, Ruby responded, "Let me put it this way. If you choose not to do them, you will lose credit for a completed assignment sheet. It is your choice." Students may become accountable for their behavior when they know the consequences they face as a result of decisions they may make. They may perceive they have influence over what happens to them.

These teachers are firm, fair, and consistent in enforcing consequences. Even Dale and Dean, who tend to be more permissive than the other teachers, are adamant about firmness, consistency, and fairness in discipline as a technique to hold students accountable for their behavior (Glenn, 1982; Glenn & Nelsen, 1988; Nelsen, 1987).

Attempts to empower students appear to promote social and emotional development. They show respect for students by communicating, "I know you are capable of handling this situation." It facilitates bonding by building mutual respect and conveying caring. It also places responsibility for student behavior in the student's lap, where it belongs, thus relieving teachers of an unnecessary responsibility in an already demanding job (see Box 5.8, Appendix C).

Problem-Solving Skills

Problem-solving skills involve a critical-thinking process in which one focuses on possible solutions by identifying the pros and cons of an action or decision and weighing these pros and cons before deciding on an action plan or solution. These teachers not only practice good problem-solving skills but also model these skills for their students. They take time to lead a student through the thinking process rather than simply telling him or her the answer. They use the Socratic method when teaching. Tom says,

> They know they may ask me a question. I come back with a question—but they can pretty much guarantee I'm not going to just ask one of them. It's a series of questions. I'm setting up one question for another question later on.

Tom knows this helps develop critical-thinking skills. For another example, Dale says,

> When they ask me a question, rarely do I try to just tell them the answer. I try to make them think for themselves and come up with the answer by themselves. And then I'll say, "Well, you see how you can do that." And then I'll remind them it's just kind of a way to know which questions to ask yourself. And if you get that down, you're okay.

Dean provides a good example of modeling problem-solving skills as a method of teaching students how to resolve problems.

> When they come and confide in me that they have done this or that, I just kind of help them guide their way into confronting the problem or situation like a young man or young woman . . . as an adult should. . . . "Maybe you want to think about not coming across like this. Maybe you need to take responsibility and do this. If you are having problems with this teacher and this teacher is dogging you, you really need to go up and have a talk with them."

Pam vividly demonstrated her problem-solving skills the day I observed her working with students on a simulated archaeological dig exercise. As described in Chapter 3, students had forgotten to bring the required equipment for an archaeological dig exercise they were to do that day. Modeling problem-solving skills, Pam had her students sit in small groups and brainstorm how they would help each other remember to bring the required supplies the next day.

Then she had the small groups share their ideas with the whole class. Some great suggestions came out of the process, and students learned a problem-solving technique plus felt empowered in the process.

Problem-solving skills may support bonding by creating a respectful process in which two or more people may work together on a task. They enable the teacher to include students in a critical-thinking process and to empower students. They also eliminate stress by not making the teacher responsible for knowing the answer to everything.

Conflict Resolution Skills

Conflict resolution skills involve not only a rational process like problem-solving skills but the ability to deal with intense emotional issues *as they occur.* Conflict resolution strategies involve a greater variety of communication skills than problem-solving strategies. Although these teachers' styles for resolving conflict differ, they are confident of their ability to resolve conflict situations. Some teachers deal with conflict using mediating and negotiating strategies; others use diffusing strategies. Several of the observed teachers perceive themselves as key mediators for conflict situations that arise within their buildings. For instance, at Inner-City High School, Dean is often called on to break up fistfights or to confiscate weapons from students. During the three observation days alone, Dean was called on to break up two arguments with students. Besides his communication skills, Dean has the advantage of his physical size and the respect he commands on campus. (He was a college football player.)

Several teachers use conflict resolution skills with conflicts that arise at meetings they are attending with their peers. As an example of her conflict resolution skills, Pam describes intervening at the team meetings at the beginning of the school year.

> [Last year] there was a lot of problems with this team issue
> and people took it very personally. When I came in this year,
> the first meetings I ever attended with all the seventh-grade
> teams, they were personally attacking each other. And these
> people didn't know me at all, and I just stepped in and said,
> "Wait a minute. I'm real uncomfortable with the tone being
> set here and I don't want to start this way. . . . This is what I
> hear you saying." And it completely changed the tenor of the
> group. It just diffused it, and we got back to business in a

much more constructive way. And a lot of times I see my role as a facilitator.

When resolving conflict, communication skills are imperative. Ruby states that conflict is difficult for her, but she has developed the communication skills for dealing with it. Because of her abusive familial background, she is not really comfortable with conflict. But when there is conflict between her and a student or valued peer, she uses communication and mediation skills to resolve it. When asked to describe how she handles a situation in which there is conflict between her and a student, Ruby says,

> [I] deal with that student one-on-one and find out where the concern is, where the problem was, or where the lack of understanding was and try to paraphrase it and really focus in on where the lack of understanding came from and why.

Pam also recognizes the importance of effective communication skills in conflict resolution. Her conflict resolution style emphasizes listening and clarifying skills.

> I firmly believe that most conflict is due to lack of communication, a lack of listening or perceptions that differ. And so I try to make sure that the other people involved are listening to each other. If I'm one of them, then maybe I'm not listening to what this person is saying or maybe they're not listening to me. So I try to paraphrase, shift out of the personal front kind of feeling.

Two of the observed teachers deal with conflict primarily by diffusing the situation. Dale often uses diffusing techniques. In fact, Dale says often he will let students be angry with him for awhile because at this age, "Nine times out of 10 they'll come back and just talk like nothing happened." Dale indicates that in real heated conflicts between a student and himself, he will send the student out for a while to give them both a chance to simmer down. Then he may ask a counselor to come assist with the mediation of conflict. Dale recognizes that sometimes the anger of the students is coming from places that he does not understand. The counselor helps him to see that.

Dean believes it is important for him to resolve the conflict rather than calling on the administration. Because he values fostering student growth, he sees modeling how to resolve conflicts appropriately and successfully as part of his teaching responsibilities.

> I really believe that one of my roles is not just to teach but also to resolve some of the conflict too. Because, you know what? I'm not really teaching biology. I'm teaching them— hopefully I'm teaching them how to resolve conflicts as well, in the workplace and in life. And if I've shown them that the only place that they can resolve the conflict is down in the office, then I'll never teach them how to resolve it within themselves.

The ability to resolve conflict successfully eases stress by giving teachers confidence that they can deal with the uncomfortable situations that arise when two individuals work closely together. It also encourages bonding. Students are comfortable that conflict will be handled in a dignified and respectful manner. The teacher is viewed as someone safe to get close to (see Box 5.9, Appendix C).

Accountability Skills

Accountability skills refer to one's ability to acknowledge mistakes, accept ownership for one's behavior, and verbally make amends. They involve not only recognizing that a mistake has been made but also apologizing and then working together on a solution. These teachers view mistakes as opportunities to learn and welcome feedback that helps them to improve. Pam provides a vivid example of accountability when she acknowledged to students that she was guilty of harassing a student the very day she led a discussion on harassment.

> Pam sent a student who had picked at a hangnail until it bled to the nurse's station to get a Band-Aid. She began to joke around about how she hated blood. Several students joined in. They started poking fun at the trivialness of the "injury," making fun of the student for wanting medical attention for a hangnail. Suddenly one student noted that they were harassing the student. "We are doing the very same thing we

were talking about." Everyone was immediately quiet. There was a pregnant pause as individuals realized the truth in the statement. Then Pam said, "I was doing it too. What a jerk you have for a teacher!" A student piped up, "A cool jerk." (observation notes)

These teachers work hard at doing things right but recognize that it is okay to make a mistake. They see their acceptance of their mistakes as an opportunity to teach students that it is okay to make mistakes; it is okay to take risks and fail. Tom says, "The ability to make a fool of myself and show the kids 'that's okay' I think is a very good attribute of a teacher."

These teachers can laugh at their mistakes, an attitude that helps them be accountable for their behavior. For instance, one observation day Dale made a mistake in the solution he put on the board to a math problem he had asked students to work on.

After a few minutes the students started to complain that the problem was impossible. Dale glanced at the board and said, "Oh no! I forgot to carry over!" He went to the board and changed the numbers in the problem. The class groaned and playfully shouted, "You made a mistake. You are the math teacher! You are supposed to know this stuff." Dale laughed and said, "I made a mistake." The students laughed and teased, "When we make a mistake you count it against us. How come it doesn't count against you?" Dale teased back, "It does count against me. I have to put up with you guys raggin' on me. Isn't that enough?" The students laughed. (observation notes)

Making and admitting their mistakes and then having the willingness to reconcile helps these teachers "level the playing field" between student and teacher. Such accountability helps these teachers demonstrate their humanness. It makes them more approachable for students and thus facilitates bonding (see Box 5.10, Appendix C).

Summary of Personal Revitalizing Resources

This chapter and the previous chapter identify and describe personal beliefs, skills, traits, and experiences six nurturing teachers hold in common. Knowing these qualities provides a window to understanding the personal characteristics that support and advance nurturing behavior.

When these inner resources are melded together within one teacher, the synergistic effect appears to enable a teacher to competently pursue the mission of helping young people reach their fullest potential—cognitively, socially, emotionally, and morally. And these teachers are competent and effective at helping young people and making a difference in student lives. The reason for this competence becomes apparent when one reviews the counseling literature regarding the traits and communication skills of effective helpers. Many of the intrapersonal characteristics and interpersonal skills of the six nurturing teachers are the same traits and skills that the counseling literature identifies as essential to be effective helpers. In particular, the communication skills of listening, conflict resolution, and self-disclosure (Aspy & Roebuck, 1972; Wiggins, 1982) and the intrapersonal characteristics of genuineness and authenticity, respectfulness, and potency (Carkhuff, 1969, 1987; Rogers, Gendlin, Keisler, & Truax, 1967; Small, 1981) have been identified as both traits and skills for effective helping and predominant intrapersonal characteristics and interpersonal skills of the teachers observed. These characteristics and skills contribute to the teachers' ability to revitalize and sustain their professional energy by facilitating their effectiveness on the job.

The teachers observed have the skills to be effective in helping young people and making a difference in students' lives. They also have effective coping strategies to deal with the intense demands of their jobs. And they have the personal beliefs that provide strong motivation for teaching and interacting with students the way they do. Thus, a job, which for some teachers may require too intense an investment for too little emotional dividends, becomes a source of personal psychic rewards and satisfaction for these six nurturing teachers.

6

Supporting Nurturing Teachers in the Workplace

Dean is sitting across the dining room table from me. We are in the privacy of his home because conducting an interview with Dean at school is almost impossible. Students hang around Inner-City High School long beyond normal school hours, and they wander freely in and out of Dean's classroom after school. We tried the first interview at school during lunchtime in a quiet room in the library. Students still found him.

This is the fourth interview. Dean is reflecting on what it might be like for him to work in another school environment, like Suburb Junior High School, where Pam and Tom teach. "If I taught where Pam does, it would be awful. And if I taught the way I do, it would not work. It would not work. And I'd be a failure. I would be teaching maybe a year. If Pam came here and she didn't adapt to Inner-City High School, she would teach maybe a year and she would drop out in frustration. These two schools are like night and day."

Dean pauses, then continues. "Teaching is like being an artist. It is an art. So if you're going to teach, you had better be working with the medium you handle competently. As an artist, if I do beautiful, beautiful paintings, then I'm going to paint. I'm not going to be able to go and take a piece of granite and sculpture that granite and have it a beautiful finished product. It's a different

art form. It requires a different technique. Where I am and where she is . . .
both are hard. We're both artists, but we're two different types. We're both
to be appreciated."

   Dean's thoughts trigger several questions in my mind. I wonder what
really would happen if Dean taught in a suburban school and Pam taught
in an inner-city school? Would their teaching or bonding styles need to
change? How do work environments affect bonding styles? And what are
the work environments like that are most supportive of teachers making
healthy connections with students?

Supportive School Environments

   Teachers and their work environments can be highly interactive.
As such, school environments can be important resources for encouraging and supporting teachers who want to develop close and trusting connections with students. The immediate surroundings can
influence what a teacher can and cannot do and what they will and
will not do. Work environments have an impact on teachers' feelings
of effectiveness and thus their enthusiasm and professional energy
for their jobs. Because this study does not focus specifically on the
supportive features within schools, the research literature was con-
sulted to discover some of these features. From the ideas suggested
by the literature and from reflections on the three school sites in the
study, some insights emerge about school environments that support
teachers nurturing students. This chapter discusses the workplace
resources that seemed to support the six nurturing teachers' efforts
to connect with students. It presents what educational literature
contends is supportive of nurturing teachers and compares these
ideas with what the observed teachers relate is most supportive.

School Environments Perceived as Supportive

   Research literature contends that a teacher perceives a school
environment as supportive when the educational goals of the teacher

match the overall mission of the school *and* the needs of the students (McLaughlin, 1990). If this contention is true, then school environments that promote the educational goal of student personal growth can be perceived as supportive by teachers who value nurturing students. School environments promote student personal growth when fellow colleagues and administrators value student growth and making caring connections with students. In addition, the overall school mission reflects the importance and value of making nurturing connections. School policies, curriculum decisions, and problem-solving structures emerge that facilitate the nurturing of student growth (McLaughlin, 1990).

This study supports the contention that teachers feel supported when the school's overall mission and the needs of the students match the teacher's educational goals. Three teachers in the study—Tom, Pam, and Gail—perceive their schools' administrators and many of their colleagues as holding the same top educational goal for students as they do. These teachers are pleased with the support and encouragement they receive from their administrators for their efforts to make special connections with students. The teachers feel acknowledged, valued, and treated as professionals. Tom says about his work environment,

> I see this place as a professionally rewarding environment to work at. Most of the restructuring that's gone on here has been generated from the bottom up. And that's very important in terms of the realization you are being treated as a professional. Your opinion does mean something. Your expertise does mean something.

Pam concurs with Tom's perceptions of support within their work environment.

> I think this is a very professionally rewarding place to work. For example, the administrators, specifically the principal, made sure that I was, as a new hire, included in the mentoring program in which I got a small stipend for the time I put in, as well as the opportunity to go to all kinds of professional development seminars around professionalism in teaching. . . . I think also the administration is absolutely committed to improving the school environment for our

instructors in any way they can. . . . They give us release time
to plan for teams and that often comes out of the principal's
discretionary funds to pay for subs for us to do that.

The three other teachers—Dean, Ruby, and Dale—perceive their
administrators as holding educational goals for students that are
different from their own. (Although both Dean and Gail work at the
same high school, they reported different experiences with the administration. Inner-City High School hired a new principal between
the times Dean and Gail were observed and interviewed. Gail is
newly employed at Inner-City High this year. Unlike Dean, she never
worked under the administration that Dean saw as unsupportive.
Dean has more positive feelings about the new administration.)
Perceiving that the administration does not value the same educational goals affects how supportive these teachers feel their work
environments are. For instance, Dean perceives his administration as
having different educational goals than he does. He says of the old
administration,

> I think the administration views us as professional in words
> but a lot of times their actions don't support us as profession-
> als. Because it's like, "Oh, you can't do that! You're doing
> this great stuff but you can't really [do that]." They won't
> give up [control] a lot of times.

These teachers do not experience their schools as particularly supportive of their special efforts to connect with students. These teachers also do not feel treated as professionals by their administrators
(see Box 6.1, Appendix C).

It is rare that an entire school reflects a singular overall school
goal. Usually there are critical differences in educational goals among
the faculty or between faculty and administrators. As in Dean's
situation, some faculty or administrators may not see personal growth
of students as part of a school's responsibilities. Some faculty or
administrators prefer to focus on developing good work habits, basic
academic skills, academic excellence, and so on rather than student
personal growth. This mismatch of faculty or administration goals is
often further complicated by the diverse needs of heterogeneous
student bodies. Because of the many sources for complicating a singular
overall school mission, McLaughlin (1990) suggests that teachers

seeking support from their work environments may have to focus on subenvironments within the school. She encourages administrators to organize secondary schools around supportive subenvironments within the school. Also, she advocates developing strategies for integrating these diverse subenvironments so they can work together effectively.

According to McLaughlin's suggestions, if Dean, Dale, and Ruby want support from their work environment, they need to seek support from individuals within their workplace who hold the same educational goals. And this is what they have done. All three teachers talk about seeking support from colleagues who demonstrate the same type of caring and concern for students that they do. For instance, Ruby says,

> There's some faculty here that, because I've been here so long, I have some really special, lifelong friendships with some of these people and I definitely feel that I have a support system within the school. . . . Those people I tend to congregate around are really positive, upbeat people. They believe in the same things I do for kids—that we get them to experience success in the best way possible. So those are probably the two main things about [what makes this a nice place to work].

Dale says,

> I think there's a body of teachers around here, which includes Ruby and four or five others, that the kids kind of enjoy knowing. I think that helps [teachers who nurture] want to do better.

But in addition to a small cadre of supportive colleagues, these teachers talked about support coming from other individuals associated with school environments—students and parents. Student reinforcement and parental appreciation are identified as resources for support within their work environment. For example, Dean says,

> You know something? I love [Inner-City High School]. I really, really love [Inner-City High School]. I love it because it's not like a school and it's not like a district. And it's not

like the principal. I guess what I like about it and what the thing is all about is, it's about the 690 kids that go here. Because it's about the faculty members that I work with that *are* really competent and are doing some great stuff for kids. That's what it's about—it's about all those kids and making me laugh and having a great time.

Dale mentions the acknowledgment of parents as an important source of support for his nurturing efforts.

I think we get our rewards, our advancement, our kudos, I guess, from parents coming up and saying, "You did a hell of a job" or "You did a great job for us. My son or my daughter really enjoys being in your class. You're teaching them something. They've never liked math before." I get that. And that, to me, makes it worthwhile.

From these observations, it seems that teachers who bond with students need to be appreciated and acknowledged as making a difference in students' lives. If their administrators are not able to do this, then this recognition can come from colleagues, parents, or even students themselves. In fact, when considering key individuals within the school environment who provide support to these teachers, students were identified by *all* these teachers as most supportive of their efforts to nurture. Students provide teachers with the greatest psychic rewards for teaching (Lortie, 1975; McLaughlin & Talbert, 1990). Being with the students helps the teachers sustain their professional energy and their motivation to nurture healthy relationships with the students. For these teachers, the students are not a drain. For these teachers, their love for students provides them with a solid emotional context that replenishes their professional energies.

The kids themselves revitalize me. They're a real treat. There's almost never a day that when I leave, I don't have something to smile about. They make me laugh. They make me mad. They make me cry. They make me upset. But they mostly make me laugh. I really like them. (Pam)

Pam's enjoyment of students is representative of all the teachers. Ruby says, "The kids, for me, are why I went into education. I think they make [Rural-City High School] a good, good place to work." These teachers' love for kids allows them to enjoy the students rather than feel drained from the experience. Dean says,

> And if I want to really revive myself, you know what happens? After school I just hang around with some kids and talk. It's all right. I don't feel overwhelmed by them. Hanging with kids and just laughing and joking and messing with them, that's what revives me!

And Tom says,

> The kids, that is what keeps me sane. . . . Without the kids, there's so much other crap . . . the parents, the administration.

(See Box 6.2, Appendix C, for more supporting evidence.)

In summary, these six nurturing teachers perceive that students provide them with the most support within their school environments. Administrators and the school in general are also perceived as supportive by the teachers when the teacher's educational goals match the overall mission of the school and the needs of the students. Teachers who value making caring connections with students advocate student personal growth as an important educational goal. These teachers perceive their work environments as supportive when their fellow colleagues and the administration value promoting the personal growth of students along with the academic growth.

Schools That Encourage Nurturing Connections

Fellow colleagues and administrators advocating student personal growth as the primary educational goal is key if teachers are to *perceive* the workplace as supportive. There are other workplace factors, though, that can provide support to caring teachers. These factors are often indigenous to the school environment and emerge naturally because of the way a school is organized. McLaughlin and Talbert (1990) characterize the ideal school environment for teachers who nurture bonds with students. They call these ideal school environments personalized environments. Alternative schools usually are representative of a personalized environment.

In addition to having the overall educational mission of the student's personal growth, personalized school environments have several distinguishing characteristics. Faculty and administration believe that students attending the school are in need of individual attention and strong support from the teachers. The relations among teachers and students are grounded in intimate, personal knowledge about individuals' lives outside of school as well as inside the classroom. The curriculum is individually designed based on instructional scaffolding from what the student already knows.

The personalized environment embodies several organizational structures and problem-solving strategies that enhance a teacher's ability to make nurturing connections with students (McLaughlin & Talbert, 1990). These organizational qualities can be summarized into four main clusters:

1. *Schoolwide structures for communication and collective problem-solving* involve such strategies as team teaching (with teams maintaining for 3 years), weekly staff meetings, core teams, joint parent-teacher-student conferences, and "adopt-a-student" programs. School environments are often described as families or communities in which students and staff feel cared for.

2. *Norms that support diffused teachers' roles*, encouraging assumption of responsibilities beyond the conventional instructional role and beyond the classroom. Teachers' authority is based on referent power.

3. *Individualized instructional strategies* such as student-directed learning, teacher-student jointly constructed curriculum, bimonthly student progress reports, individual instruction, and so on.

4. *Organizational strategies for revitalization and recommitment* such as schoolwide weekend retreats, mutual respect for professionalism of teachers and administrators, close contact with nurturing principals, ongoing support for instruction, flexible teachers' schedules, and so on.

These organizational structures and strategies help foster relationships among teachers and students that are founded in intimate, personal knowledge about the students' lives outside as well as inside the classroom. This type of knowledge helps teachers develop close and trusting relationships with students. Neither the students nor the faculty are anonymous. Schools and classes within personalized school environments are relatively small. Students usually like school, and the school has few attendance problems. Sometimes students have even chosen to be there. Teachers are stimulated by the support within the work environment from their colleagues and from the students. Teachers who value developing close and trusting connections with students tend to thrive in these environments. Such environments are ideal for teachers who value developing close and trusting relationships with students (McLaughlin & Talbert, 1990). Thus, a personalized school environment is a strong source of support and revitalization for nurturing teachers.

Recognizing that a personalized environment supports teachers who advocate for student personal growth, the study looked for these qualities in the school environments of the observed teachers. It seemed logical that if the selected sites had some of the qualities of a personalized environment, these qualities may be providing environmental support for the six teachers' efforts at making healthy, emotional connections with students. This information could offer insights on workplace resources supportive of caring teachers.

Both Suburb Junior High and Inner-City High School contain some organizational strategies, structures, and environmental norms recognized in the personalized school environment as helpful to teachers seeking to make caring connections with students. Both schools offered the opportunity to observe if or how these workplace resources support or revitalize teachers who develop close and trusting relationships with students. The following sections describe these workplace features as they are operationalized within selected sites. They discuss the support these workplace features provide to the six teachers and contrast these environments with school environments that do not appear to provide the same workplace resources.

Familial or Communal Atmospheres
Within School Environments

Both Inner-City High School and Suburb Junior High School work environments are described by the observed teachers in familial or communal terms. Dean and Gail talk about their school and students in familial terms. Gail says, "I treat students like family members." Dean says, "Think of it like this—it is just one big family. This is my child." There is a definite feeling around the classrooms of Dean and Gail that school is like a large, extended, caring family. Students hang around the classroom to visit with each other or the teacher. Former students return to reconnect and visit.

Tom and Pam describe Suburb Junior High more in terms reflecting a sense of community rather than a sense of family.

> There's a real feeling of caring about people and helping out [among the staff]. When people have been sick and needed sick days, there has never been a problem with people volunteering sick days, giving up their sick days for that other person. . . . If you're in need, there's a lot of caring people on the faculty. (Pam)

> I've had more fun times teaching here than in any school. I could combine all the schools I've been in and this is by far [the most fun]. We've done some of the most crazy things in the world. Great practical jokers, a lot of humor. And people realize that the way we keep our sanity is through laughing. (Tom)

These teachers say that the administration at Suburb Junior High fosters a sense of community among staff. The staff feels supported and cared for and cares for each other. The administration of Suburb Junior High School bends over backward to work out flexible schedules for teachers. Teachers give up sick days to help other teachers who have extended illnesses. Colleagues enjoy one another and are supportive of each other. The familial or communal atmospheres at Inner-City High School and Suburb Junior High provide the observed teachers with strong support for their nurturing efforts by fostering a sense of mutual interdependence, teamwork, and personal affirmation (see Box 6.3, Appendix C).

There is no evidence of a sense of communal or familial relations among staff and students at Rural-City High School. In fact, the support they most readily acknowledge receiving from their school environments, other than support from the students themselves, is being left alone. Ruby says,

> I think there's definitely some fixable things to make it a better environment for everybody. I think within my own

classroom I can pretty much create the kind of climate I want, but it can be very different from my class to the class next door.

It appears that lack of interference by the administration and colleagues is viewed as helpful. These teachers are committed to making a difference in student lives and find ways to nurture students despite the lack of familial relations among staff and students.

Schoolwide Structures for Communication and Collective Problem-Solving

Both Inner-City High School and Suburb Junior High have organizational structures that facilitate teachers' talking to each other about different students they have in common. Suburb Junior High has established several different institutional strategies for teachers to talk to each other about student concerns. They have staffings, core teams, staff meetings, and team meetings. These strategies help teachers understand their students on a personal level as learners. Student-teacher-parent conferences, called staffings, are common occurrences at Suburb Junior High. Teachers, parents, and sometimes the student work together to develop helpful curriculum strategies for the student. In the 6 days of observation at Suburb Junior High School, there were three staffings involving the two observed teachers.

> [We] have staffings, which are usually either teacher- or parent- or sometimes student-generated, where you pull together the group of teachers [the student has in common]. It's a lot easier when you have [teachers] working on the team do that. For me, it's a lot more rewarding and productive to go to one where it's associated with a kid on the team rather than a kid who's not on the team. . . . [With the kid off the team], you know, you get in the meeting and everybody then compares notes and discovers what's going on, which is time-consuming. That should be done before you get to the meeting. (Tom)

Suburb Junior High School also has a program called the "Cool Cats" program. This committee functions like a core team, taking referrals from staff members on students in trouble. Twelve teachers serve on Cool Cats; Pam chairs the committee. Their objective is to evaluate the student's situation and assign an appropriate teacher for a mentor-student relationship. Suburb Junior High teachers mentor no more than one or two troubled youths. This low ratio of students to teachers in the mentor-student relationships creates an opportunity for teachers to get to know one or two students very well and provides staff with in-depth information regarding that student when needed. It also creates an advocate for that student. Approximately 35 troubled students are referred to the program annually. The staffings and the Cool Cats program meet outside the school day and are added responsibilities for Suburb Junior High School teachers. Cool Cat committee members get to know troubled students and their fellow committee members well.

Suburb Junior High also has a very active team approach to teaching. Tom is chair for a social science-language arts-mathematics interdisciplinary team that works with a block of 120 students. Teachers on a team meet daily or weekly, depending on the team. These meetings provide opportunities to discuss common concerns about students and coordinate essential learning across the curriculum. A serendipitous gain is that teachers get to know their team members well and have the opportunity to learn more about their students from another teacher's perspective. The school administration has provided substitute teachers for team members doing extensive interdisciplinary curriculum planning. Pam says, "[The administration] gives us release time to plan for teaming. That often comes out of the principal's discretionary funds to pay for subs for us to do that." Except for team curriculum planning, the committee work involved in these schoolwide structures is an overload for Pam and Tom. Yet the intrinsic psychic rewards encourage them to devote a lot of energy to this type of professional work.

Suburb Junior High's schoolwide structures for communication and collective problem-solving provide support for Tom and Pam, which they cherish in their efforts to make caring connections with students. These structures give these teachers intimate and personal knowledge about students' lives outside of the classroom. They provide Tom and Pam opportunities to learn how their students are being perceived by other teachers and sometimes by parents as well. As supported by McLaughlin and Talbert's (1990) study, this kind of knowledge helps teachers in their efforts to build close and trusting relations with students.

Encouraged by these supports within their work environment, Tom and Pam take an active part in the governance of the school. For instance, in addition to chairing the Cool Cats committee, Pam also chairs the Student Learning Improvement Committee, which is writing a grant requesting state funding for improving student learning. Tom is head of the social science department, on the faculty council, and on the committee that administers a Student Learning Improvement Grant. He is one of five faculty members that initially spearheaded the school-restructuring program for Suburb Junior High School. Both these teachers clearly see their role and responsibilities extending beyond the classroom into school governance and educational renewal. They are actively involved within their professional community with issues regarding school renewal. Both serve as excellent examples of good stewards of the teaching profession for their colleagues.

Inner-City High School also provides organizational channels to facilitate teachers talking to one another. They have core teams and staff meetings and are beginning to develop team teaching as well. But neither Dean nor Gail makes use of these channels of communication.

> There must be a friggin' thousand committees. And we have the attendance committee and we have the at-risk committee that meets every Friday and talks about certain kids. You could all become part of that but that's all in your free time. That's before school or after school and it sucks the life out of you. (Dean)

> We have an impact team here where you talk about students who might have trouble with drugs and alcohol. And you can be a part of the impact team. It meets like every Friday morning. There are quite a few things to belong to here. You could have a meeting every day if you wanted one. (Gail)

Both Dean and Gail individually tap teachers whom they know and respect and privately discuss whatever concerns they may have regarding students, curriculum, and so on. As Dean says, "You got to grab time with [a teacher]." Gail phrases it, "I've had the same concerns as other teachers, and we just got together." Although communication channels and problem-solving strategies are available, Dean and Gail work primarily in isolation, very autonomously.

Inner-City High schoolwide structures for communication and collective problem solving do not appear to be helpful to these teachers' efforts to bond with students.

On the surface, the nonuse of these communication channels by Dean and Gail seems at odds with recent research suggesting that organizational structures designed to encourage collective problem solving among teachers are supportive for teachers who nurture (McLaughlin & Talbert, 1990). Reflection shows, though, that the committee work entailed in these structures is an add-on, an overload to a teacher's job at both Inner-City High School and Suburb Junior High School. Gail and Dean are not willing to give their time to committee work. They prefer to spend all their extra time with students. One possible interpretation of these findings is that unless organizational strategies and structures designed to assist teachers in knowing their students personally are integrated into a teacher's daily workload, *some* nurturing teachers may not use these organizational supports. When teachers who bond primarily by creating one-to-one time with students are asked to choose between giving time to students and working on committees, despite how helpful committees may be, they may choose to spend their time with students. Neither Pam nor Tom depends on the strategy of one-to-one time with students as the primary strategy for bonding. Another possible interpretation is that within large inner-city schools there are so many troubled youths that participating in organized committee work designed to help individual students is not empowering for teachers and decreases their feelings of competence and effectiveness.

Tom and Pam actively use the schoolwide communication structures. Tom bonds through setting high expectations for students while conveying a belief in their capabilities. Pam uses primarily appropriate self-disclosure. The schoolwide communication structures help them to garner their personal knowledge about students and student needs. This personal knowledge helps them make meaningful connections with students using their preferred bonding strategies.

The schoolwide structures for communication and collective problem-solving strategies that draw teachers and/or students together are not evident at Rural-City High School. Rural-City High School has a committee for collectively problem solving student drug and alcohol abuse problems, but the observed teachers did not feel there was much administrative support for the committee's work.

Even the architectural design of the school does not facilitate communication among the faculty.

> We have no hallways, so there's not really a closeness [among faculty]. The only time we ever see anybody is in the lunchroom, and that's why we kind of hide in that little corner. (Dale)

The observed teachers at Rural-City High School may turn to a counselor at the school to help them problem solve difficult situations with troubled students.

> What I'll do is I'll go talk to Roy, the counselor. I'll say, "Roy, we have some problems, and we need you to talk to this person." Then, we'll both talk to this person together. (Dale)

Norms Supporting a
Diffused Role for Teachers

A diffused role for teachers refers to a more holistic view of the role of a teacher as a human service professional rather than the more conventional view of the role of a teacher. The degree of diffusion of the role can move anywhere along a continuum from the conventional teacher who is classroom-bound and assumes responsibility for only the cognitive needs of students to the nonclassroom-bound teacher who assumes responsibility for the social, emotional, and moral (and sometimes physical) needs of students as well as their cognitive needs. Teachers who assume a diffused role have more opportunities to make meaningful connections with students. Schools that have norms that accept or encourage a diffused teaching role make it easier for teachers to nurture students by expanding approved opportunities for making meaningful connections with students (see Box 6.4, Appendix C).

It appears that social norms and school policies at Inner-City High School support teachers assuming diffused roles. These norms cultivate opportunities for caring and continual mentoring of students in and out of the classroom. The observed teachers at Inner-City High School, Dean and Gail, connect with students both on and off the school grounds. They become involved in students' lives beyond the classroom and school activities. As a result, the boundaries between students' lives at school and their personal, social, and familial lives are blurred.

Both Gail and Dean perceive their school environment as supportive of their choice to define a diffused teaching role. They perceive themselves as having the approval of both their peers and their administrators. When asked to give an example of why he perceives that teachers enjoy their jobs at Inner-City High School, Dean describes social norms supporting a diffused role.

> We're always doing extra stuff with kids. And you know what? You don't do that unless you really like those kids and really like the place. . . . I mean, there's so much stuff they [faculty] do that I can't even begin to tell you. There was this woman who came here from a middle school in [another school district]. She said the faculty resented her at [her other school] because she would do extra stuff for kids. It was like, "What are you doing? You're doing that without getting paid? If you keep doing that, they are going to expect us to do that." And then she said it was more of an attitude of "We do our jobs and we don't do anymore." At Inner-City High School, it's more like, for a lot of us, a core group, we do our jobs and then what else—what more can we do? What can we do to help these kids? What extra stuff can we do?

When Gail was asked if there were any policies that encourage the teacher's role with students to be diffused beyond the classroom, she responded, "As long as it's legal, it's fine."

With this perceived support, Dean and Gail readily assume a role that at times includes being a friend, counselor, or surrogate parent to students. This enables them to connect with students on a variety of levels, creating more opportunities to nurture and bond. In fact, Dean sees the diffused role as being necessary for a teacher to be effective in inner-urban schools. Gail sees her friendship connections with students as one of the most enjoyable aspects of her job. It is the strategy she uses to bond with students.

> I spend a lot of time with students, talking to them about their personal problems or things that have happened to them over the weekend, overnight. Fun things. It's not always serious and it's not always sad. . . . And I go to their

basketball games and football games. . . . I spend the weekend with various students. They either come by the house, or I pick them up. We go to basketball games or what have you. I've been on shopping excursions with teenagers. They know my phone number. Lots of the kids are my friends. . . . Many kids have come over to the house. They've eaten dinner. The cheerleaders spent the night, which they will never do again because they stayed up all night long. I'm too old to stay up all night [laughter].

Dean's attitude toward his role as a teacher is very similar to Gail's attitude.

I really don't even set boundaries. I go with my feelings. Those kids need counselors. I do more counseling than any friggin' counselor in this whole place. As far as a parent, where I work, that comes with the job. . . . If I am just going to be a teacher, then I am going to provide just a part of the service I could provide the other way. That is my choice, though. Not every teacher should have to do that. (Dean)

The social norms and school policies at Suburb Junior High and Rural-City High School do not appear to support a diffused role for teachers. The observed teachers from these sites do not perceive the policies and norms at their schools as encouraging a diffused role with students. In fact, policies and norms were seen as discouraging a diffused role, sometimes to the disappointment of the teacher. Tom talked about how union policies prohibit personal connections with students outside the school setting. When asked about school policies that encourage a diffused role, Tom said, "You couldn't do that. You couldn't do that through the unions." Any connecting that Tom does with students after hours and/or beyond the school setting he clearly associates with school activities. And he usually connects with only groups of students, not just one or two.

Both Dale and Ruby from Rural-City High School made reference to the restrictiveness of the school policies regarding a diffused role for teachers. Ruby talks about how these restrictive policies limit teachers in reaching out and doing extra things with students. Ruby said,

You know, we're not supposed to give kids rides home after a turnout or after a game if the kid doesn't have a ride. We're supposed to wait there with them for their ride to come and get them and have somebody else around. I mean, it's almost a fear that we're living under, which is really too bad.

Dale made a similar comment.

There was a time when we used to let the kids drive our cars downtown to get something for us. I know the shop teachers have done that. You know, because I'm the baseball coach, I'd let them drive my car to get the gear and bring it back over here or something. Now, boy, you do that and you're just asking for trouble in just an instant.

The observed teachers from Suburb Junior High and Rural-City High School do not assume diffused teaching roles with the students. They establish clear boundaries between their teaching role and the role of a human service professional, friend, or surrogate parent and clear boundaries with their responsibilities associated with nonclassroom activities. Pam says,

I don't pretend to be these students' friend. . . . And you know, when I talk to them about problem-type issues, not history, curriculum stuff, but social-type issues . . . I'm pretty clear about saying, "Well, you know, as your teacher . . ." And I remind them that this is only one—I'm only one person that they can talk to about things. There are also counselors. "I know I'm not your parent; I'm not your counselor; but I am your teacher, and I care about you because of that."

Although these school environments do not appear to encourage a diffused role for teachers, which research suggests is supportive of a teacher's efforts to build effective relationships with students (McLaughlin & Talbert, 1990), the observed teachers still appear able to nurture students successfully within the more narrowly defined teaching roles prescribed by their work environment. In fact, Pam, Ruby, and Dale are quite comfortable with the narrow definition of their teaching role. They report feeling little personal frustration, limitation, or lack of support within their workplaces because of the narrow definition. And they do not describe feeling any internal pressure to assume a more diffused role because of student needs. Dale does not seem even to have in his conscious awareness the possible expectation that he should be a friend, parent, or counselor to students. It may be that these teachers' styles for bonding, plus the other workplace resources, make diffused roles less important for connecting with students for Tom and Pam than for teachers who bond through one-to-one time with students.

On the other hand, Tom, from Suburb Junior High, feels personal pressure to be a surrogate parent to students because of student needs despite the lack of school norms to support such a role. (Tom has previous teaching experience in alternative schools working with high-risk populations in which diffused roles were accepted. This experience may contribute to this personal role conflict.)

> Teaching has changed. I think that because parents are so wrapped up in their own things, you know, and accumulating the material things, like I said, teachers have been forced to become parents. I feel like I'm a parent to a lot of kids. I feel like I'm their big brother.

Tom resolves this personal conflict by clearly establishing his professional boundaries. He carefully connects all his activities with students to school-sponsored events. He clearly maintains the influential nature of the teacher's relationship with the students. And even though he feels pressured by student needs to be a surrogate parent or big brother at times, he feels no conflict when restricting his role to exclude counseling responsibilities. As a result, Tom perceives the building administration as supportive of his unique style for connecting with students (see Box 6.5, Appendix C).

In summary, the social norms and school policies of Suburb Junior High School and Rural-City High School are perceived by the teachers as not supportive of a diffused role for teachers, limiting the opportunities for teachers to connect with students. Teachers at these sites do not assume a diffused role with students, even though one teacher indicated that he felt internal pressure to do so because of student needs, despite lack of support from his work environment. These teachers are able to foster bonds with students through various strategies other than or in addition to one-to-one time with students despite the more narrowly defined role.

The norms at Inner-City High School appear to support a diffused role for teachers as expected and appropriate behavior. Teachers at Inner-City High School readily assume a diffused role and even describe diffused roles as necessary if teachers want to be effective and of service to their students. These social norms create additional opportunities for these teachers to bond with students when using the bonding strategy of one-to-one time with students. Social norms encouraging diffused roles support the bonding efforts of Dean and Gail, who attempt to bond using one-to-one time as their primary strategy. Without diffused roles, it would be more difficult for them to accumulate the one-to-one time and intimate knowledge they appear to have about their students. Because neither Dean nor Gail chooses to use schoolwide structures for communication and collective problem solving, a diffused role allows them to gather needed personal knowledge about their students. Reflecting back to the vignette at the beginning of this chapter in which Dean tries to imagine teaching at a suburban school, the freedom to relate to students from several different role perspectives is just the formula that makes Dean's teaching style so successful at Inner-City High School. Without this freedom, Dean readily admits, "It would be awful . . . and I would be a failure. I would be teaching maybe a year."

Norms within Inner-City High School are more generally encouraging of teachers assuming a diffused role with students. Without further study, it is difficult to determine what conditions contribute to the receptivity for diffused roles at Inner-City High School as compared with the other school sites. The high-risk populations in this school may require a more diffused role for inner-urban teachers to feel effective working with their students. This sounds plausible but does not explain why other settings do not encourage diffused roles as well. In essence, all student populations may be described as being at risk for negative, nonproductive behavioral patterns. The observed teachers from all three sites discuss the need of their students for the focused time and attention of a caring teacher. It may be that inner-urban schools have an environmental culture with a history that more readily accepts teachers assuming a diffused role. And it may be that Inner-City High School provides an isolated example of an environmental culture within inner-urban schools.

Organizational Strategies
Encouraging Revitalization and Recommitment

Suburb Junior High provides organizational strategies for revitalization of its faculty and recommitment to their educational goals. This school provides retreats for faculty for curriculum development and fun at the beginning of the school year. A variety of topics are covered at this retreat, from dealing with kids in crisis, to school restructuring, to curriculum planning for the interdisciplinary teams. Suburb Junior High also has institutionalized celebrations of their "community." These celebrations involve weekend gatherings. Faculty give up their weekends to attend. Every spring, there is a "fun" retreat planned.

> Every spring on the lighthearted side—and this is part of what makes this school so good—the men have, well, what's called Swamp Fest or The Male Initiation Rite at Spring as we call it. There's a guy who used to teach here . . . who owns 35 acres of swamp outside of [town]. . . . We go out there and build bonfires and do male things. [laughter] And the women have what's called the FFF, the Female Faculty Function. It rotates from place to place. It's really fun. (Tom)

The administration at Suburb Junior High has an open-door policy and provides ongoing, close support for the faculty. The principal of Suburb Junior High goes out of her way to recognize people's contributions and to support faculty for their efforts. Pam attributes the sense of community among the faculty to the principal's supportiveness.

> If you have a problem that you feel you can only get resolved through [the principal's] direct intervention or attention, you can just go in and talk to her and this is not true of all buildings. She's very approachable. . . . She's a real straight-arrow, and boy, that's a nice trait. (Pam)

> There's one vice-principal here I respect a great deal. I go to him and, you know, I ask him how he would have handled the situation. He's good at giving me feedback, and he's helped me out a lot in the past 2 years. And a lot of the time I can tell him what I did wrong first. (Tom)

Another source of revitalization for teachers at Suburb Junior High School, as briefly mentioned earlier, is the schedule flexibility provided by the administration. For example, a teacher at Suburb Junior High has multiple sclerosis. The administration arranged a part-time schedule for her, and staff and faculty do whatever they can to support her. Pam shares a good example.

We have a teacher that has multiple sclerosis that people have literally bent over backward to try and accommodate her schedule and keep her working by allowing her to do part-time work and being real flexible with that—working around her situation—giving up rooms, for example, so she would have one where she wouldn't have to walk as far. That's pretty neat.

These different strategies for revitalization provided by the organizational structure of Suburb Junior High are a source of support and renewal for Tom and Pam. There is a twinkle in their eye when they talk about their school, and there is definitely a sense of pride in their voices for the open support they receive from their workplace. Neither Inner-City High School nor Rural-City High School provides this workplace resource for supporting teachers making caring connections with students.

Summary of Supportive Work Environments

Secondary schools that support nurturing teachers are organized around efforts that encourage teacher-student relationships. These personalized environments advocate student personal growth as an overall educational mission. The organizational structures and norms encourage making caring connections with staff as well as students. These schools build in strategies for renewing a teacher's professional energies. School policies, instructional strategies, and problem-solving structures promote caring connections between students and staff. In these ideal environments, nurturing teachers can thrive, not just survive.

Of the three school sites selected for this study, the teachers from Suburb Junior High appear most supported and stimulated by their work environments. They volunteered positive feedback about their school administration and their colleagues even when it was not solicited. They speak fondly of their principal, vice principal, and colleagues and definitely identify their work environment as a source of support and revitalization. Their work environment contains several key aspects of a personalized environment, schoolwide structures for communication and collective problem solving, and organizational strategies for revitalization and recommitment. But diffused roles are discouraged. As a result of the workplace support, the teachers from Suburb Junior High School seem more actively involved in school governance and school renewal than the other observed teachers.

The observed teachers from Rural-City High School appear to be the least supported by their work environment. These teachers appear more detached from school governance and school renewal issues. They work fairly autonomously and in isolation. Even without a supportive work environment, it is clear that these teachers are committed to making a difference in student lives and find ways to make meaningful connections with students—despite nonsupportive work environments. These teachers would reach out to nurture students wherever they teach. A supportive work environment is just a plus. The study indicates, however, that the minimum level of administrative support these teachers need is classroom-level autonomy. This is especially true when the administration's educational goals are not congruent with the teachers' goal of student personal growth.

Making Nurturing
Teachers the Norm

❦ ❦ ❦ ❦ ❦

Jim is the father of one of Tom's troubled students I want to interview. I phoned Jim and his wife to ask permission to interview their son. I can tell by the tone of the telephone conversation with them that they are concerned about their son and want what is best for him. Jerry, their son, has been skipping school and is delinquent with his schoolwork. His attitude seems indifferent and apathetic, and his grades reflect his apparent lack of interest in school. Although Jerry seems to be making a turnaround in behavior, Jim and his wife are still worried about their son's low self-esteem.

During the phone conversation, it is clear that Jim has been reflecting on his role in his son's difficulties at school. He confides in me about how his experience of being raised in an orphanage affected his parenting skills: "I made a commitment to myself that when I had kids, I would give them everything. I would do everything for my kids. I now realize that, alone, I cannot give my sons everything they need to grow up to be happy and well adjusted. That was a hard lesson for me to learn."

Jim continues to talk to me about his son. "Jerry entered Suburb Junior High this fall with little interest in school. There are a couple of teachers

there, though, that have been a big help to him. He seems to have really
connected with them, and they are helping him. Tom is one of them. Tom
has made a big impact on Jerry. He gives him second chances, encourage-
ment, and support, and I see Jerry's self-esteem shooting up. I'm really
thankful for the role Tom's playing in Jerry's life."

Jim hesitates for a moment and then adds, "I would've liked to have
done it all by myself, but I know now I need other people, as well as me, to
direct his life."

Jim chats with me a little longer about the valuable help Suburb Junior
High teachers are providing him in shaping a more positive attitude toward
life in his son. Then he comments again on Tom. "You know, with all Tom
does for his students, he never crosses the line of being a parent to his
students. He doesn't take over my role. He clearly stays in his role as a
teacher. I admire that."

🦋 🦋 🦋 🦋 🦋

Implications for Educators

As an orphan, Jim had no extended family to care for him as a
child or to help him raise his own sons as an adult. Today, even
parents who do have extended family find that their kin live too far
away or are too busy to provide much support with child rearing.
Without networks of caring adults actively involved in their lives,
children have a hard time developing the social skills and feelings of
self-worth necessary to become productive, competent adults. Strong
bonds with positive, prosocial adults are essential for healthy social
and emotional development. As Jerry's parents discovered, young
people need more than one prosocial adult actively involved in their
lives. They need to be emotionally connected with a network of
caring, prosocial adults. Teachers potentially provide a large pool of
prosocial adults with whom young people can bond. As such, teachers can make a difference for students by nurturing healthy emotional connections with them.

This book examines role-appropriate ways teachers might nurture those close and trusting relationships with students. It explores
ways teachers can provide that network of caring adults needed to
raise healthy, prosocial young people, without becoming surrogate

parents or counselors. The nurturing behavior described in this book is naturally embedded within the role of a teacher. As such, this book has implications for the way educators think about their relationships with students and how they respond to students. The following sections offer comments about the meaning of this book's insights and information for practitioners, for teacher educators, and for educational administrators. The comments are organized according to questions that may concern specific educators regarding the nurturing behavior of teachers.

Implications for Practitioners

- Can the information about the nurturing roles of these six teachers apply to all teachers? Can all teachers become nurturing?
- I became a teacher to teach, not to promote student social and emotional development. I don't believe nurturing students' overall development is part of my job.
- I want to make a difference in students' lives, but I don't see myself as a nurturing person. Is there something I can do?
- I don't feel comfortable getting as involved with students as the teachers do in this book. What can *I* do and still get positive results?
- If I am always nurturing, don't I run the risk of giving up some of my control as a teacher?
- What about students who resist nurturing or respond negatively? How do resistant students affect my ability to nurture students?
- Conceivably, not all students respond equally to nurturing. How can I avoid playing favorites?

The following section addresses these questions one at a time.

Can the information about the nurturing roles of these six teachers apply to all teachers? Can all teachers become nurturing? There is something in this book that can help any teacher improve his or her ability to make healthy connections with students. The six observed teachers are not superstars; they are singular individuals who are dedicated and motivated to help young people. They have some vivid personality traits in common, but they are also different in many ways. Some of these teachers are strict, detached, and almost cool toward students; others are warm, compassionate, and easygoing. These teachers use a variety of different strategies to facilitate caring connections with students. Some hold high expectations for student performances; others push for motivation in learning but feel rewarded when students simply attend class and are respectful. Some teachers use self-disclosure; others remain private about their personal lives. These teachers also exhibit a wide variety of styles for teaching and disciplining. Some use traditional lecture modes for curriculum delivery; others use cooperative-learning or group strategies. They exhibit different tolerances for classroom noise. Some have classrooms that are rowdy; others have classrooms in which you could hear a pin drop. Despite all these differences, these teachers develop healthy, emotional connections with their students. They all earn the respect of their students. The core underlying behavioral response or attitude they hold in common appears to be respectful treatment of students, which is applicable to all teachers.

It was an awe-inspiring experience to observe these six caring teachers work with students. The resulting examples and vivid descriptions provide us with a picture of a teacher's nurturing behavior. Besides the core attitude of treating students with dignity and respect, this information provides all teachers with a way to think about their relationships with students and to understand what behavior may nurture students. It offers direction, purpose, and clarity to teachers attempting to nurture students. For some teachers, the information and insights gleaned from this book make sense of what they are already doing. Other teachers may be encouraged to try new behaviors. There is no step-by-step formula for nurturing students, but the strategies and principles outlined can be adapted to an individual teacher's style and classroom needs. Any teacher who is motivated to make a difference in students' lives can find *something* in the nurturing behavior of these six teachers that helps him or her cultivate better relationships with students.

I became a teacher to teach, not to promote student social and emotional development. I don't believe nurturing students' personal growth is part of my job. It is true that not all teachers enter the teaching profession with the intention of promoting the personal growth of students. Some teachers may be more motivated than others to work with their students' overall prosocial development. Traditionally, teachers are viewed as being responsible for promoting only the cognitive or academic development of students, not student social and emotional development. Those teachers who do not see promoting student personal growth as part of their job need only to reframe this responsibility to be developing healthy connections with students. Making healthy connections with students *is* a traditional responsibility of teachers. Just because healthy student social and emotional development is a serendipitous outcome of healthy teacher-student relationships, such outcomes need not compromise the importance of making effective teacher-student connections. Healthy teacher-student relationships are an essential component of a teacher's job.

The ambiguity about a teacher's role in promoting the prosocial development of students is more acute for secondary teachers than primary teachers. Working with the overall prosocial development of children is viewed as a more natural part of an elementary teacher's job. Unlike elementary teachers, secondary teachers are content specialists. They are trained and licensed to teach specific subjects, and many enter teaching because of their love for a specific subject. A dilemma all new secondary teachers face is finding a balance between promoting mastery of the subject about which they care deeply and the more pastoral concerns for a student's overall well-being. Each new teacher must find the balance that best fits him or her. Regardless of what balance of the pastoral and academic responsibilities a teacher assumes, making effective connections with students remains an essential dimension of his or her responsibilities—whether or not such connections enhance student social and emotional development. In the end, a teacher's primary purpose for promoting the prosocial development of students is to assist them with achieving the academic goals he or she has for students. In this day and age, those healthy connections that entail some pastoral care of students are essential if a teacher sincerely is advocating academic achievement.

I want to make a difference in student lives, but I don't see myself as a nurturing person. Is there something I can do? As highlighted by the vignette with Pam at the beginning of Chapter 2, teachers have their personal impressions and beliefs about nurturing behaviors that color their thoughts on the subject. Pam did not see herself as nurturing. To her, a teacher needed to be "mothering" the students to be nurturing. The information and insights provided by this book help us all get beyond our preconceived notions about nurturing. They provide us with tools to begin exploring what nurtures students in the caring teacher-student relationship.

The fact that six teachers with very different personalities have very different styles for nurturing students helps expose some common misconceptions about a teacher's nurturing behavior. First, nurturing does not require a teacher to touch students or to be affectionate, sweet, gentle, or warm. Several of the observed teachers demonstrated that a teacher can nurture when being stern and professionally detached. And touching students, although helpful, is not necessary. In fact, several of the teachers studied *avoided* touching. Second, nurturing is not gender-dependent. Of the two genders, the female gender is often stereotypically thought of as the nurturing gender. It is easy to assume that women can nurture more effectively than men. This study demonstrates that male teachers can nurture as well as female teachers. Third, nurturing is not synonymous with permissiveness. Some teachers believe that when a teacher is caring toward students, he or she ends up indulgent and lenient. Caring is associated with weakness or permissiveness. The nurturing teachers in the book demonstrate that one can nurture *and* still be a strict disciplinarian. The bottom line to a teacher's nurturing behavior appears to be treating students with dignity and respect.

I don't feel comfortable getting as involved with students as the teachers do in this book. What can I do and still get positive results? As affirmed by the study, the bottom line is to treat students with dignity and respect. If a teacher does not want to become involved to the degree of, let's say, Dean or Gail, just treating students with dignity and respect will make a difference. Any interaction with students in which a teacher treats students with dignity and respect will improve teacher-student relationships. Recall the story Tom shared with us regarding the teacher who made the difference in his life. When Tom was a student in high school, he was using drugs and involved in activities he should not have been. It was his literature teacher, Mr. M_____ who helped turn Tom around. Mr. M_____ was a "geek." He was not a star. He was not athletic. He didn't socialize with the students. He wasn't even a "favorite" teacher of the students. In fact, Tom said some students made fun of him. But students all knew he cared. How? He showed respect for them. In class, Mr. M_____ sought their opinions and ideas, he valued their thoughts, and he demonstrated that he believed in his students' capabilities. This recognition alone was enough to make a powerful difference for Tom. Tom credits Mr. M_____ with his life.

Teachers making such a powerful difference in student lives are not unusual or unique. The research literature on prevention of high-risk behaviors among young people is filled with similar stories. When the teacher-student interaction is caring and supportive, reflecting respect for the student, feelings of capability and significance are fostered within the child. Treating students with dignity and respect, in and of itself, will make a difference for many. Students don't necessarily need adults to be intimately involved with them or spend a lot of time with them. They need adults who care about them. Caring is shown by treating them respectfully, that is, listening to them, knowing their names, dialoguing with them, soliciting their opinions, valuing their ideas, and believing they are capable. When they need correction or guidance, showing them their mistakes only provides them with additional opportunities to learn and develop the skills necessary to be productive, successful adults.

If I am always nurturing, don't I run the risk of giving up some of my control as a teacher? The fear of losing one's control as a teacher is a common concern. As stated earlier, some teachers believe that to be caring toward students, one needs to be indulgent and lenient. They fear losing their ability to maintain control of their classrooms. With this misconception, nurturing students is associated with loss of power as a teacher.

The nurturing teachers described in this book demonstrate that nurturing can *increase* a teacher's power. In all the cases observed, the teachers had tight control over their classrooms. Three of the teachers are described as strict by their students, yet these teachers still clearly communicate caring to their students. Two teachers identify themselves as permissive; they can tolerate a high level of disruption before their patience is tried. But when they discipline, they are committed to firmness and consistency—and, of course, respectfulness. Interestingly, the students of these two teachers do not see them as permissive. Their students describe them as tolerant and understanding yet firm disciplinarians.

Understanding the power base from which these six nurturing teachers work helps explain their impressive classroom management ability. These teachers are not dependent on the legitimate power granted to them by virtue of their position as teachers. Nor do they motivate behavioral change by dangling possible rewards or threatening punishment with students, the key sources of power associated with coercive and reward power bases. These teachers' power is based on a student's admiration and respect for the teacher. It is called *referent power*. With referent power, students frequently identify with the teacher as a role model. And they are willing to adjust their behavior so as not to lose the love and respect of the teacher.

The six nurturing teachers provide vivid examples of the use and potency of referent power. These teachers use their power as teachers *to be of service* to students. They treat students with dignity and respect. They do not put down, criticize, or ridicule students. They do not coerce, threaten, or give or withhold rewards as a means of behavioral management. These teachers do not presume that their position gives them any right to treat students any differently than they treat other human beings in their lives. Such respectful treatment exemplifies an ethical use of the power accorded a teacher.

With such referent power, these teachers have a powerful influence on their students' behavior. None has problems with classroom management or chronic student disruption. Tom's student teacher, Jon, provides a vivid story of the increased potency that referent power provides teachers. He describes a situation in which a substitute came for a day when Tom was absent.

> The kids *ate him alive* . . . they just *ate this guy alive!* It was pathetic, and the kids were on a feeding frenzy. Earlier the next morning, I mentioned it to Tom. He was just furious! Tom doesn't like his class acting like that. He confronted the class with the information I had shared, but he did it in a real interesting way. He didn't tell them I told him. He said, "I hear there were some problems yesterday. What were they?" The kids immediately started confessing. And it wasn't Jimmy telling on Susie or Susie telling on Bobby. The kids who had been the problem students said, "I did this." It was the damndest thing! Their honest response showed me that they have a whole heck of a lot of respect for Tom because when they were caught, they didn't try to weasel out of it. And they didn't give excuses, like "Well, I did it because." They just said, "I did it." No prompting, no threatening. I don't know how he got them to that point. It was amazing. I had given him the names of the perpetrators, but *they all owned up!*

Tom did not make the students do 500-word essays on why students should not eat a substitute alive. They did not lose any of their privileges or have to stay after school. Tom's disappointment in his students was punishment enough. He clearly expressed his embarrassment and disappointment with them. And he had Jon share how embarrassed he felt, as a student teacher, observing the class behave so discourteously. Then together, Tom and the students worked out a plan to ensure it would not happen again.

This is a beautiful and powerful example of the potency of referent power for a caring teacher. One can also turn to the research literature for even more evidence. Studies examining the effectiveness of different power bases as means for changing behavior show referent power as the most effective, and coercive and legitimate power as the least effective (Golanda, 1990; McCroskey & Richmond, 1983; Stahelski & Frost, 1987). In influential relationships in which the distribution of power is asymmetrical and unequal, coercive and legitimate power are readily available and easy to wield. Yet these power bases alter behavior only temporarily and may not induce long-term growth, change, and learning.

Referent power is often associated with teacher charisma, but it can be developed by most teachers. How? By treating students with dignity and respect. The power wielded by Tom and the other observed teachers is nurturing and supportive of students because it is used caringly and respectfully *in service* of students. A teacher does not lose power when assuming a nurturing posture with students but may gain it. In fact, how a teacher uses his or her power in the teaching role may be the key to a teacher's nurturing behavior. A respectful and caring use of a teacher's power seems quintessential in developing close and trusting relationships with students.

What about students who resist nurturing or respond negatively? How do resistant students affect my ability to nurture students? There is no doubt student receptivity affects a teacher's capacity to nurture. In this study, several of the teachers mention that some of their students appear indifferent or unaffected by the concern and care they are shown. These teachers indicate that they just continue to nurture, whether or not the student is receptive to their nurturing.

When we reflect on this statement, it seems to indicate that these teachers nurture students because it is what *they* want to do, not necessarily because it is what students want or need. Whether or not a student responds is inconsequential to whether the teachers will continue caring or not. Knowing the personal beliefs that motivate these teachers to nurture students, nurturing for nurturing's sake makes sense—despite student response. Eventually some resistant students come around and respond to the teacher's caring, as a student in Pam's class indicates. She says, "At the beginning of the year, I didn't like her and I didn't want to be in her class. Now, I'm glad that I have her for my social studies teacher and I want to get her again next year." And some students may never come around.

If we look at this question from another perspective, one way resistant students can really impose on a teacher's capacity to nurture is by being an emotional drain. Burnout is associated with giving more than one receives and the incompletion of the caring cycle. If a teacher is working in an environment in which a lot of students are nonreceptive to the nurturing and caring of the teacher, then that teacher will not get the student reinforcement needed to support his or her nurturing efforts. Burnout is imminent unless the work environment provides many other kudos. It would be difficult for teachers to maintain their professional energy and the level of caring and involvement exemplified by the six nurturing teachers in such an environment. And practically speaking, how realistic is it for individuals whose primary educational goal is student growth to stay in a job in which they see little growth or change from their sincere efforts?

Conceivably, not all students respond equally to nurturing. How can I avoid playing favorites? Students have varying degrees of relational skills that affect their ability to make healthy connections with a teacher and to be receptive to caring. According to psychological research in the area of bonding, relational skills appear to emerge from familial bonding experiences as babies. During this time period, children develop mental sets of who they are in relationship to others and how much they can trust others (Bowlby, 1988). These mental sets affect how they respond in relationships. Children who were insecurely attached as babies have a difficult time trusting that an adult will be there for them. Thus, they have a more difficult time positively responding to a teacher's nurturing.

In fact, kindergarten teachers who are familiar with the bonding research can usually identify which students will have trouble making healthy relational connections and which will find relationships easy and natural. As one expert cleverly put it, "Whenever I see a teacher who looks as if she wants to pick a kid up by the shoulders and stuff him in the trash, I know that kid has had an avoidant [insecure] attachment history" (Karen, 1990, p. 50). Because of negative bonding experiences, these students are often difficult to give to and to love. Insecurely attached children are hard to nurture. They are more likely to evoke responses from adults that reinforce their negative sense of self in relation to others. Thus, the very students who need positive relational experiences are the hardest for teachers to nurture.

One can appreciate that it is easier for a teacher to respond to and nurture students who are receptive. When students are nonresponsive to a teacher's sincere efforts, it may be difficult to avoid playing favorites. Interestingly, some students from the study talked about one of the observed teachers as if she played favorites. Accordingly, one of her students in the interview was asked, "Does she treat all students the same?" The student's response was enlightening.

> No. . . . I mean, I think every teacher has favorites. She gives a little extra to everybody . . . she tries to spread it out. Sometimes though, she gives more to some than others. But life isn't fair. Sometimes you get lucky or whatever. But it's no joke that she gives more than most to everyone, so it is not like she has favorites.

Such wisdom from the mouths of babes! It is true. Life does not treat us all equally. We must learn to make the most of the hands we are dealt. In the real world, students are going to have to learn to work with preferential treatment. Without a doubt, teachers should try their best not to play favorites, and they should recognize they are human when they do.

Implications for Teacher Educators

- Are the skills and traits of nurturing teachers teachable? If so, which ones?
- How do we go about teaching nurturing behavior to teachers?
- There is so much that teachers need to know. How can we possibly include nurturing skills also?

The following section addresses these questions one at a time.

Are the skills and traits of nurturing teachers teachable? If so, which ones? Probably the most frequently asked question by teacher educators is, "Can we teach student teachers these skills?" The answer is yes. These nurturing behaviors are teachable. Two aspects can be presented in teacher education: (a) the conceptual framework that validates the behaviors and legitimizes their use by teachers and (b) the relational skills necessary to begin developing competence at nurturing.

When teachers are given a way of thinking about nurturing and about a way of relating to students that is appropriate to their role, they can identify guidelines within which to develop their connections with students. This book is not about techniques of nurturing; rather, it presents principles or guidelines that can be applied in a variety of ways. Knowing and valuing the principles is the first step.

Although there is no step-by-step formula for nurturing students, the strategies and principles outlined can be adapted to individual personal styles and classroom and curriculum needs. The strategies are made up of behaviors that can be learned or developed. Although some of these behaviors are innate and natural to some individuals, these traits and characteristics are still teachable. Choices of strategies used and styles employed are dependent on teachers' personalities, their personal preferences, their relational skills, and, of course, the work environment in which they teach.

Relational skills such as effective communication skills, empowering skills, conflict resolution and negotiating skills, and accountability skills are teachable, *as are* the more ethereal qualities such as genuineness, a nonjudgmental attitude, and respectfulness. These traits, as well as other "unteachable" characteristics, have been addressed for years in social work and counselor education programs. In the 1960s and 1970s, research in counseling showed that intrapersonal characteristics such as genuineness, respectfulness, empathy, and unconditional acceptance as well as interpersonal skills are essential for effectiveness in a helping profession (Aspy & Roebuck, 1972; Carkhuff, 1969; Rogers et al., 1967). Since that time, educators in the helping professions have developed and adopted curricula to train their students in these qualities. These curricula often contain an experiential component in which students practice these skills under supervision. The learning process usually begins with defining the characteristics and knowing the importance of the quality for success in the chosen profession. Proficiency, though, is a lifetime effort.

This is not to suggest that teachers should be trained as social workers or counselors. Rather, the fact that these skills are already being taught successfully in colleges and universities across the United States demonstrates that these skills are teachable. Unquestionably though, some of the same skills that counselors and social workers use are skills that teachers also need—especially in today's classroom. In fact, these good relational skills are needed by all professionals in influential positions working directly with people, such as business, the arts, or technology.

How do we go about teaching nurturing behavior to teachers? The communication skills, the conflict resolution skills, and the empowering skills necessary for nurturing behavior are already part of many in-service trainings for teachers. Continuing education courses offered through many universities and colleges contain a myriad of courses stressing these relational skills for teachers. The skills for nurturing students, though, are seldom taught in preservice education programs. Teacher education has been primarily dependent on continuing education and in-service trainings to provide these basic, essential skills to teaching professionals.

Although a viable way to reach teachers, in-service programs do not reach all practitioners. The choice to take such a course is left up to the teacher. In practice, all teachers need to know these skills. Yet not every teacher chooses to learn them. To ensure that more practitioners are introduced to these essential skills, it would be preferable for courses in a teacher's nurturing behavior to be offered by preservice education programs as part of their regular curricula. Preservice education programs interested in teaching nurturing skills can review curricula that have already been developed and implemented by the social work and counselor education programs. Courses such as "Interviewing and Counseling Skills," "Introduction to Human Service Practices," and "Theories and Methods of Intervention" found within most university social work or counseling curricula contain major components that are relevant for teacher education training. There are even college-level textbooks and training manuals available for such courses. Much of the curricula already developed is adaptable to the role of a teacher, especially considering a teacher's needs with today's students. Interpersonal and intrapersonal skills can be taught in a regular classroom format or incorporated as part of the student-teaching curriculum.

Usually making a decision to incorporate specific information into a college's curriculum means eliminating other information that seems just as essential. The question whether to incorporate new information comes down to what information is more important and what should be eliminated. If it seems impossible to add a course or eliminate another, it *is* possible to begin teaching these skills through modeling. Teacher educators can model these skills in their own classrooms and use discussion time for students to reflect on teacher behaviors that helped them develop healthy connections with their professors. In this way, no additional course is absolutely necessary. A vital aspect of teaching nurturing behaviors is modeling nurturing behaviors.

There is so much that teachers need to know. How can we possibly include nurturing skills also? This is an important question teacher educators must ask, and answer, themselves. When planning to revise teacher education curriculum, a basic concern that should shape such revisions is, What do teachers need to know to be successful in a classroom in this day and age? Placing more of an emphasis on the nurturing behavior for teachers and relational skills is of utmost importance for several reasons. First, building effective teacher-student relationships is acknowledged as one of four key dimensions of today's teaching role (Goodlad, 1990). But this dimension is often overlooked. Why? The answer is unclear. Some educators may assume that the skills are unteachable. These skills seem innate to an individual or at least acquired naturally and not teachable. As the educators in the helping professions have demonstrated, this is not so. Another possible reason that nurturing behavior of teachers is overlooked is that teacher educators themselves are unsure of the skills. Some may practice these skills naturally. But few, if any, have had the opportunity to study these skills. It is difficult to acknowledge the importance of skills one has not yet clearly identified. Without preservice education in basic theory and skills for developing healthy connections with students, some teachers do not even recognize that making caring connections is a part of their job. "I'm just here to teach," they declare.

A second reason it is important for teacher educators to place more emphasis on healthy teacher-student relationships involves the positive association between student achievement and effective teacher-student connections. There is enough evidence now demonstrating that student achievement is directly associated with effective teacher-student relationships to justify placing more emphasis on the relational skills within teacher education programs. As Noblit, Rogers, and Brian (1995) say, "Without this connection, teachers may have their subject-matter knowledge and the technical ability to teach, but the opportunities for real learning will be scarce because what the teacher does not have is the student" (p. 683). In a time of restructuring education to improve student learning and achievement scores, recognition of the positive association between teacher-student relationships and learning places a responsibility on teacher educators to help potential practitioners develop the needed skills to create better connections with students.

Finally, with changing student needs resulting from cultural and lifestyle changes, it is important that teachers and student teachers are introduced to the relational skills necessary to be successful in their chosen profession. Practitioners often express bewilderment and confusion about dealing with the emotional and social issues presented to them in the classroom. One can try to avoid or ignore these situations only so long. Often teachers are unable to attend to their primary job responsibility—the academic development of students—without competently handling immediate social or emotional crises. Placing teachers in classrooms with emotionally and socially needy children without the basic communication and relational skills to comfortably handle such situations seems preposterous. Teachers deal daily with socially and emotionally needy children in less controlled conditions and for longer periods of time than most social workers or counselors. Yet social workers and counselors receive up to a year or more of preservice training for skills to handle these situations. Teachers are given little to no training. Leaving training efforts to continuing education programs or in-service trainings seems somewhat erratic and risky at best.

The need for preservice teacher education training in these skills is clear. How teacher education programs are revised to include such training is a programmatic decision. As stated earlier, at minimum, teacher educators can begin training in these essential skills by modeling these skills in their classrooms. The place to begin may be professional development programs with preservice teacher educators, at which teacher educators can learn to identify and employ these skills themselves.

Implications for Teacher Administrators

- As administrators, should we encourage diffused roles for teachers (e.g., socializing with students outside the classroom, helping students with their personal problems, etc.)?
- What risks are involved for teachers who socialize with students outside of school (e.g., invite students to dinner, go to games with them, etc.)? Do these risks outweigh the benefits?
- Do schools with the most supportive structures for nurturing teachers encourage a greater number of nurturing teachers? How do we go about implementing a program to help our teachers become more nurturing?

The following section responds to these concerns one at a time.

As administrators, should we encourage diffused roles for teachers (e.g., socializing with students outside the classroom, helping students with their personal problems, etc.)? This is a good question for administrators to discuss among themselves. There is no easy answer. To begin the discussion, it is not absolutely necessary for teachers to assume diffused roles in order to nurture students successfully. Some teachers do prefer to socialize with students beyond the classroom or to help students with personal problems. They relate to students this way in an effort to nurture them, especially if their only strategy for bonding with students is spending one-to-one time with them. Several teachers in this book, though, illustrate that a teacher *can* successfully bond with students without assuming a diffused role—without even having one-to-one time with students. Other strategies, such as appropriate self-disclosure, building community, believing in students' ability to meet high expectations, and networking with kin, also develop healthy bonds with students. And often teachers who use these other strategies prefer *not* to assume diffused roles. For these teachers, policies restricting personally socializing with students legitimize their choice of professional roles and discourage behavior that accelerates burnout.

Considering whether or not to encourage diffused roles brings up an interesting dilemma highlighted in the book. Both teachers from the inner-urban school assumed diffused roles, and both used one-to-one time with students as their primary strategy for bonding. Is this because this strategy best fits the personalities and teaching styles of these teachers, or is it because the strategy works best with the student population with whom these teachers are working? Or is it because the social norms of the school encourage diffused roles? These concerns are not clarified by this book. Would Dean's informal, easygoing style of socializing one-to-one with students, including helping students with personal problems, fraternizing with them after school, and eating lunch and sometimes dinner with them, work in other school environments with other student populations? Would Dean be able to make effective connections with his inner-city students without assuming such a role? In reverse, Pam at Suburb Junior High explicitly chooses not to assume a diffused role as a teacher. If Pam worked at an inner-urban school, would she be able to make healthy connections with students without assuming a diffused role? Would her strategy for bonding, using appropriate self-disclosure, work well with students from inner-urban neighborhoods or primarily working-class or lower-class neighborhoods? In other words, are diffused roles more effective with certain student populations than others? Administrators considering a policy of encouraging diffused roles may want an answer to this key question before making the decision.

What risks are involved for teachers who socialize with students outside of school (e.g., invite students to dinner, go to games with them, etc.)? Do these risks outweigh the benefits? Sadly, we are all too aware of the risks involved in socializing with students simply from watching the evening news. It is clear that we need to be careful when assuming a diffused role. Socializing with students can evolve to potentially inappropriate behavior on the teacher's part, resulting anywhere from producing confused students to sexual harassment or sexual abuse charges. Sometimes a teacher's caring behavior is misinterpreted by a student. In any account, both the teacher *and* the student are placed in precarious positions.

Because of possible threats of sexual harassment and abuse, some administrators may overreact. Dale and Ruby's situation is such a case at hand. These teachers expressed that they are living under a fear perpetuated by the administration. They are not supposed to give a student a ride home if he or she is stranded at school; they are to wait until the student's ride comes, if ever. And while they are waiting, they are to make sure someone else is waiting with them. If a student is hitchhiking, they are not supposed to stop and pick him or her up. Both teachers talked about how these severe restrictions limit their ability to give students extra support.

The situation for Dean and Gail is just the opposite. The administration trusts their staff to behave appropriately and their students and parents to accept the teacher's nurturing behavior in the light it is intended. They allow teachers to relate to students in whatever way they feel comfortable, as long as it is legal. This liberal policy does give these teachers many more opportunities to make meaningful connections and to show students that they are cared for. It does provide these teachers with additional "teachable moments" but at a high risk for the school's administration.

The risks with diffused roles are onerous, complicated by the fact that appropriate boundaries are often liberally defined with diffused roles, allowing for easy misinterpretation of a teacher's behavior. Gail, from Inner-City High School, demonstrates how liberally boundaries can be defined in her statement, "As long as it is legal, it's fine." With risks so high, the benefits may not outweigh the risks. Clearly defining the boundaries may be a way to minimize the risks yet not critically minimize the opportunities for nurturing.

Tom's situation at Suburb Junior High provides an excellent model of clearly defined boundaries that lower the risk of misinterpretation yet do not critically interfere with opportunities to nurture. Tom, a social studies teacher, has taught in an alternative school in which diffused roles are accepted. But at Suburb Junior High, where he now teaches, policy restricts a teacher from socializing with students beyond school activities. Tom and his administrators have worked out a plan that appropriately accommodates Tom's teaching style and his inclination for assuming a diffused role. Boundaries for his diffused role are clearly limited to events that are associated with school and to group events. These boundaries *prohibit* socializing with students at dinner or having students stay overnight at a teacher's house for a social activity. These boundaries *do* encourage attending with students afterschool events sanctioned by the administration. And the school can liberally sanction off-campus events. For example, the administration could sanction a dramatic play in town or a major league sporting event. Arrangements for such events are made prior to the happening. The teacher then attends the event, along with a group of students, as a chaperon. Students attend with parental permission. With these boundaries, a teacher maintains his or her professional position in the influential relationship, and there is little danger of misinterpretation of the teacher's intentions. Every year, Tom takes students to major league baseball games and to Washington, D.C., for a week of sightseeing and touring of the nation's capital.

Social activities for the sake of socializing with students, such as asking a student to dinner or having students stay overnight, as Dean and Gail have done in the past, present a very high risk. Many would agree that, in present times, the benefits may not outweigh the risks. This is especially true when this type of socializing with students is not absolutely necessary to develop healthy teacher-student relationships. Both Dean and Gail are able to develop close and trusting relationships with students with whom they have never socialized after school hours. These teachers, and the other teachers in this book, demonstrate that it is not absolutely necessary for teachers to socialize with students in risky ways in order to make healthy connections with students. For teachers who want to develop healthy connections with students, it may be helpful to be aware of the many other ways available to do so.

Another aspect of this same dilemma of risk versus benefits involves socializing with students after they graduate or advance to a higher grade. As discussed in Chapter 1, becoming friends with students after they are no longer officially a teacher's student still presents problems. Even when a student moves on, the teacher holds a place of honor and esteem in the student's eyes. Once the hierarchy in a relationship is established, it may never completely fade. Teachers remain role models for students, which carries a lot of influence with the student. As such, the power distribution in the relationship is still asymmetrical and unequal. The responsibility that comes with this asymmetrical power needs to be acknowledged by the teacher. Teacher-student relationships are more easily moved to confirmatory or instrumental relationships than to friendships (see the section in Chapter 1, "Four Types of Social Relationships").

All and all, the decision to encourage diffused roles for teachers is complicated by a host of confounding variables, from teacher preference to threats of lawsuits. For many, the risks involved with a liberal definition of a teacher's role may not outweigh the benefits. There are less liberal positions that administrators can advocate that involve less risk of misinterpretation yet still offer extended opportunities for nurturing. In any event, whatever role a teacher assumes, the teacher should remain cognizant of the unequal power distribution in a teacher-student relationship.

Do schools with the most supportive structures for nurturing teachers encourage a greater number of nurturing teachers? How do we go about implementing a program to help our teachers become more nurturing? Certainly, it makes sense that caring, nurturing environments encourage a greater number of nurturing teachers—and discourage those teachers who are uncomfortable with nurturing relationships with students.

Nurturing behavior is motivated by personal values and belief systems that determine how we relate to other people. As such, there is no set program to be adopted by schools for promoting nurturing behavior by teachers. Practitioners can be taught the basic skills for nurturing, but there is no step-by-step program for actually implementing the nurturing behavior within the schools. As many administrators already know, top-down programs are often easy to implement but seldom bring about significant change in the school environment. If implementation is attempted in such a way, the practice often is only grafted onto the school as another add-on, ineffectual program. This is especially true when the needed behaviors are based in personal values and beliefs of the teacher. Nurturing comes from a genuine and authentic center in the individual that can be encouraged, validated, and supported by the environment in which he or she works.

Administrators who want to encourage a greater number of their teachers to become nurturing teachers may want to model the nurturing behaviors themselves. By doing so, they begin to affect positively the customs and beliefs within their own school environments. Nurturing teachers are encouraged by caring cultures within schools. Encouraging nurturing teachers requires the development of caring cultures that are built on treating students (and staff) with dignity and respect. Such caring environments *can* begin anywhere but need to be cultivated by the administration. Administrators need to model nurturing relational skills and support school norms and organizational structures that assist teachers in their efforts to develop healthy relationships with students. Nurturing behavior does not necessarily emerge from radical restructuring, mandates, budgets, or changes in policies. Rather, it emerges from subtle changes in the attitudes and behaviors of educators. Administrators can model this behavior and *be* the change they want to have happen.

Summary of the Book

This book examines the nurturing behavior of six teachers. It reveals the skills, understandings, and sensitivities that teachers employ to form healthy relationships with students that are naturally embedded within their role. The implications for educators of the insights and information garnered from these six teachers were just discussed. What follows is a summary of the book's major themes about a teacher's nurturing behavior. For simplicity, these themes are clustered around three categories: (a) the nurturing behavior of teachers, (b) the personal resources needed for renewal, and (c) the workplace resources that support nurturing teachers.

Major Themes About
Nurturing Behavior of Teachers

The six nurturing teachers demonstrate six different ways teachers can build close and trusting connections with students in role-appropriate ways. First, teachers can create one-to-one time with students. This one-to-one time can be created by remaining accessible to students before and after school, between classes, during extracurricular activities, or during the class period. It can be created by using a delivery style for the curriculum that maximizes individual or small-group contact, by writing personal comments on student papers, or by giving nonverbal cues such as touching or eye contact.

Second, teachers can use appropriate self-disclosure to nurture closeness and trust with students. With this strategy, teachers disclose personal information about themselves that is pertinent, in both content and context, to the needs of the students. When using this strategy, teachers exercise discretion regarding the personal information they share and have some idea of how students can use the information to enhance their learning process.

Third, teachers can hold high expectations of students while clearly conveying a belief in their ability to meet those expectations. This strategy for bonding requires two distinct behaviors: (a) Teachers have to establish and maintain high academic standards for their students, and (b) teachers need to believe that students can meet these high standards.

Fourth, teachers can bond with students by networking with parents, family members, friends, and neighbors. These intergenerational networks create a sense of familiarity and a common ground with common histories on which a teacher can build healthy connections with students.

Fifth, teachers can build community among their students. A teacher builds community by encouraging students to take risks within the classroom, make honest self-disclosures, and share among class members. By inclusivity, the teacher is drawn into this community of students.

Sixth, teachers can use rituals and traditions within the classroom. These rituals and traditions foster a sense of familiarity and belongingness.

These six strategies suggest that there are several options for teachers to nurture the development of bonds with students both in and out of the classroom but still remain focused on their primary academic goals. These strategies do not appear to interfere with a teacher's academic instructional role. In fact, in most cases, they are embedded within the teacher's academic instructional role. The six strategies may not be the only way teachers can build close connections with students. Further research may uncover other strategies.

Among the teachers studied, one-to-one time with students was the most prevalent strategy for bonding. All six teachers in the study relied on this strategy in some form. Some teachers employed one-to-one time as a primary strategy; others used it in conjunction with other strategies. Styles for employing this strategy also vary. For instance, along with one-to-one time with students, the observed teachers used one or more of the following styles: (a) designing curriculum to enhance opportunities to connect with students individually or within small groups, (b) interspersing personal and academic talk within a lecture to create one-to-one time with students, (c) using direct personal dialogue during free time and between classes, (d) connecting with students on a one-to-one basis by writing personal comments on student papers, and (e) using nonverbal communication to establish personal contact. A teacher's style of connecting on a one-to-one basis is based primarily on teacher preference. The subject taught does not influence how a teacher can create one-to-one time.

Although the bonds between the teachers and their students were formed prior to the study, the bonding strategies identified are very likely to be the basis for the close and trusting relationship that has developed between the six nurturing teachers and their students. The student inventories confirm that a close and trusting relationship has been established between these teachers and their students. Different educational and psychological theories and research studies establish that these strategies or techniques foster close and trusting connections between parents and children, counselors and clients, or individuals such as friends or group members. Therefore, although not studied directly, it is likely that the bonding strategies discussed in this book, if effectively implemented, build close and trusting relationships with students.

Treating students with dignity and respect was discovered to be fundamentally necessary for students to perceive that a teacher cares. Students seem able to perceive and be receptive to a teacher's caring when treated with dignity and respect. Therefore, a teacher's ability to build close and trusting connections with students is enhanced when teachers treat students with dignity and respect. These teachers are respectful of students when talking about them to administrators or fellow staff members. They use a considerate tone of voice and receptive manners when speaking to and about students. These teachers take time to listen to students and treat the students' concerns seriously. They provide opportunities for students to make themselves known in ways that might elicit positive regard from others. They acknowledge that they learn from their students. They help students perceive themselves as capable, responsible, and significant. In summary, they treat students with dignity and respect when disciplining, maintaining order in the classroom, teaching, advising, or just playing with students.

The study identifies two key related and mutually reinforcing opportunities for treating students with dignity and respect: (a) using discipline as an opportunity to teach and (b) creating a safe learning environment. Showing respect to students when disciplining helps to create a safe learning environment in which to make mistakes, to take risks, and to grow. With the observed teachers, disciplining students is viewed as another opportunity to teach students. Styles of disciplining run from strict-authoritative to permissive-authoritative, but all styles of disciplining are employed with respect for the parties involved. Expectations for behavior are clearly established and discipline is administered fairly, consistently, and firmly.

The six nurturing teachers prefer to do their own discipline rather than depend on the discipline structure of the schools. Personally handling the discipline needs of their students helps establish and maintain the clear, professional boundaries ascribed to teachers in influential relationships. Disciplining students offers nurturing teachers an opportunity to provide moral guidance and appears to be a strategy for maintaining professional boundaries when in close and caring relationships with students. Even in the more diffused roles assumed by two of the observed teachers, one way they establish and preserve their professional boundaries is by maintaining their moral authority and right to discipline students.

Finally, a strong quality in a nurturing teacher is the ability to focus on what is right about students rather than on their imperfections. The six observed teachers continually demonstrate acceptance and unconditional regard for every student. They believe in children's innate capabilities to be successful despite the high-risk situations in which they live. Seeing what is right about students rather than seeing their imperfections builds positive attitudes in them and strengthens their resiliency to the adversity. These six teachers' deep respect for their students' capabilities empowers students, encouraging them to act on their own behalf.

In order to empower a student, a teacher must see a student's strengths and capabilities. By focusing on students' strengths, treating students with dignity and respect, holding high expectations of students, believing in students' capacity for personal growth, and valuing time spent with students, these teachers empower students to act on their own behalf. Even when disciplining, these teachers empower students by focusing on a student's potential for growth and ability to self-adjust. Such discipline affirms a student's personal power and motivation to change his or her behavior as needed. These teachers see the positive qualities in students when teaching and in all their daily interactions with them.

Major Themes About
Personal Support for Teachers

Developing close and trusting relationships with students makes considerable demands on a teacher's energy. A teacher's motivation and energy for nurturing students is likely to be sustained by belief systems that give their nurturing behavior purpose and direction. The observed nurturing teachers hold in common six predominant beliefs: (a) student growth is a primary educational goal, (b) the purpose for teaching is to be of service to young people and to help make a difference in students' lives, (c) a teacher is in a powerful position to influence young people and that power must be handled ethically, (d) curriculum is a vehicle for teaching personal growth, (e) teaching is a valued and valuable profession, and (f) classroom teaching is more desirable than an administrative position. These six beliefs encourage and support these teachers' motivation to bond with students. Their belief system gives purpose and direction to their commitment to work closely with students in a caring manner. It helps these teachers make sense of what they are doing. And it serves as a source of energy that fuels a mission they have—to make a difference in student lives.

The fact that all six teachers share these beliefs suggests that nurturing teachers hold student personal growth as their primary educational goal. They believe a student's social, emotional, and moral development is as much a part of their teaching responsibilities as is a student's academic development. They view teaching as an opportunity to be of service to young people. They acknowledge and respect the powerful role they play in student lives. And they enjoy their jobs.

Certain intrapersonal characteristics appear to enhance a teacher's ability to nurture and their attitudes toward students. The common intrapersonal characteristics associated with these teachers' nurturing behaviors are the following: genuineness and authenticity, inner locus of control, tolerance for ambiguity, sense of humor, nonjudgmental attitude, potency, enthusiasm, and androgyny. Among these characteristics, the most vivid and pervasive intrapersonal characteristic shared by these teachers is genuineness and authenticity. When relating to others, these teachers present themselves as human beings first and teachers second. They are unpretentious and unassuming. They are aware of their frailties, easily acknowledge mistakes, and assume accountability for their behavior. The qualities of genuineness and authenticity appear to be prominent, overarching, intrapersonal characteristics that give potency to a teacher's nurturing attitudes and behaviors toward students. These qualities appear to provide an intrapersonal context that enhances the expression of the other intrapersonal characteristics held in common.

In addition to these intrapersonal characteristics, certain interpersonal skills appear to enhance a teacher's ability to nurture students. The interpersonal skills the six nurturing teachers hold in common are the following: effective communication skills, empowering skills, problem-solving skills, conflict resolution skills, and accountability skills. Among these skills, the most pervasive interpersonal skill shared by these teachers is effective communication. Effective communication skills include listening, reflecting, paraphrasing, summarizing, and clarifying. These communication skills are dynamic tools with which to express caring and are the basic competencies necessary to effectively employ the other interpersonal skills held in common by these teachers.

Effective communication skills are also identified as essential to be successful in the other helping professions such as counseling. Good communication skills increase one's effectiveness when working with other people. For teachers, proficiency with interpersonal skills increases their personal sense of competence, a key to professional rejuvenation. Possessing and practicing these skills appears to be one of a combination of factors that help to sustain and revitalize the professional energy of nurturing teachers despite the demands made on their time and energy.

Major Themes About
Supportive Workplaces for Teachers

The workplace resource claimed most supportive by the six teachers are the students themselves. Students provide teachers with psychic rewards for their work. These teachers' love for and commitment to students is a key to their revitalization. It provides them with a solid emotional context for replenishing their professional energies. Free time spent with students inspires and reenergizes them. The company of students provides support and revitalization for nurturing students.

Another potential workplace resource for support is the school's administration. When these nurturing teachers believed that their administrators valued nurturing the personal growth of students, they perceived their immediate work environment as supportive; when these teachers perceived that their administrators placed priority on other educational goals, their perceptions of support within their work environments were clouded. These observations suggest that when both nurturing teachers and their administrators hold the personal growth of students as the primary educational goal, nurturing teachers feel strongly supported by their administrators.

Research literature identifies the personalized school environment as an ideal supportive environment for teachers who nurture students. This type of environment has specific organizational strategies and social norms that are supposed to provide special support for teachers who want to develop healthy relationships with students. These organizational structures include the following: (a) schoolwide social norms fostering the development of familial or communal atmospheres within the schools, (b) schoolwide strategies for revitalization and recommitment, (c) school norms that support diffused roles for teachers, and (d) structures for communication and collective problem solving.

According to the information gleaned from this study, a familial or communal atmosphere within the school and schoolwide strategies for revitalizing staff are supportive environmental resources for nurturing teachers. Social norms supporting diffused roles for teachers are supportive for teachers who want to extend themselves socially to students beyond the classroom and workday hours. For nurturing teachers who prefer to define their role more conventionally to include only responsibility for school-sponsored activities within workday hours, social norms that encourage diffused roles are irrelevant and may, in fact, be unsettling for the teacher. The bonding strategy used by the teacher appears to mediate how helpful diffused roles are for teachers. Teachers who bond using primarily self-disclosure, community building, belief in student capabilities, networking with kin, or rituals and traditions may not find diffused roles as helpful as teachers who bond with students primarily through one-to-one time.

Organizational structures for promoting communication and collective problem solving such as core groups and teacher-parents-student problem-solving groups appear most helpful when they do not absorb the time a teacher could otherwise spend with students or when there are a limited number of deeply troubled students. For instance, in Inner-City High School or Rural-City High School, collective strategies for dealing with students could easily absorb all of a teacher's time because there are so many troubled students. When a teacher bonds primarily through one-to-one time with students, collective problem-solving strategies are not viewed as helpful. In fact, these strategies are viewed as a burden, taking away from the teachers' time with students. However, teachers who bond primarily through one-to-one time do value being able to assume a diffused role if they wish and, if they choose such a role, feel supported by norms that encourage it.

If we focus on the minimum administrative support necessary for nurturing teachers to feel comfortable teaching the way they prefer, it appears that nurturing teachers need classroom-level autonomy—along with the respect of (not necessarily agreement with) their chief administrators. The six teachers in the study appear to be driven by a mission, although none states so directly. The intense desire of these teachers to make a difference for students propels them beyond many negative blocks within their environment, for example, apathetic or even hostile supervisors, coworkers, and/or communities. As long as they get time with students and the professional respect to work with students in ways they deem important, these teachers perceive their work environments as supportive.

The six nurturing teachers reach out to students despite negative aspects about their work environments. A supportive environment, though, makes their jobs much easier, as evidenced by Dean. Last year, Dean had a different principal who was not supportive of him. But she stayed out of his way because she knew students had respect for him. Dean acknowledged and appreciated the freedom and autonomy the principal gave him. Despite lack of encouragement by the administration, he still loved his job. This year with a new principal who is supportive of his efforts to nurture students, Dean is even more energized and enthusiastic about his job.

Closing Thoughts

When discussing school restructuring and reform, the importance of the relationship between teacher and students is often overlooked. Yet *it may be key*. Maguire says, "If relationships are wrong between teachers and students, for whatever reasons, you can restructure until the cows come home, but transformation won't take place" (cited in Rothman, 1992, p. 1). We can no longer afford to overlook this essential relationship. Schools, as the most important extrafamilial environment for young people, can become arenas for caring and making meaningful connections with young people. They can house a network of caring adults who want to be actively involved in student lives, enhancing the overall healthy development of young people. In so doing, schools can play a central role in the healthy social and emotional development of young people—without taking time from a rigorous academic agenda. And healthy teacher-student relationships can play a key role in advancing restructuring efforts.

Nurturing caring connections with students is a teacher's investment in the ongoing development of young people. Healthy, caring relationships take work. They have a history and a future. When talking to Dean about how he deals with the large number of students who have become bonded to him over the years, he said,

> How do you deal with it? You just keep going. They come back into your life, and you're there to help them a little bit. You're there sometimes when they just want to say hi. It doesn't matter, It's just part of the job.

To Dean, it's just his job. To the students, it may be a lifeline. Teachers have no way of knowing the impact they are making. Even after 15 years of teaching, Dale is not fully aware of the impact he may have made in students' lives. He says,

> I still have kids that come back. I would say a couple of years out of high school. There's a lot of kids that come back for homecoming and talk to you and they're still . . . they appreciate where I was coming from. . . . I can't remember half of them. That's the trouble . . . I'm bad with names.

Dale may not remember their names, but there are, most likely, many students who can remember his. Graduates may return to high school for a couple of years and then move on with their lives. Not many of us as mature adults take time to go back and acknowledge the teachers who made a difference for us. As a first-year teacher and a mature adult who keenly remembers the few teachers who made a difference for her, Pam says,

> The impact that we have on students we might not even begin to understand or realize what that is, but it's there. And it may surface in 20 years down the road somewhere for that

student. So I think we have a moral responsibility to be cognizant of how we treat them at all times. I think the moral dimension of teaching is really overlooked a lot by teachers and teacher training, but it is such an integral part of the whole teaching experience.

A teacher's role in students' lives can be powerful. Teachers who choose to nurture young people may redirect some to grow up to be productive and successful. The nurturing teachers in this book represent a whole cadre of our nation's teachers who are making a difference in young people's lives.

Afterword

Throughout my reading of *Teaching With Heart* I found myself continually feeling gratitude—gratitude for the heart and humanity of these six wonderful teachers who are, indeed, making a difference in the lives of the youth in their "care," and gratitude also for my friend and colleague, Judy Deiro, for "care-fully" and insightfully capturing and recording their voices. Being one of those "prevention specialists" Judy described early on as "theorists and researchers who seek . . . to understand and identify factors that protect young people from high-risk behaviors," I heartily concur with the theme of this book, that establishing caring, respectful, inviting relationships with young people is not only the bottom line for promoting their healthy emotional and social development but also the number one prerequisite for student learning.

When I listened to the voices of these teachers, I was reminded of the words of Naomi, an adolescent girl living in a troubled family and a dangerous community: "School was my church, it was my religion. It was constant, the only thing that I could count on every day . . . I would not be here if it was not for school" (Children's Express, 1993). What Naomi and thousands of other youths growing up in "high-risk" environments have told us in interviews, in qualitative studies, and in longitudinal developmental research is the power of a nurturing teacher, classroom, and school to transform their life experience from despair to hope and from chaos to meaning.

Teaching With Heart delineates just what is going on in the classrooms of schools that have this transformative power. When Naomi has teachers like these six that convey—albeit each in their own individual style as Judy has so clearly shown—the deep belief in their students' innate capacity for learning, wisdom, and positive development; that "trust students are doing the best they can, given their developmental level and life circumstances"; that acknowledge that a shining light exists within every student—no matter the rough exterior; and that see their primary teaching mission as the personal, social, and emotional growth of their students, we can feel confident that school will be Naomi's sanctuary and beacon of light.

I finished this book feeling both regret—at having to part with these teachers I clearly bonded with—and a renewed commitment to get this book's fundamental message out to preservice teachers and administrators, to educational policymakers, and to the general public. Judy's well-chosen quote from one educational researcher sums up this message: "If relationships are wrong between teachers and students . . . you can restructure until the cows come home, but transformation won't take place." *Teaching With Heart* gives us even more compelling evidence that excellence in education begins with making heart-to-heart connections between school personnel and the youth they serve.

Bonnie Benard

Reference

Children's Express. (1993). *Voices from the future: Children tell us about violence in America.* New York: Crown Publishers.

Appendix A:
Notes on Research Strategies

Appendix A describes the research strategy I chose to study the nurturing behavior of teachers. The description begins with the characterization of the six nurturing teachers and the places where they work. It goes on to depict the research design, the data sources, and the selection process for the nurturing teachers and their students. Finally, it reviews the safeguards that were used to counterbalance the negative impact of my personal biases and to ensure the integrity of the study. The reader can find a more detailed explanation of the research strategy and other aspects of the study in Deiro (1994), *What Teachers Do to Nurture Bonding With Students,* an unpublished dissertation.

Six Nurturing Teachers

The following are nutshell characterizations of the six nurturing teachers. They are categorized according to the school at which they work. All names cited in the book are fictitious.

Inner-City High School

Dean. Dean is a 38-year-old Lebanese American male. He teaches biology at Inner-City High School, where he has been teaching since the beginning of his teaching career 7 years ago. Prior to teaching, Dean worked as a chemist for 5 years in private industry. He returned to school at age 31 to become a teacher. Dean has won the Public Broadcasting System's Golden Apple Award for being one of six outstanding teachers in his state. Just recently, he was chosen to teach in Japan for one year in an overseas teacher-exchange program.

Dean readily admits he is an easygoing disciplinarian. He feels this is the best approach when working with inner-city students. Sometimes his classes are as large as 36 students. Filled with incredible energy, Dean seems always to be moving. Once a college football player, he is a husky, charismatic, masculine personality with remarkable devotion and love for kids. Dean is assistant football coach and junior class adviser at Inner-City High School. He describes his childhood familial experiences as happy and filled with love.

Gail. Gail is an attractive, 36-year-old African American female. She has taught language arts at Inner-City High School to freshmen and sophomores for one year. Altogether, Gail has taught for 12 years at both the junior and senior high levels. She is a firm disciplinarian with high expectations of her students. Her counterpart, Dean, describes her as "tough as nails." Gail provides strict moral guidance with a compassionate and empathetic heart. Stylishly dressed, Gail is poised and sophisticated. She moves gracefully about the classroom.

Gail offers a culturally relevant curriculum for students of color, who make up 77% of the Inner-City High School student population. She is the drama club adviser and the adviser to the cheerleaders. Gail really enjoys spending her free time with students. She recognizes her influence as a teacher in her students' lives and uses that influence to try and make their lives better. Except for the racial discrimination she experienced as a child, Gail describes her childhood as happy and filled with love.

Rural-City High School

Dale. Dale is a 37-year-old European American male. He has been teaching mathematics in Rural City since the beginning of his teaching career 14 years ago. For the first 4 years of his teaching career, Dale taught at Rural-City Middle School. For the past 10 years, he has been teaching at Rural-City High School. Dale usually teaches the advanced mathematics courses, but this year he is teaching the Fundamentals of Mathematics to freshmen and sophomores. About 20% of his students are mainstreamed students with special needs. Dale assumed the task of teaching Fundamentals of Mathematics to see if he could help increase mathematics achievement scores within this special population.

Dale readily admits he is an easygoing disciplinarian. Of average height, slim, and wiry, he moves quickly about the classroom. He seldom is seated. Once a college baseball player, Dale is the varsity baseball coach at Rural-City High School. For many years, he also coached varsity basketball. Dale has a powerful commitment to helping kids be successful in their lives, and he uses his teaching and coaching skills to achieve this goal. Although his father died when Dale was young, Dale believes he had a happy childhood.

Ruby. Ruby is a 38-year-old European American female. She has been teaching health and physical education at Rural-City High School since the beginning of her teaching career 16 years ago. For the past 6 years, she has been teaching only health classes at the high school. For several years at the beginning of her career, Ruby taught part-time in a Rural City middle school as well as in the high school before moving to full-time teaching at Rural-City High School. She is a firm but soft-spoken disciplinarian. Physically fit and with a quick smile, Ruby conveys a potent but gentle and steadfast persona. She is the girls' varsity volleyball coach and assistant track coach.

Ruby is committed to the personal growth of her students and her own personal growth. She has a deep, abiding love and concern for children. Her own childhood was abusive and unstable. She was moved back and forth between her mother, her maternal grandmother, and foster home caregivers as a child. Both her mother and grandmother had drinking problems. She never knew her father. From these experiences, Ruby knows how important it is to be available for students and provide a stable, caring role model.

Suburb Junior High School

Pam. Pam is a 39-year-old European American female. She has been teaching social studies for 6 months at Suburb Junior High School. This is Pam's first year teaching. For 14 years prior to returning to school to become a teacher, Pam was a successful businesswoman in a glass-manufacturing company. In midlife, she made a change in careers in order to be of service to people, a core value for her. Working in the business world, she did not feel she was honoring this core value. As a teacher, she still carries the matter-of-fact, businesslike persona, although she dresses casually and moves sprightly among the students.

Pam is a strict disciplinarian with high expectations of students. She coaches varsity girls' basketball and chairs "Cool Cats," a team of teachers who are responsible for providing special attention and services to troubled students. Pam has made the transition from businesswoman to teacher well, taking with her important communication and negotiating skills learned in the business world. Her innate brightness, humor, and love for children help make her an excellent teacher. Pam describes her childhood familial experiences as abusive and difficult. Her father was prone to fitful rages and was often physically abusive.

Tom. Tom is a 37-year-old European American male. He has been teaching for 14 years. Short-haired and clean shaven, Tom dresses in a pressed shirt and tie for work. For the past 6 years, he has been teaching social studies at Suburb Junior High School. Tom has the educational preparation and experience to teach both highly capable students and special education students. He has taught in alternative schools, special education programs, and accelerated programs. Tom is a firm disciplinarian with high expectations of his students. He supervises afterschool detention weekly and annually sponsors a field trip to Washington, D.C. A social activist, Tom approaches his job with intensity and heart, yet he does not lose his sense of humor. He is actively involved in the governance of his school and in the promotion of school renewal programs such as interdisciplinary team teaching and teaching to multiple intelligence.

Tom has a personal history as a rebellious teenager. He used drugs throughout his high school experience and dropped out of school his senior year. Tom knows what it feels like to be on the outside looking in. Bright, creative, funny, and extremely dedicated, he believes in his students and nurtures their capabilities. Although his father died when Tom was 5 years old, Tom describes his familial experiences as loving and supportive.

The Schools Where They Work

Inner-City High School. With a student population of 860, Inner-City High School is located in an ethnically diverse area of a large metropolitan city. The socioeconomic class of the area is lower- to middle-class with approximately 40% of the student body on a free- or reduced-lunch program. About half the students do not live with both parents. Some of these students are living with a single parent, and some are living in alternative homes such as foster care homes or with friends or relatives. Seventy-seven percent of the students are students of color. For 25% of the students, English is their second language. Approximately 30% of the students are bused from other parts of the metropolitan area. More than half the graduating class apply to postsecondary schools during their senior year according to student services estimates. About one half of the students are on a vocational track, whereas the other half of the students are on an academic track.

Rural-City High School. With a student population of 1,150, Rural-City High School is situated in a small, self-contained, rural community of approximately 5,000 people. The high school draws from a general population area of 13,000 people. The socioeconomic class of the area is primarily lower-middle-class or working-class, with approximately 10% of the student body on the free- or reduced-lunch program and probably another 10% eligible if they would submit an application. The student population is primarily European American, with less than 5% of students of color attending the high school. The counseling center estimates by tallying student requests for transcripts that 40% of the graduating class applies to postsecondary schools. The large geographical area the high school serves generates a student population with diverse educational needs and varied parental expectations. Student demographic data indicate that student enrollment is equally divided between the vocational and academic tracks.

Suburb Junior High School. With a student population of 993, Suburb Junior High School is nestled in the suburbs of a large metropolitan area. Within the past several years, the community surrounding Suburb Junior High has rapidly transformed from a rural setting to a suburban setting. The socioeconomic class is primarily middle- to upper-class with only 5% of students on free- or reduced-lunch programs. Only 7% are students of color. The student population is composed of primarily European American students. Curriculum at Suburb Junior High is college oriented. The counseling department estimates that 85% to 90% of the students plan to go on to college; most students move into the college preparatory track at the local high school.

Research Strategy

Nurturing behavior is not easily quantified for measurement or observation. In order to understand the behaviors of teachers that nurture students, the teachers needed to be observed in their classrooms actually relating to students. I needed to talk to these teachers and their students, step into their world, and seek to understand their experiences from their point of view. In research terminology, this research design is called a case study using a qualitative methodology.

Six nurturing teachers served as key informants in the study. A key informant is a primary source for data and information for a research project. The six key informants worked in three distinctly different secondary-level settings. Limiting the study to six key informants gave me sufficient variety and diversity of teachers while still allowing the study to be completed within a reasonable time frame. In addition, two students of each key informant were interviewed.

Data Sources

Data were gathered through three different techniques: predesigned, open-ended, and semistructure interviews with the six teachers and 12 students; observations of the teachers in the classroom; and student inventories and other pertinent documentation. I conducted four interviews with each teacher. Interviews covered such topics as general family background, professional training and experiences, descriptions of work environments, perceptions of high-risk students, opportunities for nurturing, view of students, discipline techniques, and so on. In addition, I observed the teachers in their classrooms for 3 full days as a nonparticipant observer.

For supplemental data, I interviewed 12 students, two students for each key informant. These loosely structured interviews covered a range of topics, including general family background, the student's attitude toward school, information on the student's perception of how the teacher perceived the student, and qualities the student particularly liked in the teacher. The decision to interview only two students per teacher was based on experience with a pilot study that demonstrated that interviewing two students for each teacher provided sufficient supporting data.

Both teacher and student interviews were recorded on audiocassette tapes and later transcribed verbatim. Depending on what was most convenient for the teachers, some of the interviews were conducted in the teacher's home and others were conducted at school. Student interviews were all conducted at school. Data clippings from observations and interviews are located in the boxes throughout the text.

In order to triangulate data, I also reviewed appropriate documents or papers, such as student inventories measuring closeness and trust with the teacher, curriculum materials, and feedback notes on student papers from the teacher. (A copy of the inventory measuring closeness and trust with a teacher is in Appendix B.)

Selecting the Teachers

The selection of the key informants was based on four criteria regarding their skills at teaching:

1. Excellent reputations among peers, students, and staff as teachers who develop healthy, nurturing connections with students
2. Excellent reputations among peers and staff for expertise in their subject areas and their ability to teach their subject specialties
3. Commitment to the teaching profession as exemplified through their commitment to their own professional growth and advocacy for school renewal
4. Content specialists in a traditional subject area, such as biology and social studies

It was reasoned that selecting teachers on the basis of these multiple criteria would ensure that they nurture students in ways that do not compromise the primary responsibility of a teacher for the cognitive development of students.

Teachers of the experiential, elective courses such as shop, driver's education, and home economics were eliminated from the selection process. Faculty in these subjects often work closely with students on a one-on-one basis in order to build skills. Because experiential, elective courses require more hands-on, one-on-one time with students, it was assumed that it is easier for teachers in these subjects to build close relationships with students. For the purpose of this study, it seemed important to explore how teachers with less opportunity for one-on-one time with students, such as the teachers of the traditional academic classes, developed healthy connections.

In addition to the above criteria, one male and one female were chosen from each site—three males and three females altogether.

It was believed important to have an equal number of male and female teachers in order to avoid the possible interpretation that bonding with students was gender-bound. With both male and female teachers included, it is more difficult to assume that one gender can nurture students better than the other. Ethnic diversity also was considered in the final selection process: One of the male teachers is Lebanese American, and one of the female teachers is African American.

All of the key informants selected met the criteria listed. Prior to final selection, each potential key informant was discussed with his or her supervisory staff and several teaching colleagues to ensure that selection was appropriate. A self-designed, pretested inventory reflecting levels of closeness and trust developed between teacher and student was used to verify that students were truly bonded to this teacher. This inventory was administered to *all* the students of each teacher (see Appendix B). Student input on the inventories was used not only to verify teacher selection but also as an additional source for data.

Selecting the Students

Although the variables that students bring to the teacher-student relationship were not the focus of the study, student input about the teacher's behavior was vital. To get the students' perspective on what teachers do to develop healthy, caring relationships with their students, two students for each key informant were interviewed. Each student was perceived by his or her teacher as having a close and trusting relationship with the teacher.

Specific criteria for the students selected were developed. Because bonding to schools and teachers has been associated with a decrease in delinquency or behavioral problems as well as an increase in academic skills and higher scores on standardized achievement tests (O'Donnell et al., 1995), one criterion was that students be picked who had recently exhibited a reversal in negative behavioral patterns in the teacher's classroom (e.g., acting out in class, noninvolvement or low motivation, chronic tardiness). These students were called "turnaround." If there were no turnaround students in the teacher's class, an alternate criterion for student selection was students who were living in high-risk environments (e.g., high-crime areas, abusive home environments) but had made successful adjustments to the role of a student. Their successful adjustment was demonstrated by their motivation, academic achievement, and prosocial behavior. These students were called "resilient."

The selected teachers were asked, based on their perception of and knowledge about their students, to identify students who fit the category of either turnaround or resilient. For Suburb Junior High School students and Rural-City High School students, these criteria worked well. The key informants at these schools handed me a list of students who fit the criteria, and I arbitrarily chose two students for each teacher, usually one male and one female.

At Inner-City High School, however, these criteria did not work. Dean, the biology teacher, just laughed when I described for him the criteria for student selection. He said, "That just about covers every single student in my classes." He identified two students based on the additional criteria. One student was someone who knew him personally, and the other student was someone who did not know him as well, although she was clearly bonded to him. Gail, the other key informant from Inner-City High School, just smiled when told the criteria for student selection and said, "Just grab any student." Then she turned around and asked two students standing close to her at the time if they would be willing to be interviewed. They eagerly agreed. This quick selection process seemed too haphazard to me. Because all four students from Inner-City High School selected to be interviewed were students of color, I asked Gail to identify a European American student. She gave some thought to this request. In the end, five students from Inner-City High School were interviewed, one of whom was European American.

Protecting Against Bias of Researcher

Analysis of qualitative data involves an inductive thinking process. The researcher becomes an "instrument" in the research design as well as a "filter" for the data (Owens, 1982). To minimize the negative impact of the personal bias on the findings, interpretation of the data was continually double-checked with professional peers and the key informants. Sometimes at the end of an interview or after school, points of confusion or shared thoughts were discussed further with the key informants. Sometimes while analyzing the data, I would phone a teacher to clarify a point regarding that teacher's behavior and ensure a clear understanding.

An outside data reader was also employed to minimize the negative impact of personal bias. This data reader was asked to read through the coded interviews and observational data and double-check the reliability of the interpretation and coding of the data. After reading through random samples of the data for nearly 4 hours, he agreed with my interpretation.

My professional training as a counselor predisposed me to view bonding as being associated with warmth, empathy, and gentleness. Remaining conscious of that bias throughout the data collection and analysis time period, I purposely observed and interviewed two teachers who challenged my bias toward these components of bonding. One teacher was described by her colleague as "tough as nails." I was confused by her style for nurturing, and I had considered dropping her for another key informant, but I knew from student inventories that she did develop close and trusting relationships with students. Another female key informant was detached and abrupt with the students. Again from the student inventories, I knew students were bonded to this teacher. Both these teachers (the "tough as nails" teacher and the "detached and abrupt" teacher) enriched my findings by forcing me to winnow irrelevant data colored by my bias and allowing me to begin uncovering the more essential components of the bonding process.

Appendix B:
Student Inventory Questionnaire

Please describe your relationship with your teacher and class-mates. Fill in the blank with the number that comes closest to how you think or feel. Please put N/A if the statement does not apply to you.

1	2	3	4	5	6
Strongly Agree				Strongly Disagree	

_____ I feel close to and trust this teacher.

_____ I feel my teacher listens to my concerns when I talk to him or her.

_____ There are qualities my teacher has that I would like to develop within myself.

_____ Even when I schedule time to talk to my teacher, I get the feeling I am taking too much of his or her time.

_____ My teacher has high expectations of me, but I am capable of achieving them.

_____ When I have done something wrong, my teacher doesn't listen to my side.

_____ I trust that my teacher will help when I need help with school problems.

_____ I do not like my teacher.

_____ My teacher embarrasses me for not knowing the right answer.

_____ My teacher is fair in dealing with students with their school problems.

_____ In solving classroom problems, students' suggestions are followed.

_____ I do not look forward to being in this teacher's classroom.

_____ If some of my friends want me to ignore a fellow classmate and my teacher asked me to help this classmate with homework, I would do what my friends want me to do.

_____ I do not feel safe sharing my thoughts and feelings with my teacher.

_____ My teacher can control the classroom without embarrassing any students.

_____ My teacher is interested in what I do outside of his or her classroom.

_____ I do not feel respected by this teacher.

_____ This teacher does not help me to enjoy learning.

_____ I usually enjoy school.

_____ I feel my teacher really cares about me as a person.

_____ I enjoy spending free time with my teacher.

Appendix C:
Supportive Data—Boxes 3.1–6.5

Box 3.1

Treating Students With Dignity and Respect

Dale   Dale addresses the students as "ladies and gentlemen." "Ladies and gentlemen, I am glad to see you. I am really glad to see you. We need paper, pencils, and books today."

When talking about experiences from his high school years that influenced who he is today, Dale says, "The only thing I really carry with me [is] treat the kids with respect. I tell them at the first of the year, I say, I'm going to earn your respect. I'm going to work really hard to earn your respect. And I will respect you just as much as you respect me."

Dean   In talking to Dean at lunch, he said, "These kids are adults. They've already made more decisions in their life than you or I have had to. You can't treat them like kids, but like adults. Take for instance the kid sitting up there studying. [Dean points to a small boy quietly studying.] He's a gang member and has been faced with situations you or I have not dreamed of." Surprised, I commented on how small he was to be a gang member. Dean said, "The gun is the equalizer."

Gail   When asked what she assessed as her strength as a teacher, Gail said, "My ability to empathize with the students, to put myself in their place. . . . I see them as little people. I see them as independent thinkers, as very nice people. Even the ones that are sort of rough. They are really nice but you have to cut through the roughness to get to the nice part. I think I have the ability to cut through the edges and get through to the nice person, or at least find out what's wrong, what's going on in that person's life that perhaps has made that person what society perceives as a mean person or a bad person."

Gail calls students up to the podium to talk to them individually. When asked what she says to students, she responded, "It is usually something that you don't want to say out loud in front of students. Even praise—some students don't like you to praise them in front of their friends because they will be seen as teacher's pet. So I kind of do it quietly."

Pam   When asked what the qualities of a healthy, caring relationship between a teacher and a student are, Pam responded, "One is mutual respect. Another is clear boundaries. Another is clear expectations and clear consequences. That's pretty easy, huh."

"I relate to them as people. . . . I don't talk down to kids. I never have, I don't think, you know, in a condescending way. 'Oh, this is a child who wouldn't understand.' I expect kids to understand the question and be able to communicate with me—their needs and wants and that kind of thing."

"I don't speak in a different language. I never talk down to them. I use words that sometimes I know they don't know the meaning of. And I try to either have them work it out in context or if someone asks me, I have them look it up. It's like I don't alter how I speak to these guys."

Ruby   One of the ground rules for teacher and student behavior in Ruby's class is respect. "I think we have four of them [ground rules]: respect, set a goal, think positive, and make up work. I think those are the four posted up there."

Ruby suggests that students get up and move around to exchange their strength inventory with other students. Two students don't get up. She says, "Don't you guys get tired of sitting all day long?" The answer, "No." She says, "That is amazing. When I am in meetings all day, I get real tired of sitting." They answer, "Yes, but we are used to it. You are not because you are standing most of the time." Ruby pauses. "Well, that is right," she says. She allows them to remain in their seats.

"I do my very best to never confront kids in front of other kids if it's a thing where I have to get on them about their behavior. So a lot of times I'll take the two kids outside."

Tom   Tom addresses the boys "sirs" and the girls "ladies." One student responded, "We treat him with respect because he treats us with respect" (Shawn).

The student teacher said of Tom: "I think it comes down to respect. There is a definite two-way respect in that classroom. You know, a lot of teachers expect the kids to respect them, but it's not reciprocated."

Box 3.2

Student Recognition and Reaction to Respectful Treatment

Dale   I commented to a student that when Dale disciplines, students seem to adjust their behavior without grumbling or resistance. The student's response was, "Because he gives us a lot, and I think the students know that we owe him at least our attention" (Danny).

Annette knows Dale sees her as a resource rather than an object. She says, "Some teachers think 'I'm the boss and you're the student and no matter what you say you're wrong and I'm right.' . . . You can't connect because you feel like they're superior to you. Mr. _____ has always told us that teachers and students are the same and to learn from the students because they can teach you things too" (Annette).

Annette feels respected. "After being suspended for a while, you come back and it's like totally weird being in school again. And you know, I walked in [Dale's] classroom and he's like, 'Hey Annette! You're back! Congratulations, you made it!' You know, he is like, 'Have a seat. Come on. We're waiting for you' and stuff. You know, he like welcomed me." Annette admits trying harder and doing better in Dale's classes. "I mean, he's the only math teacher I've learned from. I'm good at math but I usually don't get good grades in it. All my life I've gotten Ds and stuff, and this year I'm finally getting Bs in his class."

Dean   "Well, everyone respects him. Like if people don't respect you, the teacher, and the teacher tells them to do [something], they'll just talk back and then the teacher will have to make them leave or something. And the people won't care. But people don't really like it when [Dean] gets mad at them, I don't think" (Rosie).

      "Just when he tells you, people got enough respect for him just to quit, to stop doing it right when he says it" (Vinnie).

Gail   When asked how he thought Gail saw him as a student, Jake replied, "I think she respects me as a leader . . . because she asks me a lot for opinions and advice. Sometimes she has me help other people because she knows I'm capable of believing in them and responsible enough to help them without screwing around." Jake believes another teacher whom Jake does not like sees him as "irresponsible and not willing to do his work" because that is the way Jake treats his class.

Pam   "She doesn't really have to do a lot of discipline in our class because I'm pretty sure that our whole class loves her, you know" (Kathy).

      After describing how much fun it was to cause trouble in a class of a teacher he doesn't respect, Rick said, "I don't really like to get into trouble in her [Pam's] class, really. I'm not really trying for it [to get into trouble as in other classes]. I don't like to deal with getting in trouble in her class."

Ruby   When talking about a teacher she *does not* like, Sally believes this teacher would describe her as "a kind person but not willing to respect [the teacher] and not willing to do as much work and stuff as she would like me to do." Sally is a good student in Ruby's class. Sally says, "She [Ruby] is a really caring teacher and she is a lot better than all the other teachers. And it's not just caring; it's about the teaching too.

She's a really good teacher. She makes it where you learn something and you always will have it."

Peter knows that he is more than a job to Ruby. "She seems to enjoy being here. I think she would probably still do this job if she wasn't getting paid. I think she likes it enough that she'd do that."

Tom   "We treat him with respect because he treats us with respect" (Shawn).

"He just takes a special interest in each one of the students. He tries to help each one of them. . . . He treats everybody fair. [He] tries to be fair with everybody. . . . I think everybody in our class knows that he could be strict but he's just nice to us, so I think that's why everybody's nice back to him" (Shawn).

"He doesn't have to threaten. He doesn't have to yell and scream. He doesn't have to do anything. I think it comes down to respect. There is a definite two-way respect in [Tom's] classroom. You know, a lot of teachers expect the kids to respect them, but it's not reciprocated. . . . He treats them like they're young adults, to a certain extent" (student teacher).

Box 3.3

Student Receptiveness and
Perception of a Teacher's Caring

Dale   "He understands, you know, that we're teenagers and stuff. And he just cares. I don't know why, you know, he doesn't really have a reason to, I guess. But he just does. He shows it to us by, you know, he makes it a point to talk to us before class starts and after class ends. And it's not just like math for him. It's life and math put together" (Annette).

"He's the kind of person where, you know, that if you tell him something he's not going to tell it to everybody" (Annette).

When asked what he would tell student teachers on how to develop a close and trusting relationship with students,

Danny responded, "Stay in [Dale's] classroom for a bit and watch him work."

Dean "He cares about all the kids, not only the ones he knows. He cares about all the kids. So it's like if anybody has a problem, usually they'll go to Mr. _____ and Mr. _____ will then try to help them out" (Vinnie).

"He's just . . . he's there if you need something. He knows how to make time. If he can't talk to you in school, during class, he'll like come back after school. He's always there" (Rosie).

Gail "One quality that I see is that she is a caring person. She cares a lot about kids" (Abe).

"She's easy to talk to. She tries to understand your problems. She jokes with you. She's just . . . she's open. You can talk to her and that's the teacher who cares" (Abe).

When asked what makes Gail a caring teacher, Susan responded, "[Other teachers] don't ask you, like, if you're having a bad day. They don't ask you if you're okay or anything like that. It's like . . . I'll tell her such and such is happening and I'm really worried and she'll tell me . . . The other teachers just don't ask."

Pam "Well, there are teachers that will always say, 'If you have a problem you can come to me' but you never really go to them. . . . I knew it was all right to talk [to Pam] about . . . my things, about my friends and stuff like that and she's really caring" (Kathy).

Rick was in some serious trouble at school. "Like, I had this thing going on with the school and stuff, and this one girl thought we did something but we didn't do any of it. Me and my friends . . . we really didn't. I didn't want to talk to the counselor because the counselor was, like, all on their side and so he wouldn't even listen to us. So then, Ms. _____ said I could talk to her and then I just went and talked to her."

"Well, like, she'll let you talk about [stuff]. If you have any problems, she'll talk about it with you. I think everyone likes Ms. _____ except people like _____. He has, like, an attitude toward Mrs. _____" (Rick).

Ruby "The way she talks and the way she's really caring. Just the way she goes out of her way to get to know some people. . . .

She kind of lets you know that she is there to listen to you and she's just, like, a real sweet person and she goes out of her way to get to know kids. . . . Just that I really like her a lot and that she's just a really caring teacher" (Sally).

"She just [holds] out her arms. If you ever wanted to talk to anybody, whenever you wanted to. She's always there for you. She's pretty cool. She gives you good advice . . . the different choices that you could make. Like . . . she's just really cool. Always there when you need her" (Peter).

Tom   "He's talked to me a few times. When he found out that I can't talk to my parents, he gave us a counselor that he used to go to that we went to. . . . He takes a special interest in each one of his students. He tries to help each one of them" (Shawn).

"He's nice and he'll listen to you if you have anything to say. He's honest" (Jerry). When Jerry was asked what he would tell other students who were planning to take Tom's class, he responded, "I would tell them that he's a nice guy. He has homework, lots of homework that's sort of simple, but you have to think a little harder than you would in a regular social studies class . . . all I know is that he's a real nice guy that someone can trust."

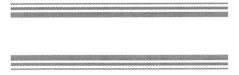

Box 3.4

Discipline as Moral Guidance

Dale   One student, Bill, a troublemaker, came up behind Dale and put his paper on Dale's back and starts to sign it. Dale says, "Don't write on my back. There are plenty of desks around here to write on." Bill tries to jive with him by saying, "Shut up man." Dale smiles, looks him directly in the eyes, and says, "What happens to you when you say that to your dad?" Bill stops and says, "He pops me." Dale quietly quizzes the student, "Maybe I should pop you?" Bill looks apologetic. He then continues more appropriate social banter with Dale. Dale immediately joins in as if nothing had happened. Within minutes, Dale is teasing Bill about greasing his hair. Bill and the students laughs.

Dean   Dean tells his student assistant, "Hey, you know what? We need to clean this fish tank up." She says, "Oh no! I'm not going to do that. You are the one who killed the fish." Dean says gently, "I want you to empty the water out of there into the sink." She said, "I am not going to stick my hands into that water with all those dead fish!" Ignoring what she just said, Dean says in a light tone, "I want you to do this." He demonstrates how she is to take a container and transfer the water out of the tank to the sink. She says again, "I am not going to stick my hands into that water." Dean responds, "Then go to the nurse's station and get some rubber gloves." She retorts, "The nurse is never there when I go down there." Dean calmly replies, "Then I will go with you to get the gloves because this is your job and I want you to do it. This is your responsibility." Dean and the student leave the room for the nurse's station.

Gail   Gail walks around the room in between the desks, watching how people are working. She stops at one of the clusters and gently says to a female student wearing a beautiful new parka, "How did you get that coat?" The female student looks up and says, "It was on sale." Gail softly says, "Take it back." The female student ask, "Why?" Gail says, "You don't keep what you can't pay for." The student was numbly quiet. Gail moves on without another word.

Pam   Pam is working in an assimilated archaeological dig with the students huddled around her. Someone says, "This sucks." Pam looks up and says quietly, "Who said that?" The culprit immediately identified himself. She asked him to step out-side. After the demonstration, Pam stepped outside with the student for a moment. She asked him if he knew why he was sent out of class. "Yes, I was disrespectful." She said, "Do you have anything to say to me?" He said, "I am sorry" and they entered the room together.

Ruby   One small group of boys are kidding around and one student says, "Oh shit!" (Swearing is not acceptable behavior in Ruby's classroom.) Ruby says calmly to the student, "Carl, see me after class." Carl turns to his friends and says, "I said shoot." His friend slowly shakes his head no. Carl meekly says, "Ship?" The class laughs and so does Ruby. After class, Ruby reminded Carl of the class rule of no swearing.

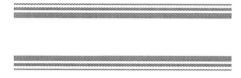

Box 3.5

Creating a Safe Learning Environment

Dale   "I call [students] by name or give them some kind of individual attention. I'm trying to get them to have confidence in me so they can ask me a question. . . . A lot of kids seem embarrassed to ask questions. So I'm trying to eliminate that feeling so they can ask me about anything and feel real comfortable."

Data from in-class observations: Dale chats with the students while they work on their homework. He seems to just accept everybody as equals, treating everyone in the same relaxed, good-natured manner. Students may start talking about something, and Dale joins in with and shares in the fun. . . . It is a very comfortable and low-key class. Students appear to be free to talk to him about almost anything, from the trouble they got into over the weekend to getting detention for passing gas in class in another teacher's class.

Danny, a student with a learning disability says, "[Dale] stays calm all the time. . . . I have never, never, heard him yell."

Dean   Rosie, when asked what Dean does that makes him such a caring teacher, said, "Well, just the way he acts. I mean, he's always making sure everything is okay, making sure you do your work, and he makes you feel really good if you do your work."

Data from in-class observations: He creates an incredible space for students to be themselves. Dean always uses a soft voice. During the whole day, I never heard him raise his voice to quiet the group or redirect their behavior. Even though less playful than the last time I observed him, he was always calm in voice. When lecturing, he often reflects questions back to the group. . . . He seldom rejects an answer all out but rather says, "a little like that" or "almost, but what about this?"

Gail   When Gail was asked for the qualities of a healthy, caring relationship with students, the quality she mentioned was providing a safe environment. "I guess . . . their knowing that they can come and talk to me, just about . . . anything. I'm not going to get mad at them or judge them."

Data from in-class observations: Gail's curriculum is relevant to the African American and minority cultures. Each day I entered the classroom, students were working with material that was relevant to their culture. For instance, the first day students were reading a short story titled *Farewell to Manzanar* about an Asian American family. The second day they were studying Martin Luther King's speech, *I Have a Dream*. The third day students were reading a play called *The Life You Save*. The play is about African American people, and it is written in the jargon of black people.

Pam   "Why do people try to sidestep responsibility? They do it because they're afraid. If you remove fear, then you're taking a huge amount of anxiety off of kids. You know, I am not going to yell at them. I'm not going to belittle them. I'm not going to ridicule them. I'm not going to embarrass them. I just want them to self-correct and they know that."

Data from in-class observations: When students forgot to bring from home items to simulate an archaeological dig, Pam had them brainstorm in teams a plan to ensure that they would remember to bring all the items for the assignment to class the next day. Pam did not criticize, nag, or tell them what they had better do to make sure the items were here the next day.

Ruby   "I want kids to feel okay to talk to me. Within the realm of the health class, we talk about so many issues in there. I guess I want them to feel safe if we're going to do a writing assignment and they're going to talk about particular issues that relate to teens. I want them to feel safe if they want to write that they've experienced something. . . . I just let them know that it remains confidential between us."

Data from in-class observation: Ruby had given the assignment of creating a 2' × 3' personal collage depicting who they are by creatively using clippings from magazines. She asked the group, "What do you think that I will not let you put on the collage?" A student says, "Tobacco and alcohol." Ruby pauses and says, "Other students also have thought that I would not permit alcohol and tobacco, but I have let students do that because if alcohol and tobacco are really that important to them, they need to express that." Another student says, "Sick!" Ruby pauses and says, "How else can we say we don't approve without putting people down?" They talk a little about this idea. She explains that "people need to feel free to express who they are . . . and that is where their lives are at." She goes on to define the guidelines as no pictures of nudity, no profanity, and no put-downs of other people.

Tom   "They generally feel pretty comfortable in here. I mean by the way they act and talk and do everything else in here. The fact that we had 81 out of 85 kids choose to come back to team-taught courses this year."

Data from in-class observations: Tom laughs and jokes with them when they make a mistake. Students are not afraid to toss out an answer. They try but are not afraid to make a mistake. They readily acknowledge when they don't know. In observing Tom's class, I was not concerned that he would shame and criticize students. I was not anticipating abrupt, angry words. Students do not hesitate to admit when they have misbehaved.

Data from student teacher: [The student teacher describes student behavior after a particularly rowdy day when a substitute teacher was there.] Tom said, "I heard there were some problems yesterday. What were they?" And they immediately confessed and it wasn't Jimmy telling on Susie and Susie telling on Bobby. The kids who had been the problem children said, "I did this." That right there showed me they have a whole heck of a lot of respect for him because when they were caught they didn't try to weasel out of it. . . . They didn't try, "Well, I did it because" or whatever it was. They just said, "I did this." Tom's response was, "We don't do that." [Then, Tom had the student teacher share how he felt watching the kids behave as they did from the back of the room.] "I think he let them 'guilt trip' themselves" (student teacher).

━━━━━━━━━━━━━━━━━━━━━━━━━━━━━

Box 4.1

Commitment to Student Learning

Dale   Dale negotiated with a student to motivate her to study her math. " 'Andrea, I will buy you a tank of gas if you pass the comp test. . . . and you can buy me a tank of gas if you don't.' Well, she did not pass the comp test, and I could have gone back and said, 'You really owe me that tank of gas.' But no, I don't care if I ever collect that. I would rather have her just pass that comp test.' "

Dean   During one classroom observation, I observed Dean working really hard to get students motivated for a test. During the last 7 minutes of class, students were coming up to Dean's desk and double-checking their grades. The upcoming test was the final test. Dean kept dogging the students to do better. One student, Steve, went up after class. Dean said, "If I am dogging you, it is because I care about you and I don't want you to fail."

Gail   "Right now I've kind of geared my language arts courses toward project based and performance based and student outcome, even in lieu of a written test. We have a lot of written work projects, so I can see exactly what the students have gotten from either the literature or some sort of assignment. They have a portfolio when they leave the classroom. So they get to look at it and say, 'This is what I have learned and this is how I understood the lesson or what it means to me.' And they get to see, they hold in their hands what they understand."

Pam   "I try real hard to be clear about what I expect, what the limits are, and what consequences there will be if those implications are not met. I do the assignments myself before I have them do them so I know what to expect. Nothing is worse than having a teacher give you an assignment that is undoable for some reason. Like maybe your library doesn't have the resources to complete the assignment and you're just stymied. Well, an eighth grader just says, 'Well, forget it. I'm just not going to do anything.' They might not communicate to the teacher that it's because they didn't have the right resources . . . so my practice is to read the lessons that I'm having them read. And I answer the questions so I know where and how it's phrased in the book. When they say, 'It doesn't exist,' it's like, okay, try this, because I've done it. I know. I've been through the process. It takes time to do that but it pays off, it really pays off."

Ruby   "I am knowledgeable about what it is that I teach. And you know, if there's something I don't know when a kid asks me, I'll get back to them. And I don't have any problem saying 'I don't know this but I'll find out and get back to you.' I think I really believe in the whole process of education. I believe it's important for kids to be here and I believe it's important for them to be taking the class that I'm fortunate to be teaching."

Tom   "I was honest with [the students], told them this is the way it's going to be and I know you can do it. And I had high expectations. And my part of the contract was I agreed to create an individual educational plan for the kids, devote time outside of school to make sure that they were able to get done if they needed any extra help, and at any point in time be there as their mentor in terms of working with the teachers at school other than me that they have to deal with."

Box 4.2

Personal Motivation to Be a Teacher

Dale   When asked what attracted him to the teaching profession, Dale answered, "See, I was a baseball player and I wanted to stay involved with the sport or just coaching in general. I thought maybe physical therapy. As I got into it, I found out I wasn't really a guy for all the muscles and all of that stuff. . . . I thought I can coach if I can get in to the teaching end. As I got into education, I found I was really comfortable. I felt good about myself when people learn things. I seemed to put people at ease and have them feel good about math. I did not want to be a PE teacher because I wanted to be challenged. . . . Anyone I figured could, hey, throw the balls out and have fun. But this was the ticket for me—still being able to be involved in sports and able to help kids."

Dean   "I had teachers at my high school who were with me. They really stuck with me. They understood a lot of times—sometimes they did not understand but they were always there for me. . . . And so as I went through life, I realized you know something, I would like to be doing this and in this profession because maybe I could actually give some [of what they gave me] back."

"Those kids are my clients. Those kids are my people whom I am serving. I got to look at their needs. I got to react to their needs. What is best for them? Everything that I do in my heart it is like, 'What is best for them?' "

Gail   When asked about her purpose as a teacher, Gail responded, "I think just to help students make it in the future, to help students have control over their lives as far as their jobs are concerned. Or if they want to further their education, then they have some sort of background. And that they have become better people hopefully because of me or something that I have said or something that I have done."

Pam   When asked what attracted her to the teaching profession, Pam responded, "Working with kids. History has long been my avocation, and [teaching] was a chance to combine my love of history with love of kids and also the opportunity to do something that is of service. Does that sound too corny? It's true. It's like I spent 14 to 15 years pursuing something that was financially very rewarding but wasn't satisfying at all on almost any other level. . . . There is this spiritual component to teaching. I was raised in a very religious household. And in the denomination I was raised in you have an obligation to be of service. I didn't feel like I was fulfilling my obligation to be of service in the business world."

Ruby   When asked what special experience can you identify that prepared you to relate with students the way you do, Ruby responded: "I would say that it was mostly different people in my life that treated me well, that encouraged me to take the next step, to go out and really accomplish what I wanted to do.

It was very impactful to me. I was like overwhelmed with 'How do I pay you back? What do I do?' Their comment always was, 'Well, do for someone else someday what we did for you.' It just fit—I am going to do this through education."

Tom   Tom recognizes that during his drug-using and drug-dealing years he hurt many kids. He sees teaching as a way of making amends. "I messed up a lot of people when I was in high school. . . . I believe that life is like a scale of justice. I have a lot of debt on the dark side. Teaching and making a difference in kids' lives helps to balance the scales on my side."

Box 4.3

Power of the Position

Dale   I am entrusted with 150 minds and the professional part of it is that it's my judgment on which way to take those 150 minds for 180 hours. I think that I take responsibility very heavily. I mean, it's not light. I understand that it's important. I understand that what I say to these kids can go a long way and sometimes I've really got to think about it."

Dean   "I just remember there were educators who really made a difference in my life. A lot of it was how they interacted with me. And I really saw—I mean they could destroy—I watched them destroy some kids, as far as their self-esteem and stuff like that. I'd think, 'Dang! I can't believe this person dogged this person like that!' Or said something that was really hurtful to that individual. 'Oh my God! How could you do that?' It was more of an awareness that I had as I go through life—whether it is in the classroom or dealing with people in general. It is how much power you have just from the words you say, whether you are an educator or not. Words are incredible. They can friggin' destroy people."

Gail   "We have a lot of power, a lot of power. [Teachers] don't realize it until they've done something damaging or until someone has come back after 10 years and said, 'I've become this because of you.' I didn't recognize it really, until 4 years ago when I did an experiment with my class—the blue eyes/brown eyes experiment. It took about 7 minutes to make half the kids really mad, really upset, and doubt their abilities. *About 7 minutes!* And these are kids that I've had 4 or 5 months and just that fast I was able to make them think they were stupid, and they couldn't do well on tests, and the other side of the room was better than they were. It took me another 20 minutes to tell them that this was all a test, not for real."

Pam   "I think that each individual really makes a difference, for one thing. And that the impact that we have on students we might not even begin to understand or realize what that is, but it's there. And it may surface 20 years down the road somewhere for that student. So I think that we have a real moral responsibility to be cognizant of how we treat them all the time. I think the moral dimensions of teaching are really overlooked a lot by teachers and teacher training. But it's such an integral part of what the whole teaching experience is."

Ruby   "You know the little things can really make a difference. A lot of the little things I am not even aware of. Kids will write to me at the end of the year, 'I really appreciated that you did this or that you didn't do this.' *Wow!* I didn't realize that this was such a noticeable thing."

"It was mostly different educators in my life that treated me well, that encouraged me to take the next step, to go out and really accomplish what I wanted to. It was very impactful to me. I was like overwhelmed with 'How do I pay you back?' Their comment always was, 'Well, do for someone else someday what we did for you.' "

Tom   "I know I've made a difference, you know, in kids. They come back to see me, like the kid yesterday. He's entering the Marines, the music program for the Marines. And yet all he wanted to talk about was his ninth-grade year. You know, and it's scary sometimes to think that you have that much impact. It's terrifying. I'm not real sure a lot of people understand that."

"This is the most important job on the face of the earth. There is nothing more important. There is nothing more important."

Box 4.4

Subject as a Vehicle

Dale "I think I hopefully try to teach more than just math in here. Some of the kids understand that and some don't. I try to teach them what it's like to grow up and to act like adults, although I'm not opposed to them being kids. Just that there are responsibilities that they need to assume."

Dean "A kid's got to be able to read; a kid's got to be able to write; a kid's got to be able to do math; he's got to be able to work in a group; he's got to be able to respect his peers and deal with people, even people he doesn't like or she doesn't like. They got to be able to have pride in themselves and self-respect and real pride and respect in their community and the people around them. My whole approach to teaching is to take a person and use the academic part to direct all of this—the reading and writing and the math and stuff like that. I use biology like a vehicle to try to make those other things occur, self-respect, all that kind of stuff."

Gail On all 3 days that I observed Gail, she used her subject matter as a vehicle to guide her students in personal growth. For instance, on day one, the class was reading the story *The Sniper.* In this story, the key characters are enemies. Gail asks the class to reflect on their personal reasons for having enemies. Gail points out that one popular reason for making enemies is jealousy. She illustrates her point by discussing how old movies often have two women fighting over one man. She comments on how insane this behavior is. She coolly suggests, "If a guy doesn't like you, move on to someone who does. Fighting about it will not make him like you."

Gail says, "I am more interested in self-esteem and happiness first and then the lesson. Because without those two, whatever I teach won't make a difference."

Pam "I mean, I love [my content area] and I believe it's real wonderful and all that. But is a seventh grader's life really going to change if they know who the rulers of Mesopotamia are? No. What's more important is that they learn how to be successful as people and they learn how to get along with each other. You know, they learn how to retrieve information that they are going to need. They learn how to work cooperatively. Those are some of the things important to me in teaching kids. That they have a sense of responsibility about being citizens and contributing and about being human beings and having compassion for one another. That's a lot more important to me."

Ruby   "I think that out of all the things that [students] come away with in the classroom, all of the knowledge and skills, I think one of the greatest things that they come away with is just the fact that there's a human being that cares about them. I really think that that makes a difference."

Tom   "I consider myself a very good source of knowledge in terms of history. But at the junior high level, how much of that is really important? It's a drop in the ocean. Everything else is much more important. When you get to the high school level, especially the type that I was dealing with in terms of advanced placement, that knowledge base is much more important. But yet I don't think it's more important than all the other affective things."

Box 4.5

View Themselves as Professionals

Dale   "I am entrusted with 150 minds and the professional part of it is that it's my judgment on which way to take those 150 minds for 180 hours. I think that I take responsibility very heavily. I mean, it's not light. I understand that it's important. I understand that what I say to these kids can go a long way and sometimes I've really got to think about it."

Dean   "This is how I view a school. I view a school as a whole bunch of firms, and the classrooms are like a business. I am in charge of the business. I am like the CEO. I am the owner of that business . . . and that is good and bad, because you know why. In order to do that and not become paranoid and weird about it like I see some teachers, you got to have a pretty good ego. You have got to realize that 'I'm alright. I am doing some good stuff.' "

Gail   "I see myself as a professional. I don't have an hourly pay. I am expected to spend time in the office outside of regular time. I have to make decisions about my job. I am able to make decisions about what I want to teach, the grade level, things concerning my job, and how it affects my life. I have a say in what my job is. Someone who is not a professional does not have the freedom to be creative with their job like I do. I do not have to punch a clock."

Pam   "For one thing, not anybody can do this job. It takes training and dedication. And those to me are the hallmarks of professionalism. It also takes a level of integrity and commitment that you don't find in a lot of industries."

Ruby   "I view myself as a professional. I think that we're all clear about what a professional is supposed to do. I think that there's a lot of reform going on with education right now and so what it means to be a teacher might look very different 10 years from now. I think for where we are right now that the majority of people definitely feel professional about teaching and are clear about what they're supposed to be doing."

Tom   "[Teaching] is the most important job on the face of the earth. There's nothing more important. There's nothing more important. There's nothing more important."

Box 5.1

Genuineness and Authenticity

Dale   Dale is authentic and genuine with the students. For instance, one student asked him why he always writes two problems on the board for the class to work out rather than one. Dale rolled off a series of reasons, "I am on a roll, besides I don't want to break up my thought process and this is easier." Then he paused for a second and said sincerely, "Actually, I don't have a real valid reason." He smiles and so did the students.

Dean   Dean's authenticity is best supported by a parent I spoke with. She said, "He lets his humanity be seen by the kids. I think he does it by being so honest and willing to let people see him make a mistake. He is not afraid to be judged, of messing up in front of people. Kids are not afraid to make a mistake in front of him." Dean says, "No matter what you do you got to be honest. You got to be yourself. You have to show them yourself. Your teaching style has got to be you."

Pam   The day of the discussions on harassment, Pam sent a student, who had picked at a hangnail until it bled, to the nurse's station to get a bandage. She began to joke around about how she hated blood. Several students joined in. They started poking fun at the trivialness of the "injury," making fun of the student. Suddenly one student noted that they were harassing the student. "We are doing the very same thing we were talking about." Everyone was immediately quiet. There was a pregnant pause as individuals realized the truth in the statement. Then Pam said, "I was doing it too. What a jerk you have for a teacher!" A student pipes up, "A cool jerk."

Ruby   When asked what she does when she is not in a nurturing mood, Ruby replies, "What I've found works really well is if I'm honest with them. Sometimes if I don't get enough sleep, I can be a little edgy. . . . I'll just tell them, 'You guys, if I appear short today or if I appear frustrated or whatever, you need to know it's nothing that you've done. I was up real late or I'm not feeling well.' A lot of times they'll be very empathetic back to you."

Tom   Tom's authenticity is evident as he describes his relationship with troubled students. "When I was evaluated, after it was written up, I took it back to class and slapped it on the table. I read it to them, explained what each part meant. So they saw my report card. And so you take it down to where everybody's equal." When asked about the characteristics of a healthy relationship, Tom says, "Well, another is when they can argue with you. Shoot. If they don't argue with you, there's something the matter."

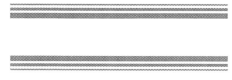

Box 5.2

Inner Locus of Control

Dale   "I used to go out and have a beer or two or three with a lot of the coach guys around here, until about 5 years ago. Then I decided that that was getting me nowhere. All they do is talk bad about the kids or this and that. I don't need that so I decided—I became so unpopular with the coaches—the older guys because they didn't invite me to the parties anymore. I mean, they looked down at me for doing that. I felt outcasted. I could have easily said, 'Hey, I'm going back. I'm going to get back into that group.' But I never did. I just never wanted to do that, I felt that wasn't the right way to go."

Dean   When asked how he handles permission slips, Dean says, "I am bad. I am bad. [laugh] Permission slips are a necessary evil. I do them, but I let kids go on field trips who do not have their full permission slips. . . . It is my choice. Ultimately, if something happened to them and a parent really wanted to be bad, I could probably be reprimanded. I would just say, 'My fault, I thought I had his permission.' " Dean does not blame the student or the school for his decision.

Gail   A student's words best reflect Gail's inner locus of control. When asked what qualities Gail has that she would like to develop, Susan said, "People talk about Ms. _____ and she does not care. She's like, 'I don't have time to worry about what other people say about me and da-da da da-da.' And I wish I could do that." After lunch, Gail goes to the closet in the back of the room. She freshens up her make-up, lipstick, and mascara. One student comes back and says, "Who are you trying to impress?" She says, "Myself. When you feel good about yourself, you always do a good job."

Pam   Pam does not say the Pledge of Allegiance because it is against her religious principles. She has the kids stand and say it if they wish. She has the boys take off their hats. Pam told me the other teachers give her grief about her stance regarding the pledge and she just shrugged her shoulders. She remains committed to her personal beliefs in the face of colleagues' disapproval.

Ruby   Ruby says regarding her traumatic childhood, "I don't know where my strength came from, but a lot of things happened to me that could have caused me to make some really bad choices in my life—in high school and earlier. I look at a lot of kids today with some of those same things happening and they have made some bad choices." Ruby refers to an individual's response to traumatic experiences as a choice, including her response.

Tom   When asked what criteria he uses to define himself as a professional, Tom said, "That is an interesting question. One is the ability to be self-directed, to be a part of the solution, to be a part of the long-range plan."
          As a social activist, Tom works hard to bring about change in situations he sees as inequitable or inadequate. Tom says, "I'm always trying to learn new things and new ways. Figuring out different ways of doing things. I'm willing to risk doing things the unconventional way. Let parents get mad. It's good for them if it brings them into the school."

Box 5.3

Humor

Dale   Another faculty member walks into the classroom. Dale says, "Ladies and gentlemen, Mr. Stewart. One courtesy clap." The students all clap once in unison. Mr. Stewart smiles broadly. He came to take the VCR.

Students walk in and ask, "What are we doing today?" Dale answers, "We have to do fractions today . . . the 'F' word." Students moan, "Oh no, the 'F' word." They work on fractions. . . . Dale says, "You guys are geniuses!" A student says, "Tell my mom that." Dale says, "You want me to? She'll believe me." Another student says, "She'd probably get you fired." Dale responded hopelessly, "I looked at my bank statement this weekend, and I've got to keep working."

Dean   After working several minutes with two students who were teaming on a project, Dean said to one student in the dyad study group. "Does your back hurt?" Both students looked at him somewhat confused. "My back hurt? What do you mean?" the one student said. Dean replied, "From carrying him through his assignment." Both students laughed.

Gail   Gail asks the students what they would do if they went home today and found they have been evicted from their home. Someone mentions they would rob an old lady. Gail hoots and says, "I take offense at that! You would have a permanent place to stay then, and you wouldn't have to worry about meals either!" She asks them the next question. "What if you go home and find that your parents are unemployed?" A group of students groan and mumble something about "as if their parents worked in the first place!" Gail rephrases the question. "OK. You lose whatever source of income you have." Another student mentions something illegal. Gail says, "You'll have a job, a job making license plates."

Pam   When Pam was facilitating the discussion on harassment, she flashed, "I feel like Oprah Winfrey!" and she proceeds into a short impromptu vignette of Oprah. She races up and down the aisles, holding a pretend microphone under the chins of different students while she facetiously asks questions.

Ruby   One student asked how she could make up the work from yesterday. Apparently they did role plays with each other on healthy ways to express anger. Ruby says, "Shall we make her do a one-person skit?" The class shouts, *"Yes!"* The student laughs because she knows Ruby is teasing.

One kid said, "That sucks!" Ruby stops and says, "We don't say that word in here." The student says, "We don't?" Ruby responds, "No, we say Hoover or vacuums." The students laugh.

Tom   It was a student's birthday. Tom goes over to her, kneels down by her chair, puts his arm around the shoulder of the male student next to her and sings *Happy Birthday* to her. First, he sings it imitating a crooner like Sinatra. Then, he sings it again as a country western crooner. The students hoot their approval. The birthday girl is embarrassed but obviously pleased. One student says, "You sound like a sick cow." Tom responds, "More like a castrated cow!" Everyone laughs.

Box 5.4

Nonjudgmental Stance

Dale   "He is really caring about people. He's not judgmental about people. You know, he doesn't judge them by the way they look or anything. He just cares about the personality and the way—he can see what's inside the person" (Annette).

Twenty minutes late, Joe walks into class. Earlier students had wagered bets that Joe would not make it to one class on time this week. Dale nods recognition of Joe and says, "Tough weekend, huh Joe?" He nods and finds his seat. Later, Joe walks across the front of the room to throw something in the wastebasket. Dale says quietly, "Hi buddy." Joe says, "How are you doing?" Dale says, "I am having a rough morning." Joe says, "Me too!" and returns to his seat.

Dean   Dean had asked his TA to clean dead fish and dirty water from a fish tank in the back of the room. The TA refused to do the nasty task but Dean insisted, explaining to her that it was her responsibility. She tackled the task halfheartedly during Dean's lunch hour. After about a half an hour with the tank still half full of water, the TA left the room and did not return. Water was splashed everywhere within the radius of 3 feet. Dean returned from lunch and asked if the TA left because she got sick from the smell. He laughed and then expressed pleasure over how well she had done with emptying the tank. He looked in the tank and said again, "She did really well, really well." Dean sees what the TA did right, not what she did wrong.

Gail   When asked how she handles a student who keeps promising to do his or her homework but comes to class every day with excuses, Gail responds, "Well, I try to figure out, maybe, if I am giving this person too much to do. Or if this person has outside interests that are taking over his or her time. . . . Maybe this person can't read and is in the 10th or 11th grade without anyone knowing that this person cannot read. And that does happen because people who can't read have mastered fooling people. They can get by. It takes a while for you to realize that a person cannot read or a person is not comfortable with reading and does not do the work." Notice Gail first thinks of barriers for the student rather than assuming resistant and inappropriate behavior on the student's part.

Pam   "I think for a lot of these students, you know, this is a period in their lives when they are going to test boundaries constantly. And what I have to always do is be real clear about what my boundaries are and have them be reasonable and have them be something that an adolescent can understand and relate to about the whys of it and just sound arbitrary. I convey to them right up front right away, 'I'm trying to be reasonable with you as I would want you to be with me.' And just tell them that and speak straight from the heart."

Ruby   Ruby asks the class, "What do you think that I will not let you put on the collage?" A student says, "Tobacco and alcohol." Ruby pauses and says, "Other students have said that but I let students do that because if that is really important to them then they need to express that." One student replies, "Sick!" Ruby says, "Well, how else can we say that without putting people down?" She says, "People need to feel free to express who they are. That is where their lives are at this time."

Tom   "I had a girl early this year who I was concerned about because she was so solemn and withdrawn. . . . She's completely different, and she just had never felt comfortablé and wasn't—you know, she didn't feel like she was the best at the subject matter. I said, 'Hey, if you could just give me what you consider to be your best shot at something and you can tell me that you tried your hardest, you'll do okay. You'll do okay in here too.' She responded real well."

Box 5.5

Potency

Dale   When asked what teachers should do to develop close and trusting relationships with students, Danny replied, "Stay in [Dale's] classroom for a little bit and watch [Dale] work."

"I mean, everybody thinks he's a good teacher. . . . Everybody, even before school starts, everybody's like, 'Oh, I want to be in [Dale's] class.' And I'll go check but his classes are usually full. Because his type of teaching is unique. I mean, he's the only math teacher I've ever learned from" (Annette).

Dean   "Mr. _____ cares about all the kids, not only the ones he knows. He cares about all the kids. So it's like if anybody has a problem usually they'll go to Mr. _____ and Mr. _____ will then try to help them out" (Vinnie).

"Well, just the way he acts. I mean he's always making sure everything is okay, making sure you do your work. And he makes you feel really good if you do do your work" (Rosie).

"I mean, Mr. _____'s work is, I mean it can be hard sometimes and he'll always help out with it. He'll always ask, but a lot of teachers are too busy correcting papers to help you out" (Rosie).

Gail   "She has turned a lot of people around and sometimes she'll respect a person more if she can see that they can come around and realize that they are screwing up" (Jake).

"I think she sees me as a leader because she asks me a lot for advice and sometimes she has me help other people because she knows I am capable of believing in them and responsible enough to help them without screwing around" (Jake).

Pam   "I think she's really understanding. When I get older, I don't think I'll be a teacher, but I want to work with little kids and stuff. And being caring like [Pam] is really great. I think it helps kids and when they see it—you know people, like I said, say 'You can come to me' and everything, but until you really see it in the person, you don't start believing them and trusting them" (Kathy).

Students are rowdy. Rick, a previous troublemaker in Pam's class asks Pam which she prefers being, a student or a teacher. Pam says she likes being a student today. Rick said, "I'll be the teacher." Pam immediately invites Rick up front to lead the discussion, and she goes to his desk. Rick starts to lead the class and turns to Pam and says, "Who are you going to be, a special student?" Pam says, "I did not give up being teacher in this class, just the leader of the discussion." Rick begins in seriousness to lead the discussion. He sits on the desk like Pam. He calls on different students and reflects their answers like Pam. Rick takes his assignment very seriously, modeling after Pam. Students get serious about the topic.

Ruby   "She just held out her arms. If you ever wanted to talk to anybody, whenever you wanted to. She's always there for you. She's pretty cool. She gives you good advice—the different choices that you could make. She is always there when you need her" (Peter).

"I really like her a lot and she's just a really caring teacher. She is a lot better than all of the other teachers. And it's not just about caring, it's about the teaching too. She is really a good teacher. She makes it where you learn something and you always will have it, you know. It is not things you learn and you just forget about" (Sally).

Tom   Shawn, a student in trouble at Suburb Junior High, believes Tom sees him as confused and "just nice in his class." He believes other teachers see him as not very well behaved, a troublemaker, and a smart mouth. Shawn acts differently in Tom's class. Shawn says of Tom, "We treat him with respect because he treats us with respect."

A powerful example of Tom's potency is the success he had working with troubled youth in an alternative school. "I pretested them all. At the end of the year, 2 years' growth average in reading and 3 years' growth average in math for every kid. I started with 15 kids and I had 15 kids at the end of the year. The year before they started with 13 kids and not a single kid was left in the program at the end of the year with the other teacher that was running it."

Box 5.6

Enthusiasm

Dale   When asked how important he thought the student-teacher relationship was, Dale responded, "I think it's very important. I don't think I could do this job if all I had to do is teach them math. I would die. If I couldn't have fun in here, I'd be out of here in a flash. . . . If I didn't enjoy it, I couldn't do it."

"I was really frustrated with what was going on in the fundamental group. . . . They were not learning anything because it was the same old, same old that they always see. So I'm inventing new ways. I'm trying to make it—I call it 'fun math.' I try to make it interesting and enjoyable."

Dean   "I just realized I really love teaching because, you know what, you're like an actor who can get up there and do your stuff and you're really the one creating the stuff that you do. And that's what I really like. I've never been caught up in the hype of money or anything like that."

Gail   Gail's enthusiasm is illuminated through her enjoyment of the students. "I like this school. It looks old and it looks like it needs a lot of work, but I like the atmosphere. I like the different activities for the kids. It doesn't seem gloomy. I've taught in schools, rich schools, and this by far has been the best experience for me because I like the—I don't know, it's the students who make up the school. It's the down-home atmosphere."

About the students Gail says, "I enjoy their company. A lot have a lot of interesting things to say. Some are really funny, really witty. I just like being with them."

Pam   "I bring a real high energy [to the job], and I'm very enthusiastic about what I do and the kids relate to that most of the time. I tire some of them out. . . . I always feel like if I can convey some of the excitement that I feel about the discoveries that I make when I read history, then I'm doing a good job."

Ruby   A student said of Ruby, "I think she would probably still do this job if she wasn't getting paid. I think she likes it enough that she'd do that" (Peter).

Tom   Tom's enthusiasm is exhibited through his commitment toward improving his teaching skills and abilities. He won a U.S. West scholarship for special training integrating Gardner's theory on multiple types of intelligence into an interdisciplinary team-taught curriculum. As his student teacher said, "He was nominated for a U.S. West scholarship . . . by one of the other teachers in the school. As a nominee, he had to write a prospectus on what he would do with the money. He wants to do a radical approach to teaching next year with the multiple intelligence, where we open up the walls 3 days a week and have a class with 90 kids using Gardner's staff."

Box 5.7

Effective Communication Skills

Dale   "I think that the things I try to do there is to stop, and if they want to talk, let them talk. If they want to hold it, then that's their choice, too. I just think that in the past when the kids come to me and talk to me, they know they can open up and say some things. There's been some things I wish some kids had not said. They've told me some things—but you can't . . . once you're there, you're there. I try to direct them to the right [person]."

Dean   "He listens, and he doesn't get excited enough to get all angry at you or nothing. He'll just help you try to figure out a way to solve that problem" (Vinnie).

Gail   "I think I'm a good listener, and I think I know when to give advice and when to listen."

Pam   "I had this thing going on with the school and stuff, and this one girl thought we did something but we didn't do any of it. Me and my friends, we did something . . . we really didn't. I didn't want to talk to the counselor, because the counselor was, like, all on their side and so he wouldn't even listen to us. So then, Ms. _____ said I could talk to her and then I just went and talked to her. And it helped. She probably told the counselor your side" (Rick).

Ruby   "I think to give kids time to be listened to is important . . . to give back to them 'this is what I heard you saying' or pull out a little bit of the phrase that they're giving the answer to and have them explain that a little bit more. Once again, just to give them the opportunity to talk about things."

Tom   "You don't have to have the answers. All they wanted to do was have somebody to talk to . . . who will listen to them instead of listening while they are doing something else. They can get anybody to listen while they are doing something else, but to really just sit and listen with undivided attention, that's something else all together."

Box 5.8

Empowering Skills

Dale   "Josh wanted to do something. I had a certain idea of how I wanted to start this lesson. He said, 'I would like to do this.' So I said, 'Okay, we'll do that.' So it kind of makes him feel like he has some control over what he's doing. . . . But I know the big picture . . . we'll get there."

Dean To a student asking Dean to move him to another study group Dean responds, "You know something, this is a free atmosphere in that you need to learn you started this project with that person and you need to end it with that person. In the future, if you don't wish to be with that person, you have to deal with how you are going to interact with that person and get out of that or not work with them."

Gail "I think some teachers want to be the one who knows all the answers, you know. And if you can kind of relax and think well, wait a minute. Someone out here may have more experience in this area than I do. Now let's all learn. And I think that's important because that gives them power over their learning and they want to learn."

Pam "We do some things where I've had them actually vote on the consequences for [classmates]. Where I've said, 'Okay, so what are we going to do you guys? So and so let us down because they didn't bring back part of their report. What are the consequences? What are the reasonable consequences for this?' So we do a lot of group consensus kind of stuff. And they're harsh. I mean, they're much harsher than I would ever be."

Ruby "I want the kids to feel that they are part of the whole process. There are obviously some things we can do and there are some things that we can't do. I think that when they have ownership in that and when they have understanding why we can't do some particular things and they help come up with rules and the enforcement of them, I think it just helps the whole process."

Tom "Sometimes I think it's just good to kind of step back and let them do the learning through the actual experience and let them go through it and then maybe later on say to them, 'You know, I was watching you two.' And then go through it with them after they kind of struggle with it a little . . . giving each one the opportunity to talk but also give them some feedback about 'This is what I see you doing.' I give the feedback more after the fact."

Box 5.9

Conflict Resolution Skills

Dale   "I'll ask them what's the problem. I'll get two different stories and then I'll try to go in and determine what really went on and the reason behind this. If it's a lot deeper than what happened in class or if they've been at each other for a while or whatever. A lot of times it's real minor and the kids get all upset right away, so then I'll call them up and I'll talk to them—separate of course."

Dean   "Yesterday there was a major conflict. And those things . . . I resolve conflict all the time. Two kids coming up and they are like talking . . . a head mounting. 'Hey! You got to come on. You guys need to chill.' Or whatever, you just resolve conflict all the time."

Gail   "I take the student that is least resistant away from it or tell them to take it somewhere else, choose another time or another place and another time. And if it is directed toward me, I use a little bit of humor sometimes, then just kind of play it off and talk to them later because I really haven't sent them to the office in a while. . . . If it's students I don't know, then I'll try to call somebody else first because sometimes it is kind of hard to get involved when you don't know the students, you don't know what is happening."

Pam   "I think if a student is having a problem, like kids will swear in my class and they just don't seem to think twice about it. Some of them become very surprised when I will hold them accountable for it. 'That is not okay to do in my class because it's very offensive to many people.' Again, we just try to handle that one-on-one. When I deal with a kid with conflict, because sometimes they will take it personally, or whatever, I will try to go out of my way to find them doing something right in the next little while and acknowledge that to them."

Ruby   "[I] deal with that student one-on-one and find out where the concern is, where the problem was, or where the lack of understanding was and try to paraphrase it and really focus in on where the lack of understanding came from and why."

Tom   "There is a lot of negative feeling between us [a student and Tom] right now. How do I deal with it? I basically ignore it at this point, right now. I let them kind of go through their feelings and a lot of times I'll sit back and kind of wait to see if they're going to take the first step forward. . . . I usually let it go about 3 days and if they don't make contact then it's usually me that does and I just give them the chance. I'll start out with, 'Okay, what are you angry with me about?' And I let them speak their mind first. . . . We go from there."

Box 5.10

Accountability With Mistakes

Dale   "I kind of like to be able to show the kids—I don't like to prove to the kids how smart I am. If I make a mistake at the board, sometimes I'll do it on purpose to see if they're watching me and sometimes I'll be going too fast and it just happens. And when I do that I go, "Dang, I made a mistake. I can't believe it!" [said humorously] Like that so it lets you know that I'm a human guy."

From classroom observations: Dale puts a problem on the board for students to figure out. After a few minutes the students start to complain that the problem is impossible. Dale glances at the problem on the board and says, "Oh no! I forgot to carry over." He goes to the board and changes the numbers in the problem. The class groans. "You made a mistake. You are the math teacher. You are supposed to know this stuff." Dale laughs and says, "I made a mistake." Students laugh and tease, "When we make a mistake, you count it against us. How come it doesn't count against you?" Dale teases back, "It does count against me. I have to put up with you guys raggin' on me. Isn't that enough?" The students laugh.

Dean   "I really don't dwell on my mistakes, because what I end up doing is I end up realizing I am going to make a thousand mistakes and just being able to say, 'My fault man, I am sorry.

I really shouldn't have gotten in your face like that.' There are times that I push too much. There are times I don't push enough. There are times when I call somebody on something when I shouldn't of because it was really kind of out of pocket for me. You just have to be able to go right up to them and say, 'You know something, I'm sorry.' "

Gail   "I apologized for whatever behavior on my part made that student feel that way. Then she realized that she was being too sensitive, and I realized that I was too. And so we hugged each other and that was it."

From a classroom observation: Several more students walk in. She calls one to the front and tells him she made a mistake on his final grade and she needs to send him down to the office with a grade change form. They tease back and forth.

Pam   "I know one time in the fourth-period class I said something to a student. And I can't remember if it came out wrong or he misunderstood me, but I could see in his face that he thought what he said was stupid. I stopped everything I was doing. And you know, walked over to him and in front of everybody said, 'You know John, it just occurred to me that maybe you think I think that that was a dumb question' or something like that. I don't remember exactly what I said. . . . And he kind of went, 'Well, yeah.' I went, 'Well, that's not what I meant. Let me rephrase what I meant to say to you.' And he just visibly was relieved."

Ruby   "Mistakes are part of life. They're part of the highs and lows of life. . . . That I am not my mistakes . . . that's one I teach to my kids. You know, I am not my mistake. A mistake is an action, not a person. . . . It's okay . . . you're going to come back and try it again, and again, and again."

From a classroom observation: Ruby asks the group if anyone had any questions about where people are. One student said, "You should have asked us earlier so that we had time to think about it." Ruby answers, "Good idea, I will give you time now."

Tom   "I like to tell the kids that I am not perfect. You are not perfect. We're going to make mistakes. I'll tell you when you make one. I hope you tell me when I make one."

Box 6.1

Work Settings and Treatment as Professionals

Perceptions of Positive Support

Gail   "You have the freedom to be creative with the curriculum,
        get together with other teachers to do creative things. . . . You
        are treated like a professional. You know what you're doing
        and you are expected to have these things done."

Pam   "I think this is a very professionally rewarding place to work.
        For example, the administrators, specifically the principal,
        made sure that I was, as a new hire, included in the men-
        toring program in which I got a small stipend for the time I
        put in, as well as the opportunity to go to all kinds of
        professional development seminars around professionalism
        in teaching. . . . I think also the administration is absolutely
        committed to improving the school environment for our
        instructors in any way they can. . . . They give us release time
        to plan for teams and that often comes out of the principal's
        discretionary funds to pay for subs for us to do that."

Tom   "I see this place as a professionally rewarding environment
        to work. Most of the restructuring that's gone on here has
        been generated from the bottom up. And that's very impor-
        tant in terms of the realization you are being treated as a
        professional. Your opinion does mean something. Your ex-
        pertise does mean something."

Perceptions of Negative Support

Dale   "The administration does not view us as professionals at bar-
        gaining time. That is one thing that has always kind of bugged
        me is the administration. You know, when it comes time to pass
        a levy, they want us right there. And I agree and I am right there.
        But it's kind of always funny when at bargaining time, how
        worthless we are or how bad they make us feel."

Dean   "I think the administration views us as professionals in
        words but a lot of times their actions don't support us as
        professionals. Because it's like, 'Oh, you can't do that! You're

doing this great stuff but you can't really [do that].' They
won't give up [control] a lot of times."

Ruby   "The administration sometimes helps to support our belief
that we are professionals. I think that some people feel that
there could be more support. . . . In my case, it's not within
this building; it's at a higher level. For some people, I think
they would like to see more support here as well."

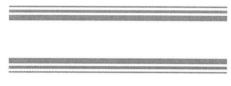

Box 6.2

Time With Students as Revitalization Strategy

Dale   "I don't think I could do this job if all I had to do is teach
them math. I would die. If I couldn't have fun in here, I'd be
out of here in a flash . . . if I didn't enjoy it, I couldn't do it."
       "The things I guess that are most attractive is the kids.
They keep me feeling pretty young. . . . I enjoy the kids.
Everyday something is different."

Dean   "And if I want to really revive myself, you know what
happens? After school I just hang around with some kids and
talk. It's all right. I don't feel overwhelmed by them."
       "Hanging with kids and just laughing and joking and
messing with them, that's what revives me."

Gail   "I like the kids, so they tend to be my source of revitalization.
. . . There are lots of fun things to talk about."

Pam   "The kids themselves revitalize me. They're a real treat.
There's almost never a day that when I leave, I don't have
something to smile about. They make me laugh. They make
me mad. They make me cry. They make me upset. But they
mostly make me laugh. I really like them."

Ruby   "Human contact is the big thing for me in terms of revitalization. This year's freshmen—I have five classes [of freshmen]

right now—are a different breed. [laughter] I really love them, but they can wear on you. . . . Something that revitalized me too is I really like all the kids that are my TAs. The kids, for me, are why I went into education. I think they make it a good, good place to work."

Tom "The kids, that is what keeps me sane. . . . Without the kids, there's so much other crap . . . the parents, the administration."

Box 6.3

Work Environments Provide a Sense of Family or Community

Inner-City High School (Sense of Family)

"[I] treat students like family members" (Gail).

"I like this school. It looks old and it looks like it needs a lot of work but I like the atmosphere. I like the different activities for the kids. It doesn't look gloomy. I've taught in all kinds of schools, rich schools, and this by far has been the best experience for me because I like the—I don't know—it's the students who make up the school. It's a down-home atmosphere" (Gail).

"Think of it like this—it is just one big family. This is my child" (Dean).

"You know something? I love [Inner-City High School]. I really, really love [Inner-City High School]. I love it because it's not like a school and it's not like a district. And it's not like the principal. I guess what I like about it and what the thing is all about is, it's about the 690 kids that go here. Because it's about the faculty members that I work with that are really competent and are doing some great stuff for kids" (Dean).

Suburb Junior High (Sense of Community)

"There's a real feeling of caring about people and helping out [among the staff]. When people have been sick and needed sick days, there has never been a problem with people volunteering sick days, giving up their sick days for that other person.... If you are in need, there's a lot of caring people on the faculty" (Pam).

"I think the administration fosters [that feeling]. Where I student-taught last year, that wasn't the case, and I didn't get the same feeling of concern for each other as people as I do at this school.... I think [the principal] really goes out of her way to recognize people's contributions, and she tries to be very fair and that says a lot right there" (Pam).

"Around here we're real good at covering each other" (Tom). "I've had more fun times teaching here than in any school. I could combine all the schools I've been in and this is by far [the most fun]. We've done some of the most crazy things in the world. Great practical jokers, a lot of humor. And people realize that the way we keep our sanity is through laughing" (Tom).

Box 6.4

School Policies and Social Norms Regarding Diffused Roles

Diffused Role: Inner-City High School

Dean   When asked to give an example of why he perceives that teachers enjoy their jobs at Inner-City High School, Dean described social norms supporting a diffused role. "We're always doing extra stuff with kids. And you know what? You don't do that unless you really like those kids and really like the place.... I mean, there's so much stuff they [faculty] do that I can't even begin to tell you. There was this woman who came here from a middle school in [another school district]. She said the faculty resented her at [her other school] because she would do extra stuff for kids. It was like, 'What are you doing? You're doing that without getting paid? If you keep doing that, they are going to expect us to do that.'

And then she said it was more of an attitude of we do our jobs and we don't do any more. At Inner-City High School, it's more like, for a lot of us, a core group, we do our jobs and then what else—what more can we do? What can we do to help these kids? What extra stuff can we do?"

Gail   When asked if there were any policies that encourage the teacher's role with students to be diffused beyond the classroom, Gail responded, "As long as it's legal, it's fine."

Nondiffused Role: Rural-City High School

Dale   Referring to doing extra outside activities with students, Dale talked about the vagueness of the general school policy and the ambiguous norms established within society. "Especially in this day and age where people get sued. Things happen. People do things legally to you if you're not versed in that area. You tend to hold off. Nowadays, people will do anything to you. Of course, [the administration] gives us our rights and responsibilities, but boy, those are pretty vague when you read through them."

Giving an example of what he was referring to, Dale said, "There was a time when we used to let the kids drive our cars downtown to get something for us. I know the shop teachers have done that. You know, because I'm the baseball coach, I'd let them drive my car to get the gear and bring it back over here or something. Now, boy, you do that and you're just asking for trouble in just an instant."

Ruby   Ruby made reference to ambiguous social norms when talking about school policies that discourage teachers from reaching out to do extra things with students. "You know, we're not supposed to give kids rides home after a turnout or after a game if the kid doesn't have a ride. We're supposed to wait there with them for their ride to come and get them and have somebody else around. I mean, it's almost a fear that we're living under, which is really too bad."

Nondiffused Role: Suburb Junior High School

Tom   Tom talked about how union policies restrict personal connections with students outside of the school setting. When asked about school policies that encourage a diffused role,

Tom said, "You couldn't do that. You couldn't do that through the unions." What he does with students outside the classroom he intimately connects with school.

Pam   About her school norms and policies on a diffused teacher role, Pam says, "I am encouraged to coach. I am encouraged to get involved with afterschool activities, but I am discouraged from having personal contact with students outside of the school setting."

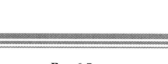

Box 6.5

Diffused Roles as Teachers

Diffused Role

Dean   "I really don't even set boundaries. I go with my feelings. Those kids need counselors. I do more counseling than any friggin' counselor in this whole place. As far as a parent, where I work, that comes with the job. . . . If I am just going to be a teacher, then I am going to provide just a part of the service I could provide the other way. That is my choice, though. Not every teacher should have to do that."

Gail   "I spend a lot of time with students, talking to them about their personal problems or things that have happened to them over the weekend, overnight. Fun things. It's not always serious and it's not always sad. . . . And I go to their basketball games and football games."

"I spend the weekend with various students. They either come by the house, or I pick them up. We go to basketball games or what have you. I've been on shopping excursions with teenagers."

"They know my phone number. Lots of the kids are my friends. . . . Many kids have come over to the house. They've eaten dinner. The cheerleaders spent the night, which they will never do again because they stayed up all night long. I'm too old to stay up all night" [laughter].

Nondiffused Role

Dale   "What I'll do is I'll go talk to Roy, the counselor. I'll say 'Roy, we have some problems, and we need you to talk to this person.' I don't have a whole lot of skills and sometimes some of these kids . . . I don't know what kind of anger they are having or they've had in the past or their background. Having a counselor that's had anger management counseling helps out a lot. . . . He is a good counselor."

Ruby   "Sometimes, if I think it's something where it might be a crisis or something really serious and they're not willing to disclose that to me, then I'm thinking that it's not going to do any good for them to be in my classroom. I will physically walk them next door and take them to a counselor and say, 'John's having some problems. Maybe you can talk with him and see what's going on. I am really concerned about him.' "

        "The only way I spend time with them outside of the classroom is if they're in some kind of extra activity such as Natural Helpers. Natural Helpers and athletic events and through coaching are the main ways in which I have time outside the class."

Pam   "I don't pretend to be these students' friend. . . . And you know, when I talk to them about problem-type issues, not history, curriculum stuff, but social-type issues. I'm pretty clear about saying, 'Well, you know, as your teacher . . .' And I remind them that this is only one—I'm only one person that they can talk to about things. There are also counselors. 'You know I'm not your parent; I'm not your counselor; but I am your teacher, and I care about you because of that.' "

Tom   "It is not my place to play counselor. I don't have a degree in that. It's like me going and doing the wiring in somebody's house and not knowing the first damn thing about wiring. [My] job, I feel, is to help people discover for themselves that there is a problem . . . and help people find the professional most suited to deal with that problem. And that is, I think, as far as it should go because otherwise you're stepping beyond what your training is and you don't play with those things."

References

American Heritage Dictionary (3rd ed.). (1993). Boston: Houghton Mifflin.

Aspy, D. N., & Roebuck, F. N. (1972). An investigation of the relationship between levels of cognitive functioning and the teacher's classroom behavior. *Journal of Educational Research, 65,* 365-368.

Baumrind, D. (1971). Harmonious parents and their preschool children. *Developmental Psychology, 4,* 99-102.

Benard, B. (1991). *Fostering resiliency in kids: Protective factors in the family, school, and community.* Unpublished manuscript available from Northwest Regional Educational Laboratory, 101 S.W. Main Street, Suite 500, Portland, OR 97204.

Bennis, W. G., Schein, E. H., Steele, F. I., & Berlew, D. (1968). *Interpersonal dynamics: Essays and readings on human interaction* (2nd ed.). Homewood, IL: Dorsey.

Bowlby, J. (1979). *The making and breaking of affectional bonds.* London: Tavistock.

Bowlby, J. (1988). *A secure base.* New York: Basic Books.

Briggs, D. C. (1977). *Celebrate yourself.* Garden City, NY: Doubleday.

Bronfenbrenner, U. (1986). Alienation and the four worlds of childhood. *Phi Delta Kappan, 67,* 430, 432-436.

Brook, J. S., Brook, D. W., Gordon, A. S., Whiteman, M., & Cohen, P. (1990). The psychosocial etiology of adolescent drug use: A family interactional approach. *Genetic, Social, and General Psychology Monograph, 116*(2), 111-267.

Burns, E. T. (1994). *From risk to resilience.* Dallas: Marco Polo Publishers.

California Department of Education. (1990). *Enhancing opportunities for higher education among underrepresented students.* Sacramento: Author.

Carkhuff, R. R. (1969). *Helping and human relations: A primer for lay and professional helpers.* New York: Holt, Rinehart & Winston.

Carkhuff, R. R. (1987). *The art of helping* (6th ed.). Amherst, MA: Resource Development Press.

Cole, M., & Cole, S. R. (1989). *The development of children.* New York: Scientific American Books.

Coleman, J. S. (1974). *Youth: Transitions to adulthood.* Chicago: University of Chicago Press.

Coleman, J. S. (1985a). *Becoming adult in a changing society* (Review literature, ISBN No. 92-64-12709-7). Paris, France: Organization of Economic Cooperation and Development Publication and Information Center.

Coleman, J. S. (1985b). Schools and the communities they serve. *Phi Delta Kappan, 66,* 527-532.

Coleman, J. S. (1987a). Families and schools. *Educational Researcher, 16,* 32-38.

Coleman, J. S. (1987b). Social capital and the development of youth. *Momentum, 18,* 6-8.

Coleman, J. S. (1988, March). *Social capital in the development of human capital: The ambiguous position of private schools.* Paper presented at the annual meeting of the National Association of Independent Schools, New York.

Corey, M. S., & Corey, G. (1987). *Groups: Process and practice* (3rd ed.). Pacific Grove, CA: Brooks/Cole.

Deiro, J. (1994). *What teachers do to nurture bonding with students.* Unpublished doctoral dissertation, University of Washington, College of Education.

Earls, F., Beardslee, W., & Garrison, W. (1987). Correlates and predictors of competence in young children. In E. J. Anthony & B. Cohler (Eds.), *The invulnerable child* (pp. 70-83). New York: Guilford.

Edelwich, J., & Brodsky, A. (1980). *Burnout: Stages of disillusionment in the helping professions.* New York: Human Sciences Press.

Farber, B. A. (1991). *Crisis in education: Stress and burnout in the American teacher.* San Francisco: Jossey-Bass.

Fielding, M. (1982, April). *Personality and situational correlates of teacher stress and burnout.* Paper presented at the annual meeting of the American Educational Research Association, New York.

Gelman, D. (1991, Summer). The miracle of resiliency [Special issue]. *Newsweek,* pp. 44-47.

Glenn, H. S. (1982). *Developing capable people* [Leader's guide]. Fair Oaks, CA: Sunrise Press.

Glenn, H. S. (1989). *Introduction: Developing capable people* [Videotape]. Fair Oaks, CA: Sunrise Books, Tapes, and Videos.

Glenn, H. S., & Nelsen, J. (1988). *Raising self-reliant children in a self-indulgent world.* Rocklin, CA: Prima Publishing.

Golanda, E. (1990, November). *The importance of the source of power in an educational setting.* Paper presented at the annual meeting of the Southern Regional Conference of Educational Administration, Atlanta, GA.

Goodlad, J. I. (1990). *Teachers for our nation's schools.* San Francisco: Jossey-Bass.

Hawkins, J. D., Catalano, R., & Miller, J. Y. (1992). Risk and protective factors for alcohol and other drug problems in adolescence and early adulthood: Implications for substance abuse prevention. *Psychological Bulletin, 112*(2), 64-105.

Heifetz, L. J., & Bersani, H. A. J. (1983). Disrupting the cybernetics of personal growth: Toward a unified theory of burnout in the human services. In B. A. Farber (Ed.), *Stress and burnout in the human service professions.* Elmsford, NY: Pergamon.

Heller, K. (1989). The return to community. *American Journal of Community Psychology, 17*(1), 1-15.

Hirschi, T. (1969). *Causes of delinquency.* Berkeley, CA: University of California Press.

Hodgkinson, H. L. (1991). *Beyond the schools* (ISBN No. 0-87652-160-X). Arlington, VA: American Association of School Administrators and National School Boards Association.

Hoffman, M. L. (1970). Conscience, personality, and socialization techniques. *Human Development, 13,* 90-126.

Hurn, J. C. (1985). *The limits and possibilities of schooling: An introduction to the sociology of education* (2nd ed.). Boston: Allyn & Bacon.

Johnson, D. W. (1972). *Reaching out.* Englewood Cliffs, NJ: Prentice Hall.

Jourard, S. (1964). *The transparent self.* Princeton, NJ: Van Nostrand Reinhold.

Karen, R. (1990, February). Becoming attached. *Atlantic Monthly,* pp. 35-70.

Kochman, T. (1981). *Black and white styles in conflict.* Chicago: University of Chicago Press.

Kubey, R., & Csikszentmihalyi, M. (1990). *Television and the quality of life: How viewing shapes everyday experiences.* Hillsdale, NJ: Lawrence Erlbaum.

Ladson-Billings, G. (1992). Reading between the lines and beyond the pages: A culturally relevant approach to literacy teaching. *Theory Into Practice, 31*(4), 312-320.

Lieberman, A., & Miller, L. (1984). *Teachers, their world, and their work.* Alexandria, VA: Association for Supervision and Curriculum Development.

Lortie, D. C. (1975). *Schoolteacher: A sociological study.* Chicago: University of Chicago Press.

Main, M., Kaplan, N., & Cassidy, J. (1985). Security in infancy, childhood, and adulthood: A move to the level of representation. *Monographs of Society for Research in Child Development, 50*(1/2), 66-104.

Marlin, T. R. (1987). *Teacher burnout and locus-of-control, sex, age, marital status, and years of experience among a group of urban secondary teachers.* Unpublished doctoral dissertation, Rutgers University, New Brunswick, NJ.

Martin, J. R. (1992). *The schoolhome.* Cambridge, MA: Harvard University Press.

McCroskey, J. C., & Richmond, V. P. (1983). Power in the classroom I: Teacher and student perceptions. *Communication Education, 32,* 175-184.

McDermott, R. P. (1977). Social relations as context for learning. *Harvard Educational Review, 47,* 198-213.

McIntyre, T. (1984). The relationship between locus of control and teacher burnout. *British Journal of Educational Psychology, 54*(2), 235-238.

McLaughlin, M. W. (1990, April). *Strategic dimensions of teachers' workplace context.* Paper presented at the annual meeting of the American Educational Research Association, Boston.

McLaughlin, M. W., & Talbert, J. (1990). Constructing a personalized school environment. *Phi Delta Kappan, 72*(3), 230-235.

McNabb, W. H. (1990). *The developing capable people parenting course: A study of its impact on family cohesion.* Unpublished doctoral dissertation, Pepperdine University, Malibu, CA.

Moskovitz, S. (1983). *Love despite hate: Child survivors of the Holocaust and their adult lives.* New York: Schocken.

Nelsen, J. (1987). *Positive discipline.* Fair Oaks, CA: Sunrise Press.

Noblit, G., Rogers, D., & Brian, M. (1995). In the meantime the possibilities of caring. *Phi Delta Kappan, 76*(9), 680-685.

Noddings, N. (1988). Schools face crisis in caring. *Education Week, 8*(4), 1-32.

Noddings, N. (1992). *The challenge to care in schools.* New York: Teachers College Press.

O'Donnell, J., Hawkins, D., Catalano, R., Abbott, R. D., & Day, L. E. (1995). Preventing school failure, drug use, and delinquency among low-income children: Long-term prevention in elementary schools. *American Journal of Orthopsychiatry, 65,* 87-100.

Owens, R. G. (1982). Methodological perspective, methodological rigor in naturalistic inquiry: Some issues and answers. *Educational Administrative Quarterly, 18*(2), 1-21.

Peck, S. M. (1987). *A different drum.* New York: Simon & Schuster.

Pedersen, E., Faucher, T. A., & Eaton, W. W. (1978). The new perspective on the effects of first-grade teachers on children's subsequent adult status. *Harvard Educational Review, 48,* 1-31.

Rist, R. (1970). Social class and teacher expectations: The self-fulfilling prophecy in ghetto education. *Harvard Educational Review, 40,* 411-451.

Rogers, C. (1961). *On becoming a person.* Boston: Houghton Mifflin.

Rogers, C., Gendlin, E., Keisler, D., & Truax, C. (1967). *Therapeutic relationship and its impact.* Westport, CT: Greenwood.

Rogers, D., & Webb, J. (1991). The ethics of caring in teacher education. *Journal of Teacher Education, 42*(3), 173-181.

Rothman, R. (1992). Study "from inside" finds a deeper set of school problems. *Education Week, 12*(13), 1-9.

Rutter, M. (1987). Continuities and discontinuities from infancy. In J. D. Osafsky (Ed.), *Handbook of infant development* (pp. 1256-1296). Oxford, UK: Oxford University Press.

Sergiovanni, T. (1993). *Building community in schools.* San Francisco: Jossey-Bass.

Small, J. (1981). *Becoming naturally therapeutic* (2nd ed.). Austin, TX: Eupsychian Press.

Stahelski, A., & Frost, D. (1987, March). *Modern managers move away from the carrot-and-stick approach.* Paper presented at the annual meeting of the Western Psychological Association, Long Beach, CA.

Werner, E. E. (1990). Protective factors and individual resilience. In
    S. J. Meisels (Ed.), *Handbook of early childhood intervention*
    (pp. 97-116). New York: Cambridge University Press.
Werner, E. E., & Smith, R. S. (1992). *Overcoming the odds: High-risk
    children from birth to adulthood.* Ithaca, NY: Cornell University
    Press.
Wiggins, J. D. (1982). Improving student behaviors with Carkhuff-
    model counseling. *School-Counselor, 30*(1), 57-60.

Index

CORWIN
PRESS

The Corwin Press logo—a raven striding across an open book—represents the happy union of courage and learning. We are a professional-level publisher of books and journals for K-12 educators, and we are committed to creating and providing resources that embody these qualities. Corwin's motto is "Success for All Learners."